KEEPER
OF THE MOON

Also by Tim McLaurin

THE ACORN PLAN
WOODROW'S TRUMPET

For Cardinal Gibbons High,

KEEPER OF THE MOON

A Southern Boyhood

1/25/95

TIM McLAURIN

Best,

T. Mc

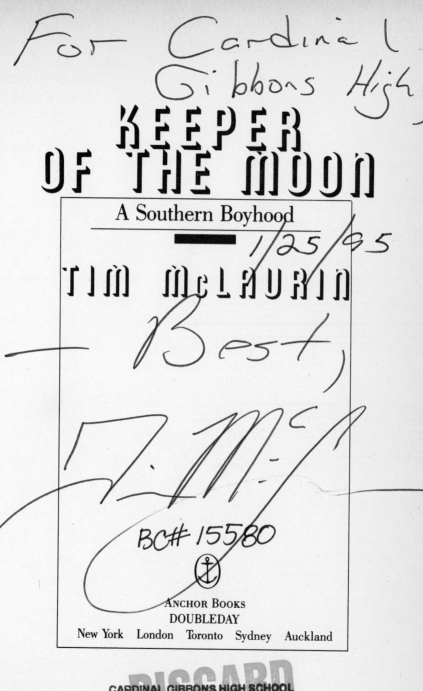

ANCHOR BOOKS
DOUBLEDAY
New York London Toronto Sydney Auckland

AN ANCHOR BOOK

PUBLISHED BY DOUBLEDAY

a division of Bantam Doubleday Dell Publishing Group, Inc.
1540 Broadway, New York, New York 10036

ANCHOR BOOKS, DOUBLEDAY, and the portrayal of an anchor
are trademarks of Doubleday, a division of Bantam Doubleday Dell
Publishing Group, Inc.

Keeper of the Moon was originally published in hardcover by W. W. Norton & Company in
1991. The Anchor Books edition is published by arrangement with W. W. Norton &
Company.

Lines from "Easter Sunrise" in *The Light as They Found It* by James Seay. Copyright 1990
by James Seay. William Morrow & Company, Inc./Publishers. Used by permission

Book design by Margaret M. Wagner

Library of Congress Cataloging-in-Publication Data

McLaurin, Tim.
Keeper of the moon/Tim McLaurin.
p.   cm.
1. McLaurin, Tim—Biography—Youth. 2. Novelists, American
—20th century—Biography—Youth. 3. Southern States—Social life and
customs—1865– I. Title.
[PS3563.C3843Z468 1992]
813'.54—dc20
[B]   92-19733
CIP

ISBN 0-385-42600-3
Copyright © 1991 by Tim McLaurin

This book is dedicated
with much love and pride
to my brothers and sisters
Karen Lynn
Bruce Wayne
Steven Keith
Danny Michael
Kelli Dawn

We lived it

. . . I thought of how sometimes it has to be enough
to settle for the moon, any music that matches the ellipse
of our lives.
I thought of how sometimes we have
to settle for whatever view there is,
though what we believe is the water running clean
with the tide of light reappearing morning after morning.

—*JAMES SEAY*, *"Easter Sunrise"*

MORNING

An evening fog is settling on the river, and in her fingers of vapor I see the spirits of one thousand memories. The rain has stopped after three days of gray skies and pewter water; the clouds are beginning to break and I have seen a sliver of the moon in the west. This fire I have coaxed is beginning to burn—Indian-style, a small pile of flames a man must huddle close to to catch the warmth. My tent is up, the canoe turned on her gunwales to let the rainwater run out. I'm down to my last tin of stew, and already I can taste it, how the gravy will bubble and steam heated right in the can.

Beavers are sounding their warnings up and down the river. They slap the surface with their tails, and you'd think someone had thrown a large rock in the water. I saw a lot of wild geese today, ducks, a dead six-point buck caught in a log jam. The river current is up and running fast, but tomorrow I'll end this journey and will stay ahead of the really high water flowing from deep inland.

I'm listening to a little stereo headset, alternating channels between classical and country stations to suit my moods. Sun is forecast for tomorrow, a high in the fifties, which is about average for a North Carolina January. I really can't understand why everyone was so worried. I'm just back doing what I've done all my life—camping in the winter, a hundred-mile run down the Neuse River to where she loses herself in the sea. I have a thing about rivers. On that first day when the rain was falling heaviest, I was dry and warm under my poncho. I had to bail the canoe once in a while with an empty Spam can. Like a worm still in his cocoon, I have likened myself to these few days, protected against the elements by my wraps, my tent, the time drawing closer to emerge.

My mind has been like a storm, running fast and full as this water. All these thoughts: memories and stories of dead men and Christmas mornings, promises I broke and pledges I have held to, women who have affected me for the good and bad, snakes and church and cold beer and coons treed by dogs.

I like this gray water, for it gives back no reflection: I've not seen my face now in three days. When I rub what stubble I have on my chin, this new crop of hair growing, I can imagine I touch my old face before I went into the cocoon and transformed into a new man these past eight months. But this change in my bones has not altered the spirits locked in my mind. Paddling, stroke by stroke, they have surfaced to me on the gray river like looking into the bright throats of morning glories on some long-departed summer morn.

JUNE 1961. I believed I was dreaming. A few feet away, a hummingbird hovered above a gardenia bud. A scarlet-throated male, tiny wings a blur of motion, he thrust his long bill into the petals and drank. I blinked—the bird remained. Through the open screen window flooded the sounds of earth awakening, cool air that washed my face, the smell of newly opened blossoms. Under the single sheet my legs brushed against the warm flank of my younger brother. My mind rolled back for an instant toward dreams, lulled by the soft noises of sleep. But life had seized me, a bubble of awareness gathered and trembled like the hummingbird's wings. What was so important about today? I bolted up in bed. Hot damn! Summer vacation!

"Get up, Bruce," I said, slapping at the fetal form under the sheet. He groaned once and rolled to his belly, relaxed, then tore upwards from the covers. A grin split his face, and sighting on the next bed, he let sail his pillow at the dream-filled head of Keith, the knee baby of our family. Bruce leaped onto the bare board floor, naked except for tattered underwear, and announced with glee, "No school today!"

Normally my mother had to beat us from the bed, my older sister, me, and three younger brothers positioned between the ages of eleven and four. We all slept in one bedroom in a worn frame house sitting on the edge of seventy acres of rough farmland. Each school morning we were turned out of our mattresses, into a cold, heartless world. Wailing and moaning, we huddled around the kerosene heater. Now all was transformed as if by fairies, our inner clocks rewound, energy levels shifted to overdrive. Suddenly the crack of dawn was a wondrous time to be explored while the world was still cool with the night's dew, the call of summer finer than the lure of warm covers. We scrambled into cutoff jeans and T-shirts, and crept single-file through the house toward the front door.

Outside, waiting to be rediscovered each day, lay Beard Station, a few dozen houses and a country store gathered at an intersection of State road 1210 and the Atlantic Seaboard Railroad. Today, most everyone is still of close or distant kin; secrets fast become common gossip. The community survives on farming; a couple of successful farmers provide the field jobs, the blacks and white children provide the labor. The adults who don't farm travel daily the seven miles into Fayetteville, where they work as salesmen, shop clerks, utility servicemen, and laborers in factories and plants that produce electrical tools, tires, fabric, and dog food. Fayetteville is a sprawling, blue-collar town and contrasts strangely with adjacent Fort Bragg Army Base, where the 82nd Airborne Division and the Green Berets train. Over four wars, natives and soldiers have bought and sold from each other, flirted with each other's wives and daughters, and fist-fought in bars whenever two or more fellows needed to prove that the uneasy truce between town and base was kept up out of strength rather than weakness.

My family is an old and populous one in the area. We immigrated here to the Cape Fear River Valley in the 1700s, and depending upon the habits of various branches, are known as either hardworking, God-fearing people or as bootleggers, whores, and delinquents. My own branch of the family has taken the middle road.

My father, Reese, had only a seventh-grade education, but most who knew him thought him a man of good common sense. He had a knack for birthing animals and was often called out late at night to deliver a breeched colt or calf. He was a man of few words, stern by nature, his manner hardened by a life of long, boring work as a machine operator in the Merita Bakery. When he was not pushed by a machine, he worked his land, trying to wrest some extra income from the dirt. As a child, I feared his silence, his explosive temper, and his drinking binges. I feared how his gray eyes would sometimes stare for long minutes without twinkle or reflection, as if he saw visions of what could have been and what might never be. As I grew older I

learned to read some of the thoughts behind his eyes, and I
came to love him more. He died young.

My mother, Darlene, is still living, and is of the glue that
holds the world together. As a schoolgirl she was gifted at
books, but followed her heart over her senses to marry my
father when she was sixteen and he twenty-one. They
courted on horseback. In the days before World War Two,
she watched for my father from the school-bus window. She
often spied him atop his horse at a break in the forest,
racing the old bus along a forest trail, his coattails flapping,
his mount throwing up hoof-clods of dirt. On these days,
she put away her books and lingered at home only the few
minutes needed to disarm her stepmother before she sad-
dled her own horse and met him at a junction in the woods.
Mama birthed five children within a decade, then a sixth
fourteen years later. She could hug with one arm and spank
with the other, while threatening punishment that would
have shocked a drill instructor. She was a master at jug-
gling money, bills, and overdue notices, kept us fed and
clothed and considerably loved. She has the eyes and ears
of a hunting bird.

"Y'ALL better get back in that bed," she shouted just as
our bare feet were only toes away from the front door.

"Ohhhh, Mama," I complained. "Let us go out. We'll be
quiet."

"Well, y'all better stay off that road. And I catch one of
you playing in the ditch, I'll beat him to death."

The last in line slammed the screen door, Joe the hound
greeted us, wiggling from wet nose to tail, a hen or two
pecked nearby in the dirt. The sun hung as only a glimmer
in the trees.

Sounds—a woodpecker jackhammers the dead limb in

the hickory tree. The mourning doves coo from treetop to powerline, a haunting cry of solitude and eternity. Doves are lonely birds, best not listened to by the heartsick. Songbirds fill in the spaces, a constant twitter and chatter of high and middle notes. The mother birds fuss and scold over nestlings, the daddy birds sing out how good and free it is to be alive. A killdeer—they are liars—runs through the pasture with one wing lowered, crying as if wounded to lead the cat away from her babies. Who would eat a killdeer; my Grandma McLaurin said they taste bitter. On foggy mornings, the ducks swoop in, a male mallard, his two frowzy hens, they circle our irrigation pond, squawking, lowering, alight for seconds only to be startled by a train whistle, the moo of a cow, lift with an explosion of spray from the water and fly into the deep woods.

Hear the hammer pound the nail into the new fence a mile distant, the drone of morning traffic as tires dry the asphalt on the big road that leads into town. One of Miss Eva's dark-skinned daughters is singing as she hangs up the diapers to dry for her new bastard baby. A jet howls overhead, her rockets churning clouds as she lifts and flies to one of those picture places like New York or Paris. It might as well be the moon.

Smells—honeysuckle, sweet honeysuckle wet with dew. Bite off the end of the flowers and suck out the nectar, only a flash of sweetness, but the flavor cannot be matched in a sugar bowl. Bury your face in the strands of purple wisteria blossom—the fragrance wraps your face like fingers. Don't sniff a bumblebee, for they love wisteria, too. Stand erect and smell the musk of the field that has been turned to seed wheat. The odor is rich, primeval with plants that grew when fishes swam where quail now nest. Catch the scent of bacon—pig meat crackling in its own grease, eggs slowly scrambled in butter. We've been too noisy and Mama is up and cooking breakfast.

I am six foot tall, a solid 185 pounds, and owe it mostly to a sound rearing and plenty of scrambled eggs and pork. The Merita Bakery supplied us with plenty of day-stale bread, the land gave us eggs and fatty pork. Mama cooked in a huge black skillet, made toast in the oven, soggy in spots where gobs of butter melted through the bread. Fold the eggs between a slice of toast, add a slice of bacon down one side, a dash of salt and pepper. Simple fare, two will fill the belly of any child, washed down with raw milk if the cow is fresh, powdered milk if she is dry. We spurned the table, grabbed up our meal, and carried it outside to the coolness of the porch. The dog begged for scraps. The meal powered us up tree limbs and through creek bottoms, honed imagination and sparked invention from that first morning of summer vacation through the dog days of late August, autumn, and the return to school.

Even today as a man of thirty-six with children of my own, I am still joined by something sacred to Southern country mornings. If indeed there exists a physical heaven, I hope it is patterned after North Carolina between the summer hours of six and eight A.M. The haunting call of doves, leaves jeweled with dew, the glint of the sun in oak branches, robins and roosters in duet, fog—something eternal exists in those minutes that a person carries in memory for life. On that first day of summer vacation, five liberated children stood at the center of the universe, with a romping black-and-tan coonhound in an hour and age heedless of the measure of time.

"*GO GET* a switch right this minute!"

Mama stared at me with venom in her eyes, one hand cocked on her hip, her frock stained from work and sweat. On the floor lay the shards of a sugar bowl. I had been warned twice to quit pushing it around on the floor like a truck. My brothers stared at Mama, a finger stuck in one's mouth, another scratching an imaginary itch on his head.

"And don't get no little ole twig, neither," she continued. "I told you fifty times to put that up. Now there'll be ants all over the place."

I hung my head and pushed out my lip, trying to look as pitiful and remorseful as possible. But there was no getting out of it. When Mama decided on a whipping, no last-minute reprieve appeared. Worst of all, instead of jerking you up and flailing you with her hand immediately and getting it over with, she sent you to cut your own switch, giving you ample time to consider your fate. I turned slowly and walked out the door, knowing her eyes were burning holes in my backside.

Not any switch would do. The switch had to be one of those limber jobs from the hedge bush, big enough that it would not break when she whipped it back and forth, but slender enough to pucker the skin and draw a welt. If you came back carrying something ridiculous like a milkweed stalk or a honeysuckle vine, you were sent back till you got a switch that was right.

My siblings waited and watched like crows on a fence. They had all made their own trips to the hedge bush, and they were caught between sympathy and the excitement of viewing another's pain. Finally, with a long breath, I snapped off the branch that was the least presentable and walked with slow steps for the back porch.

My older sister, Karen, opened the door for me, her brown eyes holding true pain. She disappeared to a back room. Bruce, Keith, and Danny, their ages and heights like descending rungs on a ladder, ringed my mother where she worked at some chore, scratching and bumbling and trying to get her attention. She had forgotten the whipping at that point. Keith fidgeted until he could bear it no longer and muttered, "He's here." She looked up at me; her eyes focused and the memory returned. Her anger was gone, but a finality shone in her eyes that said if she was to ever have sugar bowls, that if I was to grow up without becoming a rapist or mass murderer, I must receive that whipping.

Mama wiped her hands carefully on a rag as if cleaning her soul of guilt. Then she took the switch, whipped it back and forth to ensure its strength, gripped my left arm high up, and began thrashing. I started yelling before the first blow fell, ran in a circle, my free arm held behind my back to ward off blows. My brothers stepped backwards, half laughing and half crying themselves, afraid my mother would get caught up in her enthusiasm and yank them into the fray.

It ended in seconds; she hugged me to her bosom while I cried and swore to be forever good.

A FINE LINE exists between being loved and being beaten to death. The two have always gone hand in hand in the South, and many are the times that physical violence replaces physical love. As children are often told before being disciplined, "This whipping is only because I love you and will hurt me more than it hurts you," the good parent in the era of my childhood believed strongly in the use of the rod to dispel evil. Or the switch or the mop handle or the palm of the hand—whatever was handy when a child's butt needed smacking.

My parents were of two schools of discipline. My father rarely whipped one of us, but when he did, it was an "asswhupping," a violent, barely controlled release of anger and frustration that left marks on one's legs, back, and memory. Once he picked up a hound that had chewed the corner of his boot and slung the animal against the base of a tree. The dog's hipbone snapped. The fury that had glazed his eyes as quickly changed to shame and pain; he rubbed the dog's head as it whimpered and licked his hand. He lifted the dog and carried it to a veterinarian for a cast, although a quick bullet to its brain would have fit much better within our budget.

I was never beaten by my father. I did watch him whip my sister and younger brothers, their screams of true pain far beyond the exaggerated sobs we allowed my mother's switchings. My father sat on his feelings and subdued them most of the time, the dam bursting occasionally. In release, he might wound an animal, pick up an electrical cord instead of a switch, or punch another man in the nose. One night he came home following an argument with a neighbor, stormed into the bedroom, picked up the rifle, and asked my mother if it was loaded. When she hesitated to answer, he fired through the window glass. The few whippings I watched him administer to others taught me never to breach certain boundaries.

WE WERE at the supper table; I could tell by my father's few words he'd had an especially hard day. An argument started between Keith and Bruce; Bruce flung out his arm and spilled his glass of tea. The cold liquid flowed across the table and onto my father's lap.

My father lifted eight-year-old Bruce with one hand by his collar and rushed him toward our bedroom, using his free hand to unbuckle his belt. The door slammed and I heard the smack of leather against skin, Bruce's screams like animal howls. Not being able to see the violence was worse, for in the screams, bumps, and curses, I imagined he was being killed. My mother rushed from the table, shouting "Reese! Reese!" over and over again. She paused at the door, clinching and releasing her fists. She reminded me of a brood sow when we castrated one of her young, slobbering and pushing against the fence that separated her. Mama burst into the room—more shouting, and the smacks of the whipping stopped, but then I heard a heavy thud as Mama was shoved against the bed. The belt started again, the collection of sounds like a door opened into hell. We were all whimpering or crying then.

As suddenly as it started, the violence stopped. My father walked from the bedroom into his own room and closed the door. I pretended to study my homework, but watched him pass through the house a few minutes later in his coat and disappear into the winter night.

My mother was a "spanker" quick to discipline with words and her wrist, the pain minor, she as quick to forgive as we were to repent. She was best at uttering the most god-awful threats. "I'm gonna stomp the living snot out of you" was a common phrase, "Boy, I'll cut the pure blood out of your legs with a switch" another favorite. But we all knew she wasn't serious, that whatever the living snot was, she loved that part of us, too.

If I never received many whippings during my childhood, it was not from good behavior. From early in my life, I was a schemer, one who considered the risks of whatever action I might attempt, then committed it with as little fanfare or attention as possible. Often concealment, secrecy, or an outright lie was called for to get my way without getting a thrashing in return. Even today as an adult, my tendency is to act on swift decision, ask for as little assistance as possible, and hope later I have mashed no toes.

EARLY JUNE, I was nine years old, the Japanese beetles were eating the wisteria vines down to nubs. School had only been out a couple of weeks, but already we were bored. Keith, Bruce, and I walked the dirt roads near home, searching the ditches for pop bottles, box turtles, snakes, or frogs. An idea seized me as I looked upon a tobacco field, the chest-high stalks planted in rows straight as soldiers.

I led the way as we ran up and down several rows, knocking off the brittle leaves with our hands and sticks. At the end of several minutes we were panting for breath and had broken off enough leaves to fill half a trailer. I realized then the extent of our vandalism and instructed Bruce and Keith to help me gather armloads of the leaves and toss them in the woods. We went on with our day.

Twilight was creeping over our farm, my father was home from work, when I saw a pickup slow and turn into our driveway. The man who got from the truck I recognized as the farmer who owned the tobacco field. My father's face grew grim as I watched the two men talk at the edge of our yard.

"You boys get over here now," my father said.

We came with heads down.

"Mr. Blackman says someone's been tearing up his tobacco field. He said there are footprints all in the sand. Looked like little boys."

We were the only white children living within miles of the field. Keith had already begun to whimper. I knew we were in for it.

"Did y'all tear up his tobacco?" my father asked.

"We weren't trying to tear it up," I blurted out. "We were over there, Daddy, but we were just practicing cropping. I'm old enough to start cropping this summer, and I wanted to be able to show I knew how."

Bruce and Keith stared wide-eyed. My father's pulse throbbed in his neck as he studied me.

"Honest. We weren't trying to tear up his tobacco. We were just trying to get good."

"Y'all get on in the house," he said. We retreated quickly. From the window I watched the two men talk. They parted by shaking hands. That summer I worked for Mr. Blackman.

My next brother, Bruce, has always been a case study of how opposites exist in families. My tendency to consider, conceal, or dodge has always been counterbalanced by Bruce's head-down reaction toward life, willingness to charge forward and butt his way through, regardless of his own pain or scars. In many ways I have always held him as a model of the Southern man.

BRUCE found a nickel in the old washer-wringer on the front porch. The cool of morning had slowly yielded to a vertical sun; we children had busied ourselves in play that required no sweat. The day was Saturday; my father was home, resting as he seldom did in the breeze from a rotary fan, my mother busy with the endless chores that go with keeping a family clean and fed.

A nickel, shiny and fat, worth in trade a Sugar Daddy at Smith's country store that sat a long mile away on a narrow road that wound through a pine thicket. Two choices lay upon Bruce's six-year-old mind—strike out in secret and walk there alone and enjoy the gummy candy bar in solitude, or risk having Mama make him buy hard candy with the coin for all us children to share. Bruce swept the yard with his eyes and struck out alone as any normal child should do.

The community store, a small cinder-block building, was owned by the Smith family, successful farmers who employed many of the community's blacks. The store was filled with canned and dry goods, a slab of sharp hoop cheese warm as the fan-curled air and usually sold in nickel or dime slices to be eaten with an apple or sandwiched between graham crackers, household necessities, a chest-type soda cooler containing frosty eight-ounce Cokes, grape Nehis, and Royal Crown Colas, and a candy counter. Seasonal fresh produce and eggs were sold. This was in the days when a soda cost seven cents and the average candy bar was only a nickel. As Bruce rounded the curve and walked away from home, his mind was set on that Sugar Daddy, and hell or an ass-whupping was pushed to the back of his mind. He had probably gotten no more than a quarter mile when Ma came outside to count heads.

"Tim, you seen Bruce?" she called to me, where I was stirring a hurricane in a mud puddle while june bug sailors clung to a shipwrecked stick.

"He was on the porch," I answered, interrupting only momentarily my sound effects of a great storm. I heard footsteps on the porch, my mother's shrill call, then silence. When she came into the yard and called us together, her face had already drawn tight the way it did when she worried.

"If y'all are playing a game with me and he's hiding, you better tell me now," she said, her voice only faking humor. "Where is Bruce?"

"I swear, I ain't seen him," I answered. "Maybe he went in the house and went to sleep."

She turned and headed for the back door. I stared at Keith and Danny, but their blank eyes showed they didn't know his whereabouts. Danny was barely three years old and still in diapers. We all were barefoot. I walked to the back door and heard Mama searching the corners of our small house, calling my brother's name. Finally, she stood on the back steps and let loose a holler that swallowed the yards and filled every space between atoms.

"Brruuuccceee! You better answer me if you hear meeeeeeee."

The sound of her cry rolled to the edge of the woods and returned in diminishing echoes. My father appeared at her shoulder, his cool gray eyes sweeping the pasture, then staring a hole through me as if he was scanning my mind for the last glimpse I held of my brother.

We circled the house, searched the barn, the chicken coop, inside the large doghouse where the hounds slept. The circles grew larger and my mother's face grew tighter and more deeply lined. I knew where the search was pointing, and my stomach began to knot up. No one would say the word, even look that way yet, but if Bruce didn't show up soon we would go to the creek and look into the deep water of the fishing hole. It was forbidden ground without company of an adult, but always alluring as a piece of ripe fruit.

BRUCE never resisted the fruit, always reached out for the candy bar, without regard for later penalties. At age eighteen, fresh out of high school, the wide world at his feet, he got married to his sixteen-year-old girlfriend, a beautiful blue-eyed cheerleader. He confided in me about shinnying up the drainpipe on late nights to her bedroom window. A baby girl was born within a year. They settled in a small trailer on a large cattle farm where he worked as a hired hand. Later, he was accepted to fireman's school, hung up his boots and cowboy hat, and began to ride a truck for the city. The little boy with black hair swirled by cowlicks grew into a lean-cut, handsome man with dark brown eyes. He worked his off-time driving a truck for Roadway, long hours that often stretched late into the night. A second baby came, a son, money was always short, his wife took a job with an insurance agency, and ends were met. Seven years rolled by and what had begun as a teenaged calamity seemed to shape into a testimony of how love could conquer adversity. They purchased a new brick house and had lived there less than a year the night Bruce sat his wife down and told her he was leaving her for another woman. He wept through his words.

"WE BETTER go and see if he went to the creek," my father said finally when every square inch within shouting distance of the house had been searched. Until now, I had figured we would find him either asleep under a bed or hiding out of fear of not having spoken up.

"Well, he knows he ain't supposed to go to that creek alone," my mother answered, the lines in her young face like wounds. "I'm gonna beat him to death if he went down there."

On the rare days when we had visited the creek as a family, the creek was a magical place. Dragonflies skimmed the surface, the current was lazy, the water reflected oak boughs and the clouds in the sky. The creek harbors one of my earliest memories of my father as a young man. I was in first or second grade, the day probably Saturday in the late weeks of spring when bream bed in shallows. My mother packed a lunch of fried chicken and deviled eggs and sweet tea in a gallon pickle jar. My father had gone days before and cut the reeds and briers back from the bank with a bush ax so we would not get tangled or tread upon snakes. On his way home from the bakery, he had stopped at one of the little beer and tackle stores close to the river bridge in east Fayetteville and bought several fishing lines that were already strung with corks, weights, and small, sharp hooks. My brothers and I had dug fishing worms in moist soil beside the tub where the cows watered. We squirmed while waiting turn for my father to tie our lines to reeds we chose from where he had cut back the brush, watched in amazement as he instructed us once on how to skewer a worm on a hook. We gnawed on chicken, laughed, and yanked in enough perch, bream, and catfish to fill a foot tub. I recall my father's eyes were clear and peaceful and trained on us and the water, his arm often wrapped around Mama's waist where they sat close on a log.

But the creek had her dark side—a migrant child had drowned there when I was a baby. My mother had lost her prized pinto horse when he mired in the mud and sank and suffocated. If I awoke late at night when a storm thundered in the distance or the wind whistled in tree branches, I sometimes imagined the creek as a wide, dark mouth that beckoned children and animals to wander knee-deep into the water, only to be sucked under the quagmire of silt and decaying leaves.

Without words, we started across the road for the creek, my father leading. The banks of the channel began a quarter mile across a field, obscured by a tangle of hardwood trees undergrown with brush and vines. My mother's face was turned slightly skyward as if she was praying she would find no small footprints in the dust of the field, no broken milkweed stem a young boy had snapped off while skipping to see the water.

We were halfway across the field when a car rounded the curve, slowed, and tooted the horn while turning into the driveway of our house.

"Who the hell is that?" my father asked, stopping our march across the field.

The door opened and a woman stepped out. She was followed by the figure of a small boy. My mother shaded her eyes, then gasped.

"It's Bruce. That's Mrs. Smith and Bruce."

She began running, and we children followed. My father stood and watched.

The muscles and sinews in my mother's calves, as she ran, worked like parts of a well-greased machine. How vibrant and alive she looked now when moments before she feared she was going to reel her son in dead. I jumped the road ditch, saw Bruce standing slump-shouldered beside Mrs. Smith, his lips brown with caramel where he had forced down all the candy before arriving home. As my mother bore down on him, he lifted his head and fastened his eyes on her, a gesture of pride as if saying, "I made the decision, I'll face the consequences, the candy is already in my belly. It was good."

"He came in the store all by himself, and I figured you probably was worried 'bout him," Mrs. Smith said. "I thought I'd just run . . ."

My mother nodded once, flashed a smile at Mrs. Smith, then was upon my brother, her arm already cocked and lifted. She grabbed Bruce by his shirt collar.

"We thought you had drowned in the creek," she cried shrilly, "and you had gone to the blame store."

She began thrashing his bottom with her free hand. Bruce tried to run, but could only go in a circle, his hands thrust behind him to fend off blows; they spun around and around like a small tornado. Bruce cried, my mother scolded, Mrs. Smith looked quite shocked by the whole affair.

"If you ever do anything like this again I'll kill you," Ma cried.

We children knotted together and watched, afraid my mother would fly into us next and discipline us for any thoughts we might possess of wandering off. She stopped thrashing Bruce abruptly and hugged him, he grabbed her neck and sobbed. They clung to each other and rocked back and forth, my mother's face flushed, but the wounds gone, her flesh filled out with peace.

SHE hugged Bruce just as tight years later on the night when he tried to explain why he was walking out on a wife of seven years and two children. Somewhere down the line in working two jobs, always worrying about making bills, trying to live the life of a man who had grown up much too young, a sweet offering had come along, the nickel too fat and shiny again to turn down. And as always in the buying, he had to pay up, and later weigh whether the sweetness of the event was worth the pain.

He still drives a truck today, is married to another woman, but she is not the one he left his family for. He smokes his Winstons and chooses not to think how lung cancer killed most of our menfolk before sixty. In the lines on his face he hides his feelings, stores them in some deep place where probably on dark nights he debates them, examines them. He pays his taxes and generally stays within the law, and when he does stray, knows his sins ache the heart of his God and his mother. I suspect he would rather rob banks, drink good whiskey, and replace his women when they grumble than drive a truck for twelve-hour shifts and worry about his children and the bills. But he was "raised right," and in this part of the country that is a description that limits a man's list of excuses.

———— ▬ ————

"MERCY ," the second-grade kid cried, his eye glued on the cool eyepiece of my telescope. He lifted his head, squinted one eye, and stood for seconds staring at the half orb of moon hanging in the sky.

"Mercy" was only one of the exclamations I heard the

night I brought my telescope to the school Halloween carnival. The scope was my prize possession, a fine German glass given to me by my Uncle Ken, who had purchased it while on military service in Europe. It stood on a wooden tripod; the steel-and-enamel tube held lenses powerful enough to draw a laughing moon into an expanse of craters and mountain ranges, could split Jupiter into a pea-sized orb circled by five satellites and reveal a small yellow star as Saturn cut with rings.

I had volunteered to bring the scope to school and help our class raise money. The moon was in the right phase, half full, her glow not so bright that it drowned all surface features, the night sky clear and cold and hinting of frost. The principal announced over the intercom that the star machine was set up outside, and a tentative few came first to trade a dime for a cool view of the sky. Word spread. That smooth, dim coin of light that everyone but hunters or lovers took for granted now loomed into focus as a craggy, gnarled world of dramatic brilliance and shadows. Suddenly, I had become the keeper of the moon, the kid who knew how to turn the knobs and gears that lowered the sky till you felt you could reach and cradle it in your palm. I knew the answers to both kid and adult questions—how far away was the moon, what was it made of, did stars really fall; simple fare for a fourth-grader who had read every book on astronomy in the school library. Over the next few years on clear nights a farmer returning late from the fields, a mother and child, might knock at our door and ask for a quick sight of the moon or stars. I would swell out my chest and rush to get my coat, already telling the visitor what planets were in the sky.

Education has come to me through the years unconventionally in fits and starts. I am of the working class, and education beyond high school was never stressed, in fact, was actually discouraged. Daydreaming of going off to college when each paycheck had to be stretched to meet the current bills seemed a waste of time. Most of the McLaurins had built up a reputation as dependable, hard workers and were usually able to get a steady job right out of high school. If you worked hard enough, you could have a nice car and maybe someday build a house. That was the basic dream, and for many people it is a fine one. My father was in his last days of life before he ever told me he wanted me to finish my college degree. I was fresh home from two years of living in Africa, and was not fond of the thought of sitting for a year at a desk.

"I don't want you to have to work like I did, son," he said. "I want you to go back there and finish that thing."

I was in the third grade when Ken, my mother's younger brother, brought me the scope one day. Like my mother, as a child he had traveled back and forth between two homes as the result of his parents' divorce. In high school he proved himself at the top of his class and entered the University of North Carolina. There he fell prey to the good times, soon dropped out because of lack of money and poor grades, and joined the Air Force for four years. He had been discharged and was working his way into the broadcast journalism field as a reporter when he gave me the scope. Maybe he had found better ways to fill dark nights. I like to think he had learned what secrets the glass could reveal and sought to pass on the chance for discovery. He showed me how to turn the knobs and gears that moved the scope and focused it, pointed out a few of the brighter night objects, and left me with a book of basic astronomy and a mind whetted by my first glimpse of the Sea of Tranquillity drawn closer to my backyard. I soon discovered the scope was not just a tool of learning, it also could be a weapon of defense.

"You live in a shack," James Fisher smirked, his first volley of fire whenever we argued. "It looks like a nigger house."

"Well, your mama's fat," I retorted. "She's big as a brood sow."

"But you live in a shack. You have to burn wood to keep warm and you don't even have an indoor bathroom. The fenders are falling off your dad's truck."

"Maybe so," I admitted, my voice starting out low but building with confidence as I brought forth my shotgun defense. "But I got a telescope."

James's mouth stopped before he could form his next word. He had to concede or at least stumble when confronted by that fact. I did own the most coveted object of any boy in our third-grade class. True, until I was twelve we did live in a house that more materialistic people might have considered a shack. The house was badly in need of paint—a squat frame cracker box with two bedrooms, a kitchen, and a living room. We heated with a kerosene heater and wood firebox, had only cold running water in one kitchen faucet, and did our daily business in a chipped, chronically full chamber pot. But the dwelling was dry and warm and was home. James was an only child in a neat house with a carport, watched a color television, and wore new school clothes that were in fashion. Our friendship was a shaky alliance that held together mainly because we were distant kin on my mother's side, shared a common interest in the night sky, and were the closest neighbors of the same age. My mother's people were generally a notch or two higher on the social totem pole than the McLaurins. Many of them lived in the city and at family reunions banded together and regarded us as poor country cousins. James's mama was indeed fat, and though he eventually begged his parents into buying him a scope, it was a toy compared to mine.

A clear night under an early autumn sky, low humidity, camped with my brothers in the field behind our house, the campfire burned to a bed of coals. My brothers snored as I gazed into the vast blackness of a moonless heaven. The Dipper had swung high on her axis to pour rain on some distant land. An owl hooted from the deep woods. Seconds stalled into eons. I recalled the preacher's last sermon as he told of eternity and how a million years would not equal even a second of endless life. I wished one of my brothers would awaken, even more that I might nestle under the covers beside my mother and cling to her.

A fireball plowed through the sky coming from out of the east, a large meteor that had punched into the atmosphere dangerously close to earth. The dark canopy above me was suddenly rent by a flume of fire, the head of the meteor seemed to tumble and break into splinters, the tail stretched across the curve of sky. The fireball streaked and disappeared behind the treetops in the west. The flash of illumination startled several chickens to cackle from their roosts. I leaped to my feet expecting to hear a nearby explosion, but heard only the grumble of the chickens, again the distant call of the hoot owl. Against the sky a trail of vapor glowed eerily like a new finger of the Milky Way. That flash of heat and light restarted my inner clock and rushed me forward to real time. I looked at the meteor as an omen. Life was marked by chaos, and even in the seemingly ordered expanse of the sky, there might be sudden fire. Compared to the cold drag of eternity, to travel swift and in brilliance, to burn one last image against the sky, seemed comforting.

I WAS raised caught between the differing pulls of the Primitive Baptist and Southern Baptist religions. My mother and Granny's chosen faith was Primitive Baptist. It is an old sect, the beliefs and customs dying out today. When I attended church as a child, we only came once a month, for that was as often as the church met. The other Sundays we attended a Southern Baptist church near home. The congregation of the Primitive Baptist church was made up of mostly white-haired ancients. The interior of the church was as simple and plain as the white clapboard exterior. The wooden benches weren't padded, the windows were of clear glass. The pulpit was a simple podium standing at the front. In winter the church was heated by a black coal-burning heater. Summer heat was carried away by the draft of open windows and hand fans. Hymns were sung without the accompaniment of organ or piano, the old voices mingling and contrasting as they told of eternity and redemption.

We always came with Granny. My father worked those days, but probably would not have come anyway. He always said his God lived in the fields and woods. We would be scrubbed clean and wearing our good clothes. We were the only children who regularly attended; the old people would smile at us and tell Mama how good we were. One old man always gave us a stick of gum.

The first thing we looked for when taking our seats was how many preachers sat behind the podium. On a typical Sunday two or three preachers might show up, men who were not paid for their sermons, but felt called by God to speak. The service might last two or more hours. We always hoped for a minimum. After a couple of mournful hymns, one of the preachers would stand and grasp the podium. He would begin by speaking slowly, waiting for the spirit to move him. He prepared no sermon beforehand, but believed that whatever he was moved to say would come from the mouth of God. Sometimes a preacher would talk for several minutes, waiting for his message from God, then sit down, explaining he had nothing to say. But more often, suddenly, sometimes in midsentence, his voice would change, his words would lapse into a singsong cadence, and he would preach the words put into his mouth. He might go on ten minutes or an hour, but as suddenly as he began, his chant would cease, he might mumble a few more words, then sit down. Another hollow-eyed man with calloused hands would step to the podium, his mind searching for what he might say.

Once a year, all the Primitive Baptist churches in the area would gather for what was called association. If the weather was warm, the services would be held outside under the shade of an oak. Each family would bring food. Sometime around one o'clock, the preacher would rumble to a stop and mothers would go to their cars to begin spreading the dishes down a long wooden table. A lengthy blessing would be said by one of the adults, and at last we would be allowed to dig in. Fried chicken, pastry, vegetables, sliced ham, biscuits; we would pile our plates high and go and sit on a tree root. For dessert, a smaller table was laden with lemon and cherry pies, cakes and banana pudding. Between bites of food, people spoke of family, fortune, and illness and the events of changing times.

Following the meal, after the food was put away, the members of the church performed the ritual of foot washing. Foot washing is a practice of humility taken from the Bible story where Mary Magdalene washed Christ's feet with her hair. We children did not participate, for we were not members of the church, but the adults actually took soap and water, got down on their knees, and washed each other's feet. We were allowed to sit in the car during this service. In another car sat a retarded man whose mother attended the church. He would stare at us, drool hanging on the corners of his mouth. We were afraid of him and would make up stories of what he did to people at night. We alternately played and fought and argued until we heard voices gearing into the slow words of the last hymn.

I HAVE spent much of my own life searching through the back alleys of my mind for a definition of how I might describe God. A Southern atheist, I feel, is rare, for too inscribed in our heritage and upbringing is the belief that somehow this chaos is controlled by one who knows a good bit more. Despite my lack of desire for organized religion, I am confident that my basic faith has remained unaltered and undiluted through the crusades and revivals of growing up.

Mama used to say I was going to be a preacher. Early on, I would listen to her Bible stories and ask questions. Almost nightly she would read the Bible to us just before turning out the lights—stories of battles and miracles and giants and floods and famines. I enjoyed the stories and found a great comfort lying there beside Bruce under the warm covers. She would end the devotional time with a short prayer. But my questions remained stronger than her explanations. Somehow, answers of "It is not for man to understand," or "The world was different back then," or "It is God's will" did not satisfy my need to make sense of why good people died and eternity seemed frightful and how giants and centuries-old people once walked the land. And then again, I was always caught between the pulls of the two churches I attended.

The Southern Baptists were cut-and-dry. Heaven and hell waited just above and below the earth and clouds. A person—especially a child—was apt to be swept into either one between Sundays as swiftly as on a greased slide. The decision was his and could be immediately altered by walk-

ing to the front and kneeling and repenting. I cannot re-
count all the Sundays I suffered through extended verses of
"Just As I Am" while the minister pleaded with us not to
lose our last chance.

The Primitive Baptist preacher did not say that. After
the man hammered to a stop, his spirit-influenced chant
receded to a few stammered words, he would wipe his
brow, drink water, and call for one last hymn. As the old,
dry voices rolled without music through the words, he
would say once, "If there be any person here wanting to
receive Jesus Christ, let him now come forward." Through
my childhood, I saw dozens with streaming faces march to
the front of the Southern Baptist church. I cannot recall
once seeing one come forward at the Primitive Baptist
meeting.

But I saw just as many backslide as went forward under
duress to repent. How many classmates did I have who
weekly made the pilgrimage, but talked or behaved no differently during the week than I did? How many men did I
see throw fat wads of bills into the collection plate on Sunday morning, but spend twice that much on whiskey during
the week? I cannot recall ever seeing my father put money
into a collection plate, but I remember the smell of beer or
whiskey on his breath. I remember even stronger the
nights he rose to go and help another farmer deliver a
breeched calf or pull a man's truck from the ditch without
ever accepting pay.

What I could never understand about organized religion
was why a show of faith seemed so much more important to
people than simply believing the scripture. For all the
questions and seeming contradictions in the Bible, I did
believe in its basic teachings. The Ten Commandments
made good sense. The Bible also said that if a person believed in his heart and professed with his tongue his faith

in Jesus, he was saved. I did that early on. Believing in my heart was much easier than fully believing in my head stories that stirred too much argument. I was extremely shy as a kid, and the thought of marching to the front of a church was terrifying, especially when I had done what the Bible said a kid had to do to dodge hell—especially when the kids who made public spectacles of themselves seemed no more devout than me on a daily basis.

The Southern Baptists made sure you got the message. In fact, the preacher pounded it into your head during the sermon, then appealed to your guilt during the long, unending call to the altar. A painting of a river valley hung above the baptismal of Lebanon Baptist Church and was the loneliest scene of solitude and timelessness next to the night sky. The preacher always pointed at the baptismal scene before the choir launched into the first stanza of "Just As I Am."

"Don't you want to walk in the shallows of River Jordan, rest in the shade of one of heaven's own willow trees?" he began. "Won't you come forward to Jesus now?"

Gazing into that silent river valley, time halted again. I thought about the quiet duty of angels and compared them to the flash of a meteor. I remembered Billy Van.

BILLY VANN was a good kid, serious about most things, did his homework, kept his clothes clean. He was a member of my school class, president of the Sunday-school group I sometimes attended. We weren't good friends, but knew each other enough to talk. He wore good clothes like James Fisher and lived in a subdivision of brick homes, but never made a big deal of it. He burned to ashes one Friday afternoon when his uncle's propane truck overturned. Rumor said you could hear him screaming from inside the flames.

The night after Billy died, my mother hugged me and tried to explain why a good kid had to die so young. She told me that God sometimes called Christian children home to heaven early when he needed new angels. As she talked, I wondered why God couldn't just as easily have made another angel or at least let Billy die in his sleep.

THE church choir wailed through the first stanza and into the chorus, the preacher urged sinners forward.

"Just as I am without one plea," voices mingled and rose. "God's precious blood was shed for me."

"Won't you come to him now," the preacher pleaded. "Just step forward and say those words and free yourself from sin. Tomorrow might be too late."

I had no doubt I was high on the list of sinners. Not only had I never joined the church and been baptized and publicly cleansed, but I had managed to conceal a long list of transgressions that had never been discovered by teachers, the law, or my mother. Cheating on a few tests, rocks thrown at trains, a window or two broken in the Negro school, choice cusswords and dirty jokes—I knew nevertheless that any white child was welcome in a Southern Baptist church, and would be patiently waited on by the preacher to eventually confess his sins.

"Jesus is ready to wash your heart clean, take away your burden," the preacher stressed. "He wants your name on that list of those who will walk with him beside the River Jordan."

But seeing as how I was filled with sin, I was unlikely to get called home early for angel duty. I had known many relatives and neighbors who had lived lives of drunkenness and revelry and on their deathbeds repented. At their funerals, the preacher said they were now in glory. God seemed to be pretty tolerant of sinners and usually gave them ample time, and it appeared more and more as I grew older that if a person didn't get too carried away with sin, he might get by with a few things that were fun. Leastwise, he probably wouldn't get called home early, via a truck-wreck fire.

During the last stanza, the pressure to repent grew worse, the preacher pleaded that it might be my last chance to be placed on the scroll, the choir echoed in full urgent harmony. I weighed alternatives—risk damnation in hell or repent and be placed on the list of early angels. Could I slide by one more week?

I was saved more than once by the BB-shot hole in the window. Probably using a Daisy pump-action, someone mighty brave had punched a round through a lower pane. I always made it a point to sit in a pew close to that window. Squinting one eye and sighting on the hole, I used it like a gun port, trained in on a group of houses outside the church on a hill and in my mind rained them with machine-gun fire and mortar rounds. Flashes of fire and dust kicked up around the doors and windows, women and children ran from the homes only to be cut down in the hell of smoke and shrapnel. The preacher bowed his head for the prayer as the choir hummed softly the chorus before I felt it safe to stop the hillside barrage. The brief war shut off my conscience, rolled back the water of Jordan, and spared me another week of life.

BY NOT having to report for angel duty, I got a chance during my eighth summer for adventure, my first trip of more than a hundred miles from home.

My father's side of the family was tainted with a branch of Yankees. His oldest sister had married a soldier stationed in Bragg following World War Two, and returned with him to the rocky forested hills of rural Connecticut. Three girls and a boy about my own age were born to this aunt, and the yearly visits they paid to the South each summer became the high point of our vacation. These cousins talked with a clipped, funny accent, spoke of strange foods, of four-lane toll roads, and of snowfalls that stacked to the bottom of the windowsill. Their world seemed like a page out of one of the *National Geographic* magazines I loved to thumb through.

I turned pink with excitement the day I was asked to return to Connecticut with them for a visit. My grandmother and grandfather were going, we would all drive up crowded in their station wagon, we three Southerners to return in five days by bus, an adventure as awesome as traveling around the world to a kid of my experiences. We left the next morning at four o'clock, my feet clad in a new pair of K Mart sneakers, a crisp five-dollar bill folded deep in my pocket, my eyes brimming with wonder.

Somewhere in the drone of turning wheels, I drifted off to sleep as we drove north on Interstate 95, the kids packed like canned fish in the two rear seats. Maybe it was the mystical bump of the state line, maybe the blink of low sun between the branches and power lines that awakened me, but I suddenly sat bolt up in the seat, leaned forward, and inquired our whereabouts to discover we were in Virginia. All at once the sun and air took on a different quality, a foreign luminescence that seemed crystal and clean compared to the stagnant hot air I remembered from home. Even the trees seemed taller and grander, the cars we passed sported license plates of different color and design, the angles and jawbones and haircuts of drivers looked strange. I pushed my nose close to the open window and sucked down rare air.

Neither of my grandparents had ever been above the Mason-Dixon Line, so our trip north was routed with red marker on the road atlas to draw us off the interstate through some of the East Coast scenery. I had never seen a body of water larger than a lake, and was not prepared for the magnitude of the Chesapeake Bay Bridge. For miles the columns of the bridge loomed above the tidal marsh like a skyscraper. Our bottomed-out car finally took flight at the lip of the great structure and flew above the blue expanse of bay like one of the gulls that floated beside us on air currents. To leave sight of land on a ribbon of suspended concrete, then to dip into a dark maw and be swallowed by seven miles of tunnel was an assault on the senses of a kid who was accustomed to a life as slow and paced as the march of the moon through the night sky.

During the trip north, my Southern child's ear for sounds renamed some of the more familiar landmarks of the East Coast. I was astonished by the size of the highways and the number of cars that looped the major cities on the journey north. My Uncle Frank had been raised in the car-eat-car driving school of the North, and kept one hand on the horn and choice curses at the tip of his tongue. I wondered if we would live through the race down the Baltimore Distressway. I was awed crossing the bridge over the Atomic River (Potomac), and thought indeed the steel and iron ships and structure crowding the banks glowed with an unnatural glare. Best of all was seeing the Entire State Building from the highway outside New York City. After darkness fell on a long, cramped day we finally arrived in the small town of Danbury, Connecticut, to a house built on the slopes of a small green mountain.

In the four days that followed, I learned just how different, in more than miles, North Carolina is from New England. With breakfast, I found scrambled-egg sandwiches a figment of the past, replaced by creamed wheat or boxed cereal soaked with store-bought milk. The syrupy warm mornings were also gone, the Connecticut dawn as chilly as fall. The loamy, warm soil of our farm had been replaced by scrabble, rocky soil strewn with huge glacial boulders. The oak trees and sweet gum were traded for fir and maple. Small lakes dotted the countryside, fed by swift, cold running streams. My brand-new K Mart tennis shoes were no match for such terrain and were in shreds before I left. I quickly found myself on the other end of the accent jokes. Adults and children paused over my slow Southern tongue, and either mimicked me in good nature or acted like I was dumb.

Early evening proved to be most different from home, the cool air of New England unable to filter the sunlight in her last rays into the golden shade that hung over our fields, no mourning doves to call in the swarms of lightning bugs and lure troupes of bats, no pumpkin moon magnified by plowed dust and pollen hanging in the air. Sunset over New England was crisp and stark and hurried, no time to dwell in twilight and savor the day. We were soon in from the chill, eating a supper of hot tea and strange Yankee food like sausages and baked beans and squash. I found myself wanting corn bread.

In the middle of the last night, I awoke in the small cot where I slept in the living room and stared out the window at a moon that looked shades paler and ghostlier than the one over Dixie. The wanderlust for now had leached from me. As I stared at the window, I imagined it grew smaller, that I was being swallowed up and left forever in this cool, rocky land. I found my way to the bed where my grandparents slept. In the napes and folds of their old, weathered skin I still smelled sunlight, clay, and wood smoke, and between them snuggled into a nest where I stayed until daylight opened the window again, and it was time for us to leave on the Greyhound for home.

The return trip was a blur of passing humanity, fumes, and jumbled sleep. When my uncle picked us up at the bus station sometime early the following morning, I hung my head out the rear window and sucked in the warm night air and prayed he wasn't drinking bad this night, that he might not wreck and kill me before I arrived home, was able to wick my bare feet in the dew coating the fescue and hug my mother.

I WAS walking the June fields near home one Sunday afternoon when I was ten when I first held a poisonous snake in my hands. Church was still on my mind; the preacher had raged about Satan and the serpent and how the devil still embodied himself in lust, money, and liquor. Again, I had held with white knuckles to the pew while the call to repent droned through four stanzas.

At the bottom of a dead tree lay a large slab of bark from where lightning had splintered the trunk. I hoped it might hide a rat snake or blacksnake, or if I was lucky, a coveted chain king snake.

I carefully lifted the edge of the slab, excitement tingling down my arms. As sunshine flooded the withered grass, objects and creatures came into view—fungi, white grub-worms, and coiled and tensed the distinctive orange-and-chestnut markings of a three-foot copperhead. I dropped the slab and leaped backwards.

Half a dozen voices told me to walk away—no, run. I had collected nonpoisonous snakes for several years now and was becoming a self-made expert in herpetology, but my mother had forbid me ever to touch a copperhead, moccasin, or anything venomous. I recalled my Grandma

McLaurin's stories of encountering copperheads, how they could lunge for many feet and would strike repeatedly. I remembered the coonhound we once owned that had been bitten and lay swollen and whining for several days before dying. Mostly, I heard the preacher's words of how Satan reared up where we least expected him. I stared at the slab of bark and to the forked branch I held in my hand. I feared if I walked away now, I would continue walking away from many opportunities throughout my life, and only because someone had said I should.

I lifted the slab again; the snake hadn't moved. From reading, I knew that snakes really couldn't lunge more than half their body length and knew I was in no immediate danger. The copperhead lifted his head and vibrated his tail in mimic of a rattlesnake, but held his ground. I marveled at his colors, the contrast like a new and old penny held side by side. His tongue flicked out repeatedly. Using the forked oak branch, I shoved the slab of bark till it toppled over and my hands were free.

I was more than a mile from home and knew a bite would be dangerous, possibly fatal. But I wanted that snake. I raked him with the stick into the edge of the field, where he immediately coiled again, this time clearly on defense. I circled and he turned, tail a blur, his head reared half a foot from the ground. Several times I attempted to pin his head to the ground with the forked branch, but he dodged me or pulled free. Finally, I pinned him by the small of his neck and buried the ends of the fork in the dirt.

I moved quickly and without deliberation, kneeled and grasped the copperhead by his neck just behind the forked branch. I released the stick and grabbed the snake's body and stood up. He struggled at first, but I held fast, and after several seconds the copperhead relaxed and only continued vibrating his tail and repeatedly flicked his tongue.

I held something magic in my hand—the defeat of ignorance. The copperhead was incapable of twisting free and biting me, of hypnotizing me with his eyes, certainly could not speak evil to me. He was simply a wild creature that happened to have venom to kill his prey. Books spoke truer than folk tales.

I carried the snake home and put it in one of the cages I had constructed from scrap lumber and old window frames. I did not tell my mother I had caught the copperhead for several days. One morning I led her outside, saying I had a surprise. The copperhead was much calmer by then, and I pinned it easily before her eyes. When I told her it was a copperhead, she asked was I sure, and I pointed to a book opened to a picture of a similar snake. She stared at me for several moments, then told me to be very careful and never bring it in the house. Something in the way she looked last at the book, then into my eyes let me know that although she would not say so, secretly she was proud. I released the snake that fall.

NEXT to death, snakes are probably the greatest fear on earth. They will turn three-hundred-pound football players into jellyfish, stampede horses, haunt dreams, and cause imaginations to go wild. In the South, where there are dozens of species, the fables and outright lies concerning reptiles would fill volumes.

The fear of snakes may even outweigh the fear of death, or at least it did for some citizens living in our small crossroads farming community. I remember Bandy Williams, who calmly walked home from the tobacco field and got his twelve-gauge, returned, and blew a fist-sized hole in a white man's chest for throwing a dead blacksnake around his neck. A white jury sympathized and found Bandy, a black

man, guilty of manslaughter only. Two McNair brothers
drowned in the muddy torrent of the Cape Fear River after
a water snake fell off a branch into their boat and frightened them. A third survived only because he was passed
out at the time from too much wine. He awoke to find the
boat grounded on a sandbar, his brothers gone, and the
snake curled around one of the oars. You didn't play with
snakes. You shot them with buckshot, hacked them to bits
with a hoe, or ran them down with a car, then backed over
them several times for good measure. You simply didn't
play with snakes. Not if you were sane.

I was about six years old, barefoot for the duration of the
summer and tan as an acorn, the day I ran up on my first
live green snake. There was something about seeing that
snake eye to eye, maybe the fact that Mama had told me
never to pick one up, that made me grab it by the tail. The
snake wiggled and tried to double back to my hand, so I
began twirling it like a lasso. I walked the half mile back
home, swinging that snake around and around above my
head, yelping occasionally when it lunged for my hand. I
passed a few people who gave a wide berth, but said nothing. Everyone knew the McLaurin younguns were subject
to pinworms in the summer and an occasional bout with
head lice, and by heredity were in constant struggle between the pull of the pulpit and jailhouse. One of us going
crazy early was understandable.

I put that green snake in a mason jar, and from that day
forward, read every book I could find in the library on
reptiles, plus caught every one that crossed my path. I was
nine years old when I bought my first exotic snake, a beautiful six-foot-long Brazilian red-tailed boa constrictor, with
money earned in the tobacco fields. The boa cost me only
fifteen dollars, bought from the Tote-Em-In Zoo in Wilmington. The same serpent today would cost about three

hundred dollars. The boa was shipped on air freight into Fayetteville. My mother and several freight workers watched in a circle as I opened the box with a hammer, grabbed a coil of snake, and lifted. Grown men tripped over themselves retreating from that box as I lifted foot after foot of brilliant, coiling serpent. I was as proud as if I held the keys to a new car.

The first night I owned the boa, either a raccoon or a possum tore through the screen cage to the baby chick I had placed there for the snake to eat, which freed the snake and started a legend. By the time word leaked out the next day, the snake had already grown two feet. A week later, Miss Annie outran her two dogs to the house after stepping on what she claimed was a ten-foot-long snake as fat as a Coca-Cola can. Miss Annie let her pass dry on the vine. Over the years, half the community claimed to have seen the boa. Lily Parker swore she saw it crossing the road, its tail in one ditch, its head in the other. Braxton Beard said it ate one of his coonhounds, and John Bain said it climbed into his smokehouse and gobbled three smoke-cured hams. Mike Johnson claimed the boa busted the two front tires on his pickup when he tried to run it down. Last report had this nonpoisonous tropical snake still alive and surviving twenty harsh North Carolina winters, growing as fat as a small hog, and carrying a venom more potent than ten rattlesnakes.

Throughout my adolescence, snakes assisted me in getting high marks for show-and-tell, got me suspended a couple of times from school, earned me a few bucks from selling them to biology labs, and both helped and hindered my love life.

FROGS were chirping from the banks of the old gravel pit, a local smooching retreat for the youth of my area. I was sixteen, and dating Mattie Boyd for the first time, a sweet, freckle-faced country girl who looked like she had two cantaloupes stashed in her blouse. Before picking her up, I had spent two hours trying to clean the run-down Mercury my dad owned, plucking sprouted corn and wheat from the carpet where he had hauled home sacks of hog feed.

A full moon glinted on the water, the air was heavy with the scent of honeysuckle, and Mattie kept looking at me with big, damp eyes. During a half hour of small talk, I managed to work my arm to the back of the seat, and was looking for that final burst of courage to place my arm around her shoulders. Suddenly, in the midst of a sentence, Mattie's round face split with a smile. She wiggled happily, then scooted across the seat and wedged tight against me. I paused, trying to recall what I had just said that got such a response so I might use it again. At that moment, in that silver August moonlight, I spied a snake's head and neck coming slowly and smoothly over Mattie's shoulder from the backseat.

On the drive over to get Mattie, I had caught a huge rat snake crossing the road and dumped it in a pillowcase I carried for such events. Snakes are notorious for escaping through the smallest crack or hole, and somehow this snake had done so. My mouth dropped open, but no words would come out as I watched the snake come over her shoulder. Mattie's smile was bright as moonbeams as she waited for me to lean and kiss her, the snake continuing over her shoulder, then inching down her chest toward the cantaloupes. Her smile began to wane as the rat snake reached no-man's-land, and the glint in her eye dulled as if she were thinking, "And I thought he might be different from all the rest." I was making small animal noises in my throat trying to pry loose my tongue. With a sigh of disgust, Mattie lifted her right arm to remove the naughty hand from her breast. Instead, she snatched six feet of cold reptile into her lap. Mattie leaped across me with one fluid motion, going headfirst through the window and ripping her blouse where the little knob was off the door lock. She wouldn't get back in the car, even after I slung the snake into the gravel pit. She walked two miles home while I followed behind her, apologizing and illuminating the road with my brights. Time heals all—or hazes memories—and three years later when I returned from a stint in the Marine Corps, she married me.

Four years later, she unmarried me. I've never really decided if it was the snakes, maybe the emu I bought, or the monkey, the pair of aoudads, or possibly the six-month-old lioness I purchased with a loan from Dial Finance. Maybe it was a combination of them all, or simply that what seems romantic and exotic in a person often becomes impossible in day-to-day living. Anyhow, all bridges burned and the road before me, I began touring the Southeast billed as Wildman Mac—The Last Great Snake Show.

THERE I was, crouched in a motel room in Miami, holding the tail end of an Egyptian cobra, wondering which blade of my Swiss Army knife was best for opening an air-conditioning vent. The forward three feet of the snake had disappeared into the dark hole, hisses leaking out as the cobra struggled to free himself from my grip.

I knew I shouldn't have taken the cobra from the box, but I was curious to study it after driving all the way from North Carolina to Miami to barter a mess of canebrake rattlers with a reptile importer I knew. After the deal—plus downing a couple of tall Schlitz Bulls—my curiosity got the best of me, and I emptied the cobra onto the carpet. Immediately, it rose and spread its hood, staring me down with cold blue eyes, then, true to a snake's nature, it sought escape through the slats in the air vent. Only a flying dive had kept it from escaping. As I knelt there, I studied my options: keep holding on till I either pulled the snake in half or it tired and allowed me to pull it back out; kill the snake with my knife; let it go and get the hell out of town. I could picture the look on the desk clerk's face when I called from a pay phone and told him there was a four-foot cobra loose somewhere in his air-conditioning system.

Fortunately, snakes are pliable and lack claws to hang on with. After several minutes of pulling, the snake came out inch by inch, until the hot end emerged and I was able to sling it into the corner, pin its head down with my snake hook, and put it back in the box. I kept the cobra locked up the rest of the night, while I finished my beer and was finally lulled to sleep by the angry buzzing of a large eastern diamondback rattler I had also acquired in a trade.

The Last Great Snake Show consisted of several glass-fronted cages, a garishly painted canvas tent, and quite an assortment of reptiles. As a kid I had always been disappointed by the carnival snake shows, which usually had only a large python and a few other harmless snakes. I decided to give people their money's worth. After buying, catching, and trading snakes, I built up a menagerie that included two cobras, a coral snake, assorted rattlers, two rhino vipers, an African puff adder, one fourteen-foot reticulated python, cottonmouths, boas, and a five-foot Nile monitor that gobbled whole baby chicks. For a quarter admission, folks could see it all—watch me milk venom from rattlesnakes, see the bearded snake man drink the poison, and tarry as long as they liked, telling lies about the snakes they had encountered. It was difficult for me, as I sought to tell the truth about reptiles, to stand there and listen politely to some old geezer as he raved on and on about the ten-foot snake that caught up with his pickup once when he was driving fifty miles an hour down the road.

The snake show took me to some interesting places, introduced me to many unusual people, and turned a decent profit. Along the way, I became so bold at handling snakes that I would let the coral snake crawl through my fingers and reach into a cage and lift the puff adder out by his tail—he was a very poisonous snake whose bite would probably have proved fatal. Once while driving down Interstate 95 in my beat-up Ford van, heading for another show, I noticed something moving to my left. I turned my head to see one of the cobras lying on the armrest, just inches from my wrist. I eased over into the passenger seat while driving with one hand and applying the brake with an outstretched leg. I finally stopped in the emergency lane, pinned the snake, and resumed driving.

It took two rattlesnakes to convince me finally that carelessness with poisonous snakes was crazy. I was in the sauce again—Wild Turkey bourbon—and trying to change the water dish in a cage while holding the flashlight. The two rattlers were only a foot away from my hand, cocked and loaded, but not buzzing because they were accustomed to my body odor. I'd had one snort too many and dropped the water dish, startling the snakes and causing both to strike at once. A large canebrake rattler tagged me on the back of my hand; a smaller but very poisonous Mojave rattler buried one fang in the knuckle of my little finger. I snatched my hand away and gasped at puncture marks beginning to lose blood. You're in for it this time, McLaurin, I thought. Double bites. Don't even know where the nearest hospital is. Could lose a hand at least.

Years before I had been bitten by a small copperhead, and I knew that a bite from a pit viper begins stinging immediately and swelling like a wasp sting. In a state of mild shock, I stood there staring at the bites, waiting for the pain to start. It never did.

Poisonous snakes can bite without injecting venom, and miraculously I had received what herpetologists call "dry bites." After several minutes passed, I realized I had received no venom, just a strong warning from two rattlers drawing short on patience. The next morning I released both snakes in the forest and swore off Wild Turkey. Soon after, I met the woman I married for good, the mother of our daughter and son.

We had already been out a couple of times before I brought the timber rattler to Katie's house. Someone had worked on his neck with a dull hoe, leaving a four-inch gash that was filled with maggots. I had doctored snakes before and knew that because of snakes' natural resistance to infection, the rattler had a good chance of recovering if I could stitch him up. All I needed was someone good with a needle.

I placed a pillowcase filled with rattler beside a bowl of ambrosia in Katie's refrigerator. In thirty minutes' time, the rattler had cooled to a point where he was listless and easy to handle. I cleaned out the wound with alcohol while Katie took several deep breaths to steady her hand. The wound was stitched up as tightly as needlepoint, and I released the snake to the wild several weeks later. Less than a year later we married.

Katie has proved to be a patient woman. One night, she woke me by vigorously shaking my arm. "There's a snake in the bed," she hissed.

"You're dreaming," I mumbled. "Go back to sleep."

"I'm not dreaming. I felt it crawling over my arm."

"Go back to sleep."

She proceeded then to stand up in the middle of the bed

and demand that I get up and turn on the lights. Grumbling, I obeyed. I pulled the mattress aside to find a four-foot-long corn snake that had gotten out of his cage—harmless, but a cold bedfellow.

Katie gave me one of those narrow-eyed stares that let me know I should tread lightly for a couple of days, but otherwise forgot the incident. But I have kept a mental list of the things she has endured and done—like darning a rattlesnake's neck—that will keep her beautiful to me long after she is wrinkled and gray.

Except for the boa that lives in our guest bathroom, I don't keep snakes captive any longer. I prefer to see them in the wild, scales catching the sun and flaming with iridescence, spiraling around a limb or draped over a rock like a single strand of muscle. The natural habitats are going fast, as are the snakes, and the birds and animals. I suspect that soon the sight of a barefoot child toting home his first pet snake will seem like something from a Mark Twain tale. But I hope that some of the people who watched gape-mouthed as I showed them a cobra's fangs, or marveled at the satin skin of a king snake, learned at least that a snake is made of flesh and blood and it is not something to fear because someone said to fear it.

I was working in a small carnival one weekend in South Carolina when a lady from the hootchy-kootchy came in. I had watched her for several nights from the flap of my tent as she advertised her wares on a small stage, her ample curves stuffed inside a red sequined dress, face caked with makeup, already several years past head-turning days. But tonight she was in jeans and looked like any of the timid, curious people who wanted to see the snakes.

"You don't have to pay," I told her, "since you're with the show."

Still she dropped a ticket in the box. "I just wanted to

peek in," she said, her mascara streaked under her eyes where she had sweated while doing nude gyrations backstage for a crowd of bug-eyed boys and men. "I'm scared to death of snakes."

I took a red-bellied mud snake from its box and began showing it to a knot of kids. A mud snake is glossy black-and-red, with scales smooth as butter and a temperament as mild as a kitten's. I passed the snake around to anyone who wanted to touch it. The strip queen stayed at the back, close to the door.

"Aw, come on," I coaxed her. "Touch it. You think I'd let these kids rub it if it was dangerous?"

She took a full minute to finally come within range, then reached out her arm, one finger extended. Her lips were pursed, every muscle in her body on red alert, her eyes darting back and forth between my eyes and the snake. I realized that she was a woman who had probably been lied to and fooled countless times in her life. Finally, she touched the snake with the tip of her fingernail, then the end of her finger, slowly moving the hand forward until she was rubbing the snake's spine with her palm. Suddenly, the muscles in her face relaxed and she smiled, her eyes glittering like someone ten years younger. She stood there while I put the snake away, then waited until the group of kids left.

"What'd I tell you?" I said. "Felt better than silk, didn't it?"

She nodded. "My mama always told us that snakes were slimy and cold."

She leaned forward then and kissed me softly on the cheek, barely brushing my whiskers. She smelled of Juicy Fruit, cheap perfume, and the lather she had worked up while strutting her stuff under a hot floodlight, giving some kid his first taste of the apple. But her kiss seemed almost virginal and sinless now, much like the one Eve might have planted on Adam's jaw in those innocent days before she was taught to fear serpents.

————

A GOOSE to my rear end, and I might have decapitated myself and risen headless there in the early-morning hours of Christmas. I was on my hands and knees, thrust through the broken pane of a French door that divided the living room from the kitchen. Beyond that door lay our Christmas toys set in separate piles, the wrapping paper catching the light from the tree and glinting like a small, unique galxay. I was peeping at our coveted toys without waking my mother, who slept lightly in the next room.

"What you see?" Bruce whispered loudly, nudging me with his foot. "Let me look."

What I saw was a wonderful scene of packages wrapped quickly in Christmas paper, a fir tree cut from the woods behind our house and dressed in tinsel, glass balls, strings of holly berries, and popcorn, a sock from each of our feet nailed to the mantel and stuffed with fruit and candy. The air smelled of greenery and citrus fruit. I withdrew my head reluctantly, tucking in my chin to clear the edge of the broken pane.

My brothers and sister and I all went insane each year in late November. The first holiday catalog, usually either from K Mart or Sears or J.C. Penney's, infected us. We'd rip through the pages, eyes bugging at the collection of trucks, bikes, games, cap pistols, and other cheap toys. Within the first week we wanted a hundred different things but then would have to narrow the list to fit the number of gifts my mother decided we could budget. The number usually ran around five presents of our choice, plus a surprise. Our Christmas gifts were supposed to supply our

year except for something on our birthday, maybe a toy
boat or airplane purchased in midsummer. Each selection
was made with careful thought and agony, hours spent por-
ing over the slick pages. Our choices reflected much of our
individual ages and personalities.

My sister, Karen, two years my senior, was the firstborn.
She inherited my mother's brown eyes and hair and gentle,
nurturing character. Her choices for Christmas were the
same as most other girls', baby dolls and tea sets when
little, later on LPs of the Beatles and Tommy James and the
Shondells, clothes and dime-store makeup as she grew into
adolescent and teenage years. As a female and big sister to
four younger brothers, she suffered most in the hard financial years of our youth. She was acutely aware of the ap-
pearance of our house, the lack of an indoor toilet, her
often outdated fashion in clothes. I remember her tears of
frustration and shame when my brothers and I would burst
laughing from behind a tree or fence where we had spied
on her attempts to learn the steps to the Twist or Mashed
Potato. She endured, usually behind a forced smile. When
I was thirteen and my parents built the small brick house
that stands as the homeplace today, she was rewarded with
her own room, while the brothers continued to sleep two to
a bed. Today, she has been married for twenty years, her
warm eyes and smile untainted. Her oldest son will soon
graduate from the state university, the vanguard of what I
hope is a new tradition for his brothers and cousins.

Bruce was born eighteen months following me. He has
always been a meat-and-potato man, quiet in his thoughts
and quick to anger. When eating dinner, he devours each
item on his plate in turn before changing to another food.
As a child, his toys were things with wheels—trucks as a
kid, a bicycle when his legs were long enough. Today, he
drives a semi for Yellow Freight, will give you the shirt off

his back if he thinks you need it, but is still as guarded in revealing feelings and thoughts as the tousle-haired child I slept with.

Keith, the knee baby of our family, as child and man is a curious mixture of Bruce and myself. As a kid, he also loved toy trucks and dirt, but was also the only one of my siblings who shared any interest in looking through my telescope. As a kid, he was a bit of a crybaby, a tendency that Bruce exaggerated almost daily for having bumped him from Mama's knee. Once when we were kids and piling brush my father had cut to clear a pasture, he announced with wide eyes and extreme seriousness, "We are really here on earth. We are really alive."

"Of course we're really alive, dummy," the rest of us hooted and laughed.

"But have you ever thought about it?" he continued above our catcalls. "We're really alive."

As a teenager he experimented heavily with drugs and rebelled most against my parents. The philosopher in him thrives today. He repairs heating and air-conditioning units now, owns a Harley, but is happily married and the father of two children. I talk most easily with him of life and the possible afterlife; he likes to sit in the cool of the evening and watch his nesting martins swoop in while daydreaming of riding his bike slowly across America. I doubt he ever will. He realizes his fantasy of traveling *Easy Rider*–style across the country would suffer at the reality of busy highways, hot, dry air, and bugs in his teeth.

Danny is the last of the brothers, born a year following Keith. He was a skinny, silent child, so timid he had to repeat the first grade. We'd trade him nickels for dimes by comparing the size or persuade him to do our chores with simple words of praise. For Christmas, he loved anything that was wrapped and new, but could spend hours playing with a shoe box dragged on a string. Today, all that has changed. He grew into a six-foot-three-inch electric company lineman with arms the size of my calves. He is gregarious, lives at home with my mother, loves the land, animals, and open spaces.

I never believed in Santa or the Easter Bunny or the Tooth Fairy. Even at age eight, the thought of a man who flew in a sleigh pulled by reindeer didn't hold water for me—a kid who had seen Saturn through his telescope. None of us kids believed in Santa, but that did nothing to dampen our enthusiasm. We knew our gifts were bought during our mother's Tuesday trips to town and hidden at Mrs. Bell's house. She was our closest neighbor, a quarter mile down the road. Tuesday was payday for my father, and Mama would drive into town to get his check, cash it, buy groceries, and pay past-due bills. We would sneak across the field when we saw Mama pass our house on her return, and watch through the bushes as she made a couple of trips into the old woman's home, carrying oddly shaped paper sacks.

The days till Christmas crept past agonizingly slow. Two weeks before Christmas, school let out for the holiday. I began marking the days off on a calendar. This was still in the days when television holiday specials and cartoons were pretty scarce except for maybe a Bing Crosby White Christmas Special. The Grinch and Charlie Brown and all those characters were still on comic pages or in people's minds. Chores were scarce in the winter, and with no homework there was not much to do all day but hunch over the catalogs and mentally play with our new toys. We scanned the sky and hoped for signs of snow, but I can remember maybe one real snowy Christmas in my life. With a few days to spare, my father found a shapely fir in the forest and cut it and brought it home. My mother kept a large box of tree decorations in a closet top, and the first night of the tree we trimmed her with glass globes and fake ice tinsel and those fat, nonblinking colored lights. We strung red holly berries and popcorn on sewing thread. The presents my mother bought for her brother and for my grandparents were wrapped and placed under the tree. Karen gathered us boys in the bedroom and reminded us that we'd bought nothing for our own parents. We planned a secret trip to the store. We had only a few quarters between us, maybe a wrinkled dollar, some dimes or nickels. The money was found in either the washing machine or by searching the folds of the couch and armchair. I explained to Mama that we needed another dollar, but I couldn't tell her why we needed the money or why we all needed to walk to Mrs. Smith's store. She nodded and faked ignorance.

Walking through Beard, we gawked at the Christmas trees and wreaths decorating our neighbors' houses. We bought my father a jar of Aqua Velva shaving lotion, my mother a pair of hose and a box of chocolate-covered cherries. Somehow, the money Karen held in her fist was just enough to satisfy Mrs. Smith. She nodded and smiled over our good choices, even added a few pieces of penny candy to the sack. We slipped the presents into the house and wrapped them with newspaper and baling twine.

Christmas Eve finally arrived. That day has always held a magical quality for me. The air is clear and sweet. Even cold rain beads on tree limbs and wilted grass like jewels. We always gave the animals a little extra feed, a pat on the head or scratch on the belly for the tame pig or cow. I had read that animals talked on Christmas Eve, and though I didn't believe it, I liked to imagine they would speak highly of us for the extra rations. The day dragged by impossibly slow; we scanned the catalogs again and worried that we had not chosen the right toys. We printed our names on

school paper with big letters in crayon and taped the cards
to spots in the living room where we wanted our gifts
stacked. I read to my brothers stories about the red-nosed
reindeer, the baby Jesus, and Santa. We dressed and prepared for bed early, even though usually we were as hard to
get in bed as we were to get up in the morning. The house
had no central heat; I remember glasses filled with water
and left by our beds crusted with ice occasionally on very
cold nights. Mama warmed our pillows on top of the living-
room heater, and when they were close to scorching, we
dived under the cold covers, private heaters in hand. As
always at night, she read us a passage from the Bible, then
prayed. Of course, on this night she read us again the story
of when the angels visited the Christ child. Her last words
were for us not to budge from bed until she called us the
next morning.

Soon after the lights were out in our room, I heard the
truck crank up in the yard. My brothers and I scurried from
our twin beds, Karen from her cot that sat in the corner of
the same bedroom. We all gathered at the window and
watched the taillights as my parents drove up to Mrs. Bell's
to fetch our gifts. After a few minutes, they returned, and
we heard their whispers as they brought armloads of presents into the living room. Occasionally we heard them
laugh, the clunk of heavy objects, the clink of tools needed
to put something together. The air smelled of coffee mixed
with the good odor of pine boughs and orange peel. Finally,
the noise stopped, and I knew my mother and father were
retiring for a few hours before he had to rise and go to work
at the bakery. My brothers were sleeping, air whistling
through their mouths. I tied my alarm to one of my big toes.

My alarm was made of several tin cans tied close on a
string so they could rattle. The string was looped through a
nail driven into the ceiling and bent double, then tied se-

curely to my toe. My theory was that when I slept I always pulled my knees close to my belly. If I went to sleep on Christmas Eve—perish the thought—I'd wake myself when I drew my legs up by rattling the cans. String tied in place, I lay stiff on my back, legs stretched straight, and imagined what all those gifts would look like stacked under the colored lights.

I always went to sleep, the alarm never quite worked, but always somehow I awakened in the early-morning hours, usually a couple of hours before sunrise. I bolted up in bed, jerked the string from my toe, then sneaked to the closed door and listened to hear that all was quiet. Then I woke up everyone and we trooped to the French doors.

My father always worked on Christmas Day, usually reporting to work about four in the morning. I never remember him watching us open the gifts that he worked such long hours to provide. In his youth, he had been one of seven children raised during the Depression. If the fall crops had produced well, he might get a fresh orange for Christmas, or if he was very lucky, an article of clothing. I thought that impossibly sad. My mother had grown up easier. Her mother was a nurse, her father a clerk. But their failed marriage caused her to spend many of her holidays rotating between two households. Though my father could not express his feelings in words, I know that as he cranked his old truck and drove away from our lighted windows on those early Christmas mornings he left in pride. Through the window were warm sleeping children, a wife he loved, wholesome food, and a tree surrounded with gifts.

Our whispered chatter woke up my mother. She warned us to get back in bed. We obeyed her for a few minutes, then lined up to peek again. About six in the morning, the sun still an hour and a half from rising, we begged her from bed. She made us lie down again while she turned up the kerosene fire to warm the living room. Finally, she told us to line up, opened the French door, and said, "Go!"

I hold mild contempt for people who have the restraint to open gifts by carefully removing the ribbon and unsticking the tape. We flew into our gifts, elbows and hands a blur, shredding paper and tearing through pasteboard and plastic. The first gift was pulled from the box, given about two seconds attention, and laid aside, another started on. After the last gift was opened, the socks were pulled from the nails on the shelf, contents spilled on the floor—fruit and hard candy, maybe a plastic racing car. We sat with our gifts stacked between our legs, our mouths filled with candy, and looked and touched and gaped for a few moments before sorting out which one to begin playing with first.

The scientist in me showed through at Christmas. My choices from the catalogs were plastic dinosaurs, a chemistry set, a battleship, and a launchable rocket. As the room warmed, play began, a race of toy trucks around the couch, under bombardment from my scale destroyer, GI Joe attacked by a brontosaurus. The play rocked the cluttered room while we waited for the sun to rise enough to allow us outside, and the air filled with the good smell of eggs cooking along with bacon.

Joy goes fist in hand with heartbreak. I can't remember a Christmas that a bicycle was not pulled from the crate minus the handlebars, a toy truck with a broken wheel.

When I shot a spring-loaded missile from my battleship toward Keith's truck, the missile arced across the room and landed on top of the kerosene heater, slipped between the slats on the grille, and fell on top of the scalding fire drum. Despite my frantic attempts to retrieve the missile, before my eyes it shriveled, then caught fire and burned, filling the room with black smoke and a terrible smell.

On another Christmas, dawn finally illuminated the fields and pasture. The day was blustery; a chill north wind blew that was mixed with sleet. I carried my rocket outside. The foot-long missile launched on a thick rubber band was supposed to dart skyward a couple hundred feet, then return to earth by parachute. I stood in the front yard and slung that rocket into the air, saw it leap toward the clouds, where it hung for a moment, then began to fall. The top of the rocket opened, the chute unfurled and blossomed. The launch was perfect. I jumped up and down shouting with joy and excitement until I realized how strong the wind was. The last I saw of the rocket, it was whipping back and forth on the breeze as it traveled over the tops of several distant trees.

But there were other presents inside. The loss of one rocket, a truck minus a wheel or a baby doll minus her bottle, could never spoil such a day.

We ate Christmas dinner at midday at my Granddaddy Raymond's house. He was my mother's dad, a big man with a quick temper who never was very fond of small children. He was married the second time to a woman named Mollie who was very sure she didn't like step-grandchildren. We sat on the couch like timid mice and waited for dinner. Mollie brewed tea without sugar, the bitter drink sharply contrasting with the sugary concoction my mother made. In trying to drink Mollie's tea, I gained one of my first realizations that the world had no set rules.

My granddaddy gave us socks for Christmas. All of us, even Danny when he was barely out of diapers, got socks. That was also one of my earliest lessons in learning that sometimes it was important and polite to lie.

"Oh boy! Look, Mama, I got socks," I said, holding up my pair.

"I did too," Karen said.

"Me too," my brothers sadly echoed. We waved our socks like flags.

We usually ate supper at Granny's house. She was Mama's mother, a very serious woman who didn't even give us socks for Christmas. She did have something that more than compensated. She had a color television. She picked us up in her car in the midafternoon and drove us to her house, where we watched the Christmas specials, sitting close to the screen as if we were glued there.

My father met us after work at Granny's. He arrived in his white uniform, the creases dusted with flour, his person smelling of freshly baked bread. We gave him the gift we had bought with his money, and for a few moments he let down his guard, smiled, and even joked. He shook the gift, weighed it in his hand, smelled it, and listened to it for a clue. He guessed wrong. After tearing off the paper and faking surprise he opened the bottle and smelled it and smiled.

"Your eyes may shine, your teeth may grit," he said, "but this here present you ain't gonna get."

We howled with delight. He set the bottle back down, probably never to touch it again. We glued ourselves to the next color television program while baking mincemeat and sweet potato pie filled the house with good smells. As the day fell into shadow, I realized sadly that another Christmas was rapidly passing, and that the wonderful anticipation and enchantment of awaiting Christmas Day was worth much more than a lapful of opened presents. Christmas rose high above reality, was a time when a child or parent could truly believe in Santa Claus, the Christ child, and reindeer that flew. Maybe the new year would bring a bout of flu, disease might strike the hogs, and the bills would start to roll in. But for a brief few weeks those worries seemed trivial when compared to one's dreams. My father as a boy had delighted in a fresh orange for Christmas; he and my mother gave me plastic rocket ships. But more important, in the warm glow of that kerosene heater, I possessed the security and confidence that one day I might fly a real rocket to the moon. I could give no more valuable gift to my own children today than that trust. Tear into that tinsel, child, through ribbon and cardboard, cast it all aside, and go for what you know lies inside. Worry about the future next week or the next; this charmed day, this era in your life, will pass too soon.

I BLAME Granny's color television for sparking a fear of dark clouds that I carry today. There, on the screen of that first, wide Zenith, I met the Wizard of Oz.

I was about six years old the first time I watched *The Wizard of Oz.* I knew this had to be a big deal when my mother told us we were going to Granny's to eat supper, and on a plain old Saturday, too, just for the purpose of watching a television program. Actually, I thought we were going to see something called the Lizard of Oz. I had never heard the word "wizard," assumed I was hearing wrong, and imagined a creature like the blue-tailed skinks that skittered up and down our porch walls.

I fell hopelessly in love with Judy Garland at first sight of her singing "Over the Rainbow." I was scared silly at the sight of the tornado hanging from the cloud and writhing like a snake. I was bowled over by the dazzling color when Dorothy opened the front door into Munchkin Land. I had nightmares of the witch and of the monkey men for nights after seeing them swoop down and carry off Dorothy and Toto.

A couple of years ago, I tried to interest my own daughter in that wonderful movie, hoping the same enchantment might seize her, too. I remember bringing home a video copy of the movie for her to see after telling her how special it was. She watched half the tape, then asked if she might go see a girlfriend and play. I felt crushed and betrayed until I realized she had seen movies of the likes of *Indiana Jones and the Never-Ending Story* with special effects and camera tricks so elaborate that the tornado in *The Wizard of Oz* must have looked like a dirty sock. I asked her to sit on my lap and watch it with me while I told her of the first time I had seen the movie and how it scared me. She hugged my neck and told me she would not let it scare me this time, that I had to just remember it was make-believe. Somewhere in the tunes and dances of the Cowardly Lion, the bug bit her too, and I believe at last count she has watched *The Wizard of Oz* at least a dozen times in her brief seven years. Now I tell her she can only watch it when it comes on as a yearly special so she does not become bored with it. I still get misty-eyed when Dorothy says goodbye to the Tin-man.

FOR all the enchantment and near-hysteria that Christmas brought to our household, Thanksgiving in comparison was a simple holiday, not distracted by the greed associated with gifts, but a simple union of people giving thanks for a huge table of food.

The centerpiece of the table was usually a fat hen, goose, or duck, depending upon what was most abundant in our chicken yard. They came free. I was in my teens before a store-bought turkey ever crowned the table. My father killed the fowl with an ax, cut his head off clean with one chop. Often I had to hold the fowl's head to the chopping block, and the big bird would roll his large blue eyes up and stare at me. At those times I would make myself recall how the goose had chased me in the pasture the summer before, would remember the scar on my leg where a rooster had run me into a barbed-wire fence when I was small. One clean chop, the head would fall, the body would leap and turn flips, I would stare at those blue eyes, still open and staring, but now filled with a look of awesome wonder. As soon as the goose stopped turning flips, the body would be ducked in a bucket of scalding water to loosen the feathers. My brothers and I would begin picking. As in all our chores at that age, we expended the least energy possible, more of our time spent arguing over who was working harder than actually cleaning the bird. We had a saying, "Whoever eats the most goose eats the most feathers." We knew my mother would finish the task by lighting a piece of newspaper and singeing off any remaining down.

As on Christmas, my father worked on Thanksgiving Day, so our big meal was always held at night when he was home. All day my mother would labor, cooking a conglomeration of vegetables, meats, and breads that represented nearly every meal we had eaten the past year. A goose baked brown and crisp, giblet stuffing, corn, cured ham, biscuits, butter beans, sweet potato pie, potato salad, rice, gravy, field peas, dumplings, cranberry sauce, coconut cake, iced tea, deviled eggs, all the food piled on the table and served buffet-style. We'd begin with a blessing, the same one my father or mother always said, the one I use in public even today: "Dear Lord, thank you for this food and our many blessings, Amen." If my father was in a good mood, usually spurred by a couple of beers, he might add, "Bless the meat and damn the skin, open your mouth and cram it in." My mother would scold him; we children thought it delightful. We'd eat helping after helping until we resembled round, gorged ticks. The leftovers would circulate through meals for days afterwards, the goose skeleton finally picked clean.

The most memorable Thanksgiving of my life occurred when I was a young Marine home for the holiday.

I was walking the tightwire of Marine life, polished boots and brass, living under inspections and commands. My hair was cropped short, face clean-shaven. Fighting troops had pulled out of Vietnam, and I was confronted daily with a public that had little respect for soldiers.

My brother Keith was in the midst of his rebel years. He wore his hair down to his shoulders, had a wispy beard. He smoked pot and did chemicals and constantly butted heads with my father. Midnight had passed, and I lay on the fold-out sofa bed in the living room unable to fall asleep. Keith was still out. From the creak of bedsprings in my parents' bedroom, I knew Mama was still awake and worried.

He drove a souped-up Dart Swinger that had a reputation as one of the fastest street cars east of the river. The engine was cammed and was fueled by a Holley four-barrel carburetor. I was drifting into sleep when I heard a car throttle up after crossing the railroad tracks in Beard, the same grumble as my brother's engine.

The ole boy is finally getting home, I thought, and smiled. I pictured him driving with his head out the window, trying to sober up and wash the smell of marijuana off his clothes before getting home. I had done the same on many nights.

The car came fast, whining through four gears. I listened and waited for him to let off the gas before getting to the sharp curve in the road just before our house. He kept accelerating. I sat up in bed.

Brakes began squealing as the car went into the curve. I heard several sharp bangs, then a heavy thud and silence.

The door to my parents' bedroom jerked open and Mama and Dad emerged, my father pulling on his trousers. I hopped out of bed into my own jeans.

My mother's face was white with terror. "He hit that ditch wide open," she said. "God, don't let him be dead."

Dad motioned for me to come with him. My mother followed us to the door. Dad turned and grasped her arm.

"You stay here in the house now, hear me?" he ordered. "He's all right."

The night was moonless and cold. Across the yard I spied the car upside down in the road ditch, one tire still spinning. A thin stream of smoke rose from the hot engine. The headlights burned dully.

Frost crunched under my bare feet as my father and I ran across the yard. I looked back and saw Mama coming down the front steps, the front of her housecoat twisted in her hands. No sound came from the wrecked car. My stomach was knotted in fear.

We were only a few yards from the wreck when I realized the crashed car was not my brother's.

"It ain't him," my father shouted at the same instant.

"It ain't Keith," I hollered at Mama.

We found two soldiers inside the car. They hung upside down, unconscious and suspended by seat belts. Beer cans littered the roof; blood gushed from the driver's split face.

"Call an ambulance," I shouted at Mama, who now stood at the edge of the road. Dad climbed through the smashed windshield. He talked to the men, both beginning to mumble and groan. I watched the smoke rising from the engine and prayed it wouldn't catch fire.

A state trooper arrived first; minutes later an ambulance screamed to a stop. In the chaos of flashing lights and squawking radios, Keith appeared. Mama grabbed him with both arms, as usual, fussing and hugging at the same time. Two hours later, the men had been carried to a hospital, the car pulled from the ditch by a wrecker. I lay again in bed, even more awake than before. I kept thinking of that silent car as we ran across the yard, believing my brother lay dying inside. I could not stand to cover myself with the bedsheet. I pictured the soldiers carried off by stretcher, white linen draped over their blood-soaked bodies.

The next day, little was said of the wreck as family members, in-laws, and girlfriends congregated around the table. But when we bowed our heads and my mother gave thanks, I felt for the first time how truly blessed we were, how good fortune should not be taken for granted, and how close is the boundary between mourning and thanksgiving.

YEARS later when I was invited to Memphis to sit down with my future wife, Katie, and her family for the Thanksgiving meal, I was reminded again of the diversity of customs and memories between families. Katie had told me of her fondness for Thanksgiving, and I agreed wholeheartedly, conjuring up visions of my mother's packed table.

Seated at a fine dining table, we ate with polished silver. Each dish was passed and served in turn. The meal consisted of a baked turkey, corn-bread dressing, cranberry sauce made from whole berries and orange peel, rice, and gravy and rolls. A black butler filled our tea glasses when they ran low. Dessert was a good mincemeat pie. The food was wonderful, but a far cry from the feeding frenzy at my mother's table. Later I mentioned this to Katie, but the look of hurt that rolled over her face at my criticism made me backtrack and close my mouth. I realized then that she had probably never cared for the free-for-all meal that I placed only below Christmas on my list of holiday memories.

MY FATHER had arranged a deal with the Merita Bakery where he was able to bring home leftover bakery products to feed to our hogs. Almost daily he brought home a couple of barrels of swept-up flour and leftover dough that he would mix with water and stir with a shovel blade into a thick slop. Often he would bring home several dozen loaves of bread that had passed the sale date in the company store. We ate some, the rest would be mixed into the slop. Together, the mixture made a good hog feed that helped top our hogs out early in growth and get them to market. We dreaded what concoction of hog food he would bring home, would count the barrels and boxes in the truck bed. The food was free but meant more work.

One day when I was about ten, I heard my father's truck rattle to a stop in the yard. I looked out the window, expecting to see the usual paper barrels filled with dirty flour. Instead, the truck bed was heaped to overflowing with an assortment of odd-shaped packages and bright colors. I heard one of my brothers shouting and rushed to see what had arrived.

The pickup was full of cakes, doughnuts, and pastries. The package date had passed, and the salesmen had taken them from the store shelves. After a day or two in the stale shop at the bakery, it was time to throw them away. Most every single cake or doughnut had at least a good week of freshness left; Dad had given the store manager a few bucks to let him load up. Layer cakes of coconut and chocolate, Mickey snack cakes filled with jelly and banana cream, powdered doughnuts, chocolate doughnuts, cherry tarts, and fried apple pies—it was better than all the holiday desserts thrown together at once, and all we had to do was burrow into the pile and eat our way through layer after layer before it was thrown to the hogs.

We ate till bursting, then went to get Lawrance Junior and his brothers and sisters. They were the children of a black family, playmates and our nearest neighbors. We told other friends who lived within walking distance, and for several days we filled a paper sack and took cake and pastries to school and gave them away. We ate sweets until we were sick of sugar and wished the hogs would hurry and eat it all. The sows and piglets and boar caught a new gear in their sprint to the trough when dinner was called.

For days after the sweets ended, even vegetables tasted better at the dinner table. We lost the couple of pounds we'd wrapped around our bellies. The memories of that truckload of sweets still lies in my mind like the Bible stories I heard of manna.

WITH lots of children in our family, birthdays were never too far between. The day could be counted on to deliver a homemade layer cake, a box of Sealtest Ice Milk, and a round of "Happy Birthday" sung totally out of key. A birthday was good for one present. One year I requested a scuba diving mask. As my birthday arrived in mid-December, I had no hope of swimming with the mask in the gravel pit, even less chance of the cheap glass surviving until warm weather. But I recall many enjoyable minutes spent with my head submerged in a bucket of water marveling at a penny, a colorful pebble placed on the bottom, how my own breath streamed past in bursts of bubbles, as if I was exploring the bottom of the sea.

Even today, my birthday is good for cake and ice cream, a chorus of song, and a present from Mama. Often a week has passed since the real day of my birth, but regardless, my mother calls everyone over to feast and sing. Often my present is a pair of socks, but I am happy to receive socks today. The ice cream is cold, the cake gummy and sweet, and though I protest the song each year, I pray and hope we are all together to celebrate another year.

CHRISTMAS is still magical to me, but gone is that childhood fascination with what gifts I will receive. I live the holiday more and more through my own two children, the exuberance in their eyes. I look for the spirituality in the holiday, find a growing satisfaction in what I might give to others.

Eventually, the childhood Christmas left me, and evolved into a spirit that was calmer but more lasting and real. One Christmas I decided not to use the tin can alarm, and I awoke to find the sun already peeping through the treetops. For a second I wanted to sleep even longer, but then I almost wanted to cry. I was unwilling to face the fact that we had not peeked that night for the first time ever, that we had slept while my father cranked the truck and drove to Mrs. Bell's, returned, and wrapped our presents— that we had not dared a cut throat to gaze upon the pile of gifts we had coveted for two months in hours spent fixed on the K Mart toy catalog. Or maybe I was just as unwilling to admit to myself that I was more excited now about the bottle of perfume I had wrapped under the tree to give to a girl in one of my junior high classes, or that for the first time this year I had bought my mother and father gifts with money I had earned bagging groceries—a sweater for my mother, a flashlight for my father, gifts I had chosen with thought and pride. I had to face the fact, I was a child no longer, and the job of standing sentinel on Christmas Eve had to be passed to one of my younger brothers, the legacy told one day to my own children. I slipped the string from my toe and knew I'd never wear it again, rose from bed, and began to wake my brothers.

———

THE origin of life was understood early on our small farm. All of us kids had seen a stallion led to breed with a mare, rearing and snorting when he spied his lady friend. The mare would hear him, her vagina would blink, they would be released to couple in a brief, almost fierce slapping of sleek bodies. We had all seen dogs and hogs and goats and cows breed and give birth. Our old cat Martha liked to crawl into bed under our covers where she felt safe and throw a litter of squirming kittens during the night. I remember the time my mother and sister and I pulled a colt from his mother by tying a rope to his protruding hind legs. Gasping and straining, the mare neighing with one sudden, final pain, we jerked the young stallion into the world, cleaned the mucus from his nose and mouth, and watched him stand and nurse on trembly knees. We understood why we sometimes heard noises coming from our parents' room when the door was closed and we were instructed to stay away.

With the birth of such a continued menagerie, pets were a part of my childhood and rearing that was as varied and taken for granted as the changing seasons. Puppies and cats were constant, tame farm animals usually around at least until they reached maturity. I managed to haul home a respectable number of snakes, mice, and hamsters, and the hunting season brought temporary wild creatures to our house.

A young possum was curled under my chin, his tail wrapped around a lock of my hair. Under the covers with

Bruce and me were six or seven more of the ugly marsupials, each curled warmly in a fold of cover or clothing. We were "Mama," our tits baby bottles filled with milk or sugar water.

My father brought the possums home from a hunting trip after the dogs killed the mother during a chase. He had pulled the babies from her pouch and placed them in his coat pocket, believing they would all die soon. Possums are among the oldest species of animal on earth, and their fight to survive came through. After arriving home, Dad placed the young possums in a pasteboard box next to the kerosene heater.

The possums were too young to remember their real mama for very long, so the next live body with food took her place. Anyone holding a warm bottle of milk would do. They soon learned to crawl out of the box and go searching for Mama. The season was still early spring, nights still cold; the possums burrowed down under our covers and kept warm. They are ugly, grinning creatures, slow of wit, but when one is curled under your chin, it is hard to throw from the bed. Over the years of my childhood, we raised several litters of possums until they were large enough to release. Even today, I slow my car at the sight of a possum lumbering across the road and wonder if it might be a descendant of one that warmed my bed.

Foxes were other wild pets. For a few seasons, my father and Uncle Bill trapped a couple of fox dens cut into the bank of an irrigation pond. The small spring traps were padded and set inside the entrance to snag the young kits. I realize now it was wrong to trap the animals for no other reason than the opportunity to try and tame them, but at that age I did not question my father's reasoning. He dragged the young foxes into the house tied to lengths of rope, the animals jerking against their binds, growling low in their throats and urinating on the floor from fright. Within a week, the kits ate raw meat from his hand.

A couple of the foxes died, some we gave away to other people, but we did manage to raise several until they were the size and temperament of young dogs. But they returned to the forest on their own, gradually roaming further and further from our house until the day they did not return, the call of wildness a stronger urge than the dust of our front yard.

Baby birds, young squirrels, tame piglets, bottle-trained calves. We hitched a large billy goat to a wheelchair we found in a dump and would take wild chariot rides across the pasture. We rode sleek, grass-fed ponies bareback—strung their mouths with baling twine and rode Indian-style down logging roads and through fields.

The ponies belonged to a full bird colonel who boarded them and a couple of fine horses at our farm. In return for their care, we were allowed to ride the ponies. I would command one of the ponies, Bruce the other one, and with a younger brother on back we galloped at breakneck speed, slipping and sliding and holding on to a handful of the mane. Occasionally, the pony would shy and throw us, or we would simply slide off the sweat-soaked back. We'd cuss, cry, then thrash the pony with a switch a lick or two for throwing us and climb back on.

My father had a tendency to buy and trade animals when he drank. Many times he rattled to a stop in our driveway, well intoxicated, a new billy goat or ram tied in the truck bed. He once brought a pony home in the rear seat of the old Mercury. One day he arrived with twenty-five brain-damaged ducks.

The ducks were acquired through a friend of a friend, a man who worked cleaning a research lab in Raleigh. The ducklings all had received brain surgery as part of an experiment. Their heads were shaved and they walked strangely and tilted their heads as if they too were drunk. They would have been put to death with chloroform had not my father asked for them.

Dad put the ducks in an unused dog pen in the backyard. They quickly learned to identify him as the source of food and would meet him at the wire, quacking hoarsely and flapping their wings. Over the next couple of months, he spent hours slowly feeding them corn and stale bread, occasionally talking to one that ate from his hand. He put a tin washtub in the pen and filled it with water, then put duck after duck into the artificial pond. Soon they were splashing and dunking their heads and acting almost normal. I didn't care for the ducks. They were noisy and emptied their bowels like someone spitting tobacco. I knew when slaughter time came, my brothers and I would be picking duck down for hours until we were breathing the stuff and would never get them clean enough to suit my father.

The ducks grew into fat young adults. They still walked as if they were drunk and quacked in a strange pitch that reflected their tampered-with brains. Sometimes they flapped their wings as if some primeval corner of their brain suggested flight, but their bodies were too heavy, wings too weak to actually take to the air. They began to eat a lot of food. Dad announced we would slaughter the birds the coming Saturday. I moved my garden peas around with my fork and wondered how he could feed and water and talk to an animal for months, then chop off its head or sell it on market without a hint of remorse.

I awoke that Saturday morning early as usual. I crawled from bed and went quietly to turn on our old black-and-white television set and watch the horror movie on *Sunrise Theater*. Something was odd about the morning—something missing—and I realized I didn't hear the ducks quacking and fussing inside their wire. I went to the window.

The pen was empty, the door swung open wide. I gazed across the pasture and saw my father standing a quarter mile distant on the bank of our irrigation pond. He held a paper sack in his hand. The water of the pond was alive with splashing, diving ducks, swimming circles and chasing minnows and living in natural bliss. I walked outside and watched open-mouthed for half an hour.

Finally, my father began clapping his hands and calling "Duck, duck, duck, duck" in a high voice. He tossed a couple of pieces of torn bread on the ground. A duck came from the water to eat, one followed; he walked backwards and dropped more bread. Soon the ducks exited the water in mass, too greedy to miss any food. Dad made his way across the pasture, dropping a trail of crumbs, the ducks gobbling the food at his heels. I slipped back into the house so my father wouldn't know I had watched.

Dad came inside and filled a cup with hot coffee. He gruffly roused my brothers from bed and told me to turn off the television. We ate a quick breakfast and were soon outside, grabbing ducks, getting bitten, and holding them while my father methodically chopped off their heads. Soon the air seemed filled with snow as my younger brothers grumbled and argued while pulling feathers. But I did not blame my father now for killing what had been his pets. He had given them months of life, a final treat of swimming in a real pond. As I worked, I thought of what I had seen that morning and clung to that image—a strange pied piper high-stepping and leading to slaughter a flock of thoroughly satisfied, deranged ducks.

MY FATHER'S ABILITY to communicate with and understand the animal kingdom applied even to wasps. I never once saw him get stung, while my siblings and I were always getting ambushed by yellow jackets or hornets or those fat brown wasps that made me swell like an egg.

Usually, getting stung was our own fault. A football-sized wasp nest covered with stinging varmints was extremely attractive to a boy holding a dirt clod or rock. A well-placed throw would tear down the nest and send out an avenging cloud of the insects that always set us racing ahead of the storm. Even more alluring was the danger and satisfaction in getting close enough to the nest—a matter of a couple of yards—to sling a can of gasoline on the wasps. If done right, the wasps dropped instantly dead like hailstones. If my aim was a little off, a few of the wasps escaped and attacked, sending me slapping and screaming on my way to the house.

My father simply ignored wasps. He would work within two feet of a nest and never even glance that way. The wasps or hornets would rattle their wings on standby alert, but never attack.

We were filling the barn with bales of hay one summer day. The old barn was dotted with wasp nests along the edges of the ceiling. I had been stung once already, the afternoon was hot, and we were all tired. As the bales of hay were stacked higher and higher we got closer to the nests. My brothers and I kept track of the nests from the corner of our eyes; my father berated us for our fear.

"You act like they a bunch of damn snakes," he said. "You don't mess with them, they won't mess with you."

My father's job was throwing the bales up to the top of the stack where Bruce, Keith, and I fitted them into criss-crossed layers. We stayed away from the wasp nests, often leaving gaps and holes in our work. Finally my father could stand our shoddy labor no longer and scrambled to the top of the stack, cursing and belittling us. He grabbed bales of hay and jammed them into the gaps. We huddled as far from him as possible, fearing a cloud of wasps would descend any second.

"You act scared of a wasp, it *will* sting you," Dad scolded. "Y'all walk around with your tail between your legs all your life, you won't never be shit."

He worked within inches of the nests. The wasps buzzed their wings, poised like planes on an aircraft carrier. I hoped mightily he would bump a nest and they would attack, swarm him like a plague of locusts, and sting him a hundred times, that he would have to dive from the top of the stack of hay bales, swatting and cursing and scrambling for his life.

He wasn't stung once. When the last bale slid into place, he dismissed us with a look of disgust that was worse than hard words.

FOR all the assortment of odd animals and pets we had access to, dogs and cats always took top bill. A truer pal than a black-and-tan hound is hard to find. Cats—I could have done without the whole lot, but they multiplied in our barn and hayloft and were always around whether I liked them or not.

Joe lived with us nearly ten years. He was a black-and-tan coonhound who preferred a shade tree to a hunt and never wandered off our property unless following at my heels. He gained a certain amount of fame the night he treed the four coons I shook out of the persimmon tree. He had the beautiful deep bay of a chase dog and was good at barking at strangers, and was allowed his food for no more than his watchdog capabilities. He believed in guerrilla tactics and would often bark at strangers from behind a tree. He fought my friend Lawrance Junior's dog, Tag, whenever we egged the two on—a halfhearted battle that involved more growling and snarling than biting. Tag died one afternoon after bloating from eating too many soured hog guts. Joe was given away one day to a man who lived in the next county, a decision my father made under the influence of whiskey. I was pushing twelve when the dog was loaded up, but I cried just the same. Joe ran off from the man's house the first day he was taken off a chain and headed cross-country in search of home. I never saw him again, but have wondered if the old animal met his fate under the wheels of a truck or in the gas chamber of some county dog pound.

We lived with a female Chihuahua for fourteen years. Her name was Button, a happy little red dog that loved to sleep under our covers. She probably gave birth to several hundred registered puppies over her years; they were sold by my mother to help pay the bills. As Button grew older, she liked more and more to lie in the yard on warm days and rest under the song of birds. One day a Greek restaurant owner who had come to buy and slaughter goats ran over her as she slept. We buried her in a shoe box in the backyard, prayed over the small grave, sang hymns, and discussed whether there was a dog heaven.

The cats caught hell. Between being chased by dogs, hunted by me and my brothers with homemade bow and arrows, and occasionally herded together and taken to the animal shelter, the litters of cats revolved in and out of our lives in a blur of tabby and calico fur. If such adversity was not enough, any cat that dared enter the house was subject to my mother's arm.

Cats are either extremely hardheaded or extremely ignorant. A cat that has discovered the pleasure of lying beside a warm heater will risk life and limb to get inside each time the door is opened. Most of my childhood, I had to contend with one or more cats who staked out each side of the door, and at the slightest crack slithered through, between or around my feet, and bolted under the sofa. Once under the sofa, the cat would lie low until his presence was forgotten, then slink over and eat leftovers from the counter and curl up and sleep and shed fur on top of my mother's good Sunday coat.

The cats rarely got past my mother. She learned to open the screen door and begin kicking at the same time, scattering cats to the wind. Any that did slip past were promptly poked from under the couch with the broom handle and carried by tail, writhing and squawling, to be slung back outside through a hole in the top of the screen. As Mama neared the door, she would lean back and heave that cat sometimes twenty feet into the yard, where it would scamper to the barn and lick its paws.

I remember that screen door being torn out at the top for several years. My father worked terribly hard keeping us clothed and fed, but had little time or interest in performing odd jobs around the house. Torn screens, leaky faucets, and loose boards were common.

I'm not sure why my father finally decided to fix that screen. Maybe it was the flies that were able to invade the house freely or the mosquitoes that buzzed us at night. Whatever his motivation, my brothers and I watched as he stretched and fitted the screen and carefully tacked it into place. The door looked nearly good as new. He stepped back a few feet to admire his handiwork.

With the door open, all the cats had gotten inside. My mother had been in the bedroom folding clothes and walked into her kitchen to discover a cat standing in the middle of the table, spraddle-legged, lapping at a bowl of banana pudding set out to cool. From the yard, I heard her angry scream and the sound of thudding feet.

Mama was mad. She grabbed the cat by his tail and started beating him with her free hand. The big old tomcat started yawling. Through the screen, I could see Mama coming. She was glaring at the cat, still beating him, the feline's legs locked out straight, his fur raised. Mama dropped one shoulder as she neared the door, going into her wind-up. In her fury, she didn't notice that the screen was fixed.

I had but a second to leap to one side. The brand-new screen exploded in the middle, the tomcat sailing right through it like a cannonball. The cat landed a good thirty feet into the yard, Mama's record, even with having to bust through a new screen. He bounced once and streaked for the barn.

My father's mouth dropped open, his body sagged. He turned and threw his hammer toward the pasture, and without another word, stomped away. He never fixed the screen again.

Mama also despised the chickens that ran loose in our yard. Several of the hens had a habit of roosting on the windowsills and coating the wall with droppings. But the chickens were tolerated; they brought fresh meat to the table, and eggs. However, the transition from barnyard to dinner table was a far cry from today's ease of picking up a precut, ready-to-cook fryer from the grocery store.

Our job was chasing down the chicken. The chase usually became a free-for-all, the bird squawking and running in circles, my brothers and I laughing and tripping each other. The dogs would join the chase. The chicken was finally nabbed and carried to my mother at the edge of the yard.

She would wring the bird's neck by grasping the chicken by the head and twirling it like a lasso. The spine would snap, and the chicken would be dropped to the ground to leap and turn somersaults in death throes. Mama would bring a bucket of scalding water from the house and dip the dead chicken, making sure all the feathers got wet. The steaming bird was then given to us.

The chore was one of our most dreaded. The feathers had to be pulled from the skin, and they were hot and stuck to our fingers. The hot chicken would smell strongly of manure. My brother and I would bicker over who was doing the most work. Finally, a nude chicken would be in our hands, a goodly assortment of pinfeathers still embedded in the skin. The bird would then be carried inside, where Mama would fuss at our poor work, while she began to gut and cut up the unfortunate fowl. The innards would still hold the warmth of life, only minutes departed from the easy duty of crowing at the rising sun and eating worms and bugs.

———

AN EARLY-MORNING SUN blinked between sweet gum branches upon two men holding gamecocks in the crook of their arms. I stood with my friend Bobby, sipped from a half-cold beer, and watched a Southern ballet unfold. Each bird was armed with three-inch steel gaffs which had been carefully mounted over the natural spurs on their feet. The men talked to the birds, blew air in their faces, rubbed their legs—each using perfected personal tactics to ensure that his cock was ready to fight hard and kill quickly.

"Ready, boys?" shouted Larry, a beefy potbellied man in work clothes, his jaw packed with a dose of Red Man. "Let's get 'em in the pit."

The pit was a three-foot-tall circular fence made of chicken wire, about twelve feet in diameter. At the edge of the woods was another makeshift "drag pit" made from cinder blocks where the match would be carried if it lin-

gered too long and held up other fights. Occasionally fights
lasted a couple of hours. The two cock handlers, or "cockers" as they are sometimes called, and Larry stepped over
the wire and stationed themselves at opposite sides of the
ring. A diverse crowd began to cluster around the pit, including several old men wearing shined shoes and pressed
shirts, several biker types in cutoff jeans, their arms
wrapped in green-and-black tattoos, and a former state patrolman standing beside a trucker still wearing his Roadway uniform. Small children peeked through the wire.
Young women with heavily powdered faces stood on the
fringes in tight jeans, cutting their eyes at several short-
haired guys probably from Bragg. Local farmers were scattered about, Saturday's plowing still clodded on their
boots. Bobby and I had just arrived from Fayetteville.
Bobby turned away, and ignoring the prefight rituals, he
busied himself getting his birds off the pickup and into the
shade.

Larry kicked a rough spot in the recently turned damp
soil in the ring, then used the toe of his shoe to draw lines
about ten feet apart. "Line 'em up," he said, the two men
kneeling and holding their birds by their tail feathers, one
hand against their breasts. Both roosters were Brown/Reds
and looked nearly identical, except that one had a greenish
tint to his legs, the other a pearl leg. Both were stags,
meaning less than a year in age, and both fighting for the
first time. The birds eyed each other. One cackled, bobbed
his head, and blinked. The handlers talked to the stags,
wiped dirt from the gaffs, blew air on their heads.

"Face 'em," Larry said. The handlers picked up the
birds and allowed them to peck and bite each other, becoming angrier and angrier. "Flash 'em once," Larry ordered.
The handlers took a step backwards, then swung the birds
toward each other, causing them to flap their wings. "Put
'em on the line."

The handlers knelt again, holding the stags by just the tail feathers. "Pit 'em," Larry shouted.

The stags rushed together when released, wings beating the air, their feet hooked viciously. The pearl-leg jumped higher and went over the back of the green-leg, turning a flip on the dirt. The stags whirled to face off, necks extended and feathers fluffed like dust mops. They hesitated for only a fraction of a second before the green-leg attacked, rising two feet off the ground on blurred wings, pushing the pearl-leg backwards onto his back and stabbing just under the loose skin at the base of his neck.

"Handle him," Larry shouted. The handlers rushed to unhook the birds and put them back on line.

SUNDAY morning began early for me and Bobby as he prepared to drive up to Wake County for the fight. A sliver of moon hung low in the eastern sky, and the grass outside his ramshackle frame house was heavy with dew. He carefully placed four cocks inside the "keep box," a cage with small partitions and a wire front. These select birds had been chosen from the yard two weeks ago and placed in the "keep house" in cages where they were conditioned. The birds were fed a special concoction of grains, eggs, and vitamins. On several afternoons the birds were "muffed out," a practice where the cocks are fitted with padded muffs and allowed to spar. Saturday night, the birds were injected with vitamin B-12 for energy and vitamin K to speed blood clotting. After placing the keep box in the bed of his truck and covering it with a blanket, Bobby drove north, knowing his birds were as fast and tough as any in the state.

We found the blue Vega parked beside a telephone booth at the crossroads, just as he had been told we would. The man inside nodded hello and gave him directions to where the fight was being held. Bobby found the small dirt lane a mile below the crossroads, cutting between two tobacco barns and leading into the woods. He eased down the road to the entrance of a quarter-acre clearing that had been cut of undergrowth with a bush-hog mower and raked clean. Six pickups were already there, and another seven or eight were coming. There was only one way into the clearing, and a lookout had been posted with a walkie-talkie and loud brass whistle. Cock fighting is a misdemeanor in North Carolina, and it's illegal in most states in the union. Transporting a cock across state lines to fight is a much more serious violation of the Animal Welfare Act, and is punishable by a fine of five thousand dollars and a year in jail. Bobby had been busted twice at cockfights, but still strongly defended his right to participate in the sport.

"Yeah, it's brutal. I'll admit that," he said. "But it's not one bit worse than a lot of other things. Women walk around in fur coats. It's perfectly legal for a man to gun down doves and rabbits and deer and leave them to rot on the ground. But let a man fight some chickens and the newspapers and television tries to make him look like a pervert."

Bobby is a short, muscular man in his mid-thirties. He served with the Army in Korea, and today is a machinist foreman in a large company that makes aircraft parts. He pays his taxes, votes, and except for fighting cocks and occasionally guzzling a tall Budweiser while driving home from work, stays within the law. He feels cockfighters are persecuted unfairly while many types of hunting are exceedingly cruel but legal, not to mention the thousands of animals killed for research or the clothing industry.

"Colonel Sanders got rich over killing chickens," he argues and smiles. "Thomas Jefferson and Lincoln were cockers." His face snaps serious again. "You can run a deer for miles with dogs, wound it three or four times, then lose it in the brush to die slowly, and that's perfectly legal and considered sport. At least my chickens have a fighting chance. I fight a cock five times and he wins, I retire him to a life of chasing hens. I love these birds. One of my cocks out there fighting—that's me out there. I sweat and bleed with him."

Larry counted to twenty while the handlers worked on their stags. The pearl-leg bled from his neck, but the wound was only in the flesh and of little consequence. Each handler dipped one hand in a can of water and wiped his stag's face, then pressed his mouth to the bird's lower back and blew where his testicles were located to warm them and start the adrenaline flowing. "Get hot now. Get hot," the pearl-leg's handler whispered.

"Line 'em up," Larry said when the count reached fifteen. The handlers crouched with the birds. "Pit," Larry shouted at twenty.

The stags slammed together again, each bird throwing flurries that made Ali look slow. The crowd pressed against the wire, shouted encouragement to their favorite stag. A small honey-blond girl about six years old shrieked and jumped back from the fence when the fight rolled her way. Each stag cut the other several times, but none of the cuts were deep and the fight continued, the birds feinting and slashing, each trying to keep his attack above the opponent. The green-leg lost his balance and fell on his back, and the ivory-leg cut him deep in the side before he could spring up. The gaff hung in his flesh. "Handle them," Larry shouted. The handlers leaped to separate the birds. The ivory-leg tried to cut with the other foot, and stuck his handler in the finger before the birds were separated. The gaff entered the man's skin at the first joint of his index finger and poked through at his fingertip beside the nail.

The handler pulled the gaff from his finger and moved his bird back to the line, ignoring the wound as if it were a brier scratch. Immediately he began blowing on the stag's testicles. Across the ring, the handler of the green-leg assessed his bird's wound, allowed the stag to stand loose before him while he watched his movements. The cut was deep and the bird's breath began to rattle, but he was still strong and not fatally stabbed. The handler caught the bird and heated his testicles, then sprinkled water on his head. Larry was at twelve with the count.

Bobby continued to ignore the shouts from the crowd. He weighed his cock on a scale, writing down the poundage, then handed the paper to Harold, the organizer, who was matching birds by weight. The fight was a "hack fight," in which individual breeders dicker with one another and bet whatever they agree upon. Bobby preferred hack fights to "derbies," in which there is a set entry fee with the winner of the most matches taking the prize. He agreed to fight his number two cock next against a similar bird owned by a man from Greensboro. The bet was fifty dollars.

Number two was a large Gray that had already fought twice. Bobby took the cock from his cage and talked to him. "You gonna kick ass today, fellow? I got fifty that says you will."

Bobby handed me the bird so I could hold it while the cock was "heeled" or prepared for battle. Bobby pulled his first-aid kit from beneath the truck seat. The kit contained narrow strips of gummed moleskin, a spool of dental floss, a pair of scissors, and two pairs of stainless-steel three-inch gaffs mounted on bands of leather. The gaffs had been honed until now they were as sharp as hypodermic needles. Bobby stuck strips of the moleskin to the cock's legs just above and below the spur, then wrapped the spur. Then the gaff was slid over the spur and the leather band wrapped tightly with dental floss to hold it in place. The cock remained calm while the gaffs were mounted, as if his small brain understood the necessity of wearing three-inch daggers. With the gaffs tied securely, the cock was put into a collapsible "throw pen" where he waited for his turn in the ring.

Bobby cracked the tab on a cold, tall Budweiser. If he was lucky, he would go home with a couple hundred extra dollars. If not, he could go home broke. The air was heavy with the acrid smell of charcoal still burning off a dousing of kerosene. Mitchell, the man who owned the land, would soon throw hot dogs and hamburger patties on the hot grill. The food was free. For those who had not brought a beverage, he had beer for sale and shot glasses of bonded whiskey or corn liquor by the slug. From an open door of a king-cab pickup, the amplified voice of Waylon Jennings spilled and mingled with the crowing of cocks, the shouts of the spectators, and the coo of mourning doves from the deep woods.

"Line 'em up," Larry called. "Y'all ready? Pit 'em."

The stags were released, and again they clashed together in a whirl of feathers and cold, sharp steel. The green-leg was stabbed in his mouth, but the gaff came loose and he responded with a flurry that backed the ivory-leg to the fence. The ivory-leg tried to leap in the air, but one of his gaffs snagged on the wire and he was jerked to the dirt. It was then that the green-leg stuck him deep in his breast, all the way to the hilt. As the stags struggled to stand, the gaff twisted in the wound.

"Handle that cock," Larry shouted. "Handle him."

"Hot damn, he cut him then," someone shouted.

"He's killed him," another said.

The ivory-leg was hurt, and as Larry counted, the handler did everything he could to revive the bird. He heated up the stag's testicles, then put the bird's bill in his mouth, sucking out the blood that had begun to drip. The bird was breathing raggedly, his lungs rattling where fluid filled them. Across the ring, the green-leg's handler blew air on the bird's anus in an attempt to cool him. He dripped more water on the bird's head, then blew on his back. Larry shouted for the handlers to get the stags back on line. "Pit 'em."

Bobby sipped his beer and studied the way his cock strutted around in the cage. He looked good with the gaffs on, a tough knot of feathers and lean muscles lacking enough sense to fear death. Bobby still paid no attention to the shouting. Most cockers stay with their birds until it is time to fight. Cheering for or betting on another man's cock was reserved for the many spectators who came just to get drunk and wager a few dollars. Two men and a woman walked up to where Bobby and I leaned against his truck. The men were red-eyed from smoking reefer. The woman was a mousy, skinny little thing who acted like she had been backhanded once too often. She puffed at the joint when it was passed to her, her forearms puckered with gooseflesh although the morning had already warmed above seventy degrees.

"Morning, Bobby," one of the men said and extended his arm. "This here is my brother and his wife." Bobby nodded at the woman and shook hands with them. "Fine-looking Gray you got there. He fought before?"

"Twice. Other fights didn't go past the second pit."

"Yeah?" the man said, raising one eyebrow. "Well. I'm gonna put a ten on him. Cocky-looking little sucker."

Bobby offered the men a beer, but one of them patted his back pocket where a pint of Jim Beam rested. The hot dogs were on the grill now, and the smell of meat cooking wafted

through the trees. Two black-and-tan coonhounds wandered up and busily marked truck tires. Bobby helped himself to another beer. The *ka-chunk* of the can being opened
made the cock hop and turn to look. He crowed and flapped
his wings.

The ivory-legged stag was fading fast, and already a couple of men in the crowd had passed money. The handler
held his bird on line with one hand cradled under his
breast. Blood dripped on the ground from the stag's wound,
and from where the handler was gaffed. "Pit 'em," Larry
shouted.

The ivory-leg was a fine bird and still game to fight although he could barely stand. The green-leg hit him with
both feet, knocking him on his back. He lay there for several seconds, the green-leg pecking at the side of his head.
Finally he drew on his last spark of breed and pride and
responded with a flurry, but was too weak to cut. The
green-leg stabbed him again deep in the breast, burying the
gaff. The ivory-leg suddenly looked like he had turned to
clay, in a second's passage the color lifting from his feathers, his beak and face gone ashen and gray. His neck
bowed and his eyelids slid down to half-closed. Frothy
blood came from his mouth and rolled to his back. The
green-leg hit him again, then stood over him pulling tufts of
feathers from the side of his neck. "That's it," his handler
conceded, his own face suddenly aged and drawn. The
birds were separated. The slain stag would be carried
home, where he would be cooked and fed to the dogs. The
victorious bird would go home to rest and grow and fight
again.

The spectators slowly disbanded, some hurrying to fix a
hot dog and grab a cold beer before the next scuff began.
Several people gathered around Bobby as he lifted the cock
from the pen. The bird moved his head in jerks from side to

side. The sun was high now in the branches, and the cock's tail feathers caught the light and glowed like hot coals. His eyes were wide and glittered like wet, cold bullets. Bobby drained his beer and threw the empty can into the bed of the truck.

"That's a fine-looking cock you got there," someone said, but Bobby was no longer listening. He was talking to the bird, telling him how strong and mean he was, how he was going to retire him to a life of chasing hens. He massaged the cock's legs while walking him to the pit, put his lips on the bird's back, and blew hot air on that primeval spot to start the adrenaline flowing. The pit had been raked level and wet down again, and there was no evidence that two cocks just fought. Waylon Jennings's voice was still heard above the din as he sang a ballad of good whiskey and bad women and hard living.

FOR me and my brothers, the most despised animal on our farm was the hog. Like many families back then, we kept a few sows and a boar hog and topped out a few litters each year. We would butcher one or two and salt the meat, sell the rest on market for much-needed cash. Raising hogs involves a lot of work. Also, where you find hogs, you usually find a lot of mud, hog manure, and odors. We especially dreaded slopping time.

The trick was getting the slop into the troughs without being trampled by a herd of hysterical hogs. They had to be fed away from the fence so they wouldn't bust down or hurt themselves on the wire. We were afraid of the hogs. Hogs would bite. Once I had seen the remains of a goat that had been eaten alive by hogs after getting its head hung in fence wire. I had horrors of slipping in the mud, dousing myself with slop, and being devoured before anyone could come to my aid.

We learned to pour a little of the slop over the fence upon the ground. The hogs would fight over the puddle of food, their attention diverted for several seconds. My father would hand me a bucket of slop over the fence and I would race for the trough, the swill splashing against my leg. Usually when I was about halfway to the trough, a sow would spy me, squeal, and lead the charge. I would pour slop along the length of the feeder, then leap to one side as a couple tons of hog flesh skidded to a stop.

Once the hogs were eating, we would pour a few more buckets of swill. But now the sows were too busy eating to bother us; we could squeeze between the animals to fill the trough and they saw only the food under their snouts. Some of the older sows would even grunt softly if you scratched their backs.

For all the hassles of feeding hogs, castrating young male pigs was far, far worse.

Like most chores around our farm, castrating pigs was put off until the last possible moment. The surgery is best done when the pigs are only days old, but usually when Daddy found the spare time, the pigs weighed close to a hundred pounds and were close to the mating age.

Imagine being held down, your testicles cut out with a razor blade, the wound then coated with burned motor oil. I couldn't blame those pigs for fighting against us, for squealing at the top of their lungs. My job was to hold the pig's head and try to clamp his mouth closed. Each pig tried to bite me, all the while squealing at a pitch that deafened one's ears. The other young males huddled in the corner of the shed where they were closed off from the rest of the herd. Outside, the sows crowded against the door to the shed, squealing their own rage over what we were doing to their sons. My father always got angry and berated us for not holding the hog tight enough, for letting it squeal. I gritted my teeth and wished I could tell him to shut up. If we had taken time to cut the pigs when they were newborn as most farmers did, we wouldn't be in this mess. We finished the pig and released him to the pig lot, where he walked bowlegged, his blood mingling with the oil and dripping to the ground.

———

"GET the boy up."

My father made the statement with only one foot in the door, pulling off his coat as he crossed the floor to the single cold-water spigot in our house. My mother stood watching him, a dishrag knotted in her hands, as he washed under the cold stream.

"What's wrong?" she asked.

"I ain't got time to stand here and answer questions. Get him out of the bed."

I wasn't sleeping, but had sat by the window and watched my father's flashlight bob as he came to the house from the barn across the field. The season was spring, nights still cold but wildflowers in bloom. A pastel haze of tender green sweet gum leaves muted the tangle of forest. I heard only silence in the kitchen and knew my mother was trying to stand her ground. My father was a good man in nearly every way, but was quick to anger when things weren't going right.

"That sow having trouble?" she asked.

"I wouldn't be standing here if she wasn't," he answered. "It's a breech and my hand is too large."

A moment of silence passed while my mother considered his statement.

"He can't do that, Reese! He's too young."

"He was old enough to shoot my chickens. Now he's old enough to help me with that sow."

The boards in the hallway groaned as she came to the bedroom. I was on my father's bad side for ambushing a few of his chickens with a .22 caliber bolt-action after being inspired by television coverage of the early Vietnam War. I had tried to conceal my misdeed by tying rocks to the legs of the slain fowl with baling twine and tossing them into the irrigation pond. Turtles or catfish had cut the lines and three had floated up. He didn't whip me; the disappointment in his eyes hurt worse. As my mother's steps grew closer, I pulled up the covers and feigned sleep.

She shook my arm. I whined and opened my eyes.

"Son, your daddy needs you to help him with a sow."

"Help him do what?"

"He'll show you."

I hurried to the wood-burning heater in the kitchen, where our school clothes were kept warm hanging on chair backs. My father was drinking black coffee and staring out the window at the barn. He had never been one for small talk and wasn't about to start now. I had seen plenty of animals bred and born in my years, but wondered what having a smaller arm had to do with helping a breeched sow.

I walked beside my father in the orb of light from the lantern. A waning moon was already high in the sky, and an owl hooted from the top of a pine at the wood's edge. My breath turned white in air that had cooled to near freezing. Cows were huddled close to the barn, the hogs were sleeping in layers under a shelter. We stooped and entered the door of the birthing shed. I spied the sow lying on her side on a bed of straw. Her belly rose rapidly with short breaths. The glow of the lantern reflected off the walls and tin roof and lit the shed in a pale yellow glow.

I was familiar with animals having trouble in birth. We'd found goats dead from where twin kids tried to exit at the same time. Birth reminded me of slaughter—frightened animals, pain and blood.

But hogs were more important. A sow brought much-needed cash, extra meat to the table; a twelve-litter brood of piglets was a stake in the future. A dead sow meant a backup on the bills, less ham and pork chops for supper and more chicken boiled with rice. My father pampered pregnant sows, scratched their ears, rubbed their bellies, and fought to save them when something went wrong.

Something was very wrong with this sow. The opening to her birth canal was swollen and extended, mucus glinting on the straw. Her eyes were exhausted but patient, as she sensed we had returned to help her.

"You need to take off you coat, son, and roll up your sleeve."

I obeyed silently. My father hung the lantern on a nail, then pulled down a can of lard from a rafter. He instructed me to kneel beside him.

"This sow has a pig turned wrong up in her. I can feel it but I can't get my fingers around it. I need you to stick your arm up inside her and see if you can get a hold."

Suddenly the lard made sense. The amazement, dread, and embarrassment must have showed on my face.

"I can't call no vet, and we can't lose this sow. I'll tell you how to do it."

He took my arm in his hand and began lathering it with a gob of grease. I could still hear the owl calling from his high perch.

THE first time I brought home baby chicks to feed to my python, my daughter was horrified. In years of trying to teach others to appreciate reptiles, I have run into countless people, many with advanced degrees, who stack the animal kingdom's worth according to their own sense of beauty. It took much explaining before Meghan began to understand that nature is no more kind to the beautiful than to the gnarled, and that in fact, the weak and cute are more likely to be preyed upon. I have carried home a menagerie of animals to show my children that the animal kingdom does not only include songbirds and half-tame squirrels. And as the small pup grows into a dog, the old cat grows weak and finally breaths her last, they learn that life is fleet and unpredictable and not just a figment of television.

COATED with a healthy layer of animal fat, my hand slipped easily into the sow, my father nodded, and I kept pushing until half my arm was buried. The sow only grunted once.

"You'll feel it narrow between two bones," my father said. "Right after the bones you should feel the pig's head. Watch the teeth."

Sure enough, after a few more inches, the birth canal narrowed between the pelvic bones. I felt the hard, slippery crown of a pig's head. The infant was bent nearly double and wedged tight.

"I can feel it, Dad. I feel the pig."

"Try to slip your hand around its neck and pull."

As I tried to fit my hand around the pig's neck, I felt a slight movement from the animal, a faint flicker of life.

"The pig's still alive," I shouted. "If I pull on it, it might die."

"You got to pull," he answered. "It's been hung that way a couple of hours, and they'll all die if something ain't done."

Three times I wrapped my hand around the pig's throat and pulled, and each time my fingers slipped off the slick skin.

"My fingers keep sliding off."

"Keep trying."

After the tenth attempt without an inch gained, my father told me to pull my arm out. I stared at blood spots forming on my fingers where the pig's sharp teeth had cut me. He stood and walked to the wall of the shed and came back with a coat hanger. I watched as he straightened it, then took a wire cutter and snipped off a foot-long length. He snipped one end at an angle to make it sharp.

"Son, we have to get that pig out of the way. I want you to try hooking it and pulling with this wire."

"Hooking it!"

"Yeah, I'll show ya."

He twisted one end of the wire around my wrist. The free sharp end he bent double like a talon. He tugged on the wire to make sure it wouldn't slip over my hand. The apparatus rested against my palm.

"You need to go back in there, but keep your fingers closed over the hook. When you feel the pig, try to snag it and pull it on out."

"I can't do that, Dad."

"This sow is dying. You've got to try."

I took a long breath, then went in. At the pig's head I paused again, felt a tremor of life, gritted my teeth, and pushed forward.

"Try to find the jawbone or ribs and hook it where it won't pull out." he ordered.

I felt what seemed to be the soft belly of the pig. After several attempts to grasp the hook in my fingertips, I succeeded. I touched sharp steel to unborn flesh and pressed, felt the hook push against the skin, then pop through and bury.

"I think I got it, Dad."

"All right. Now slide your arm out slowly, but pull hard."

I had just begun to retreat when I felt resistance; the wire pulled on my wrist. The sow grunted and struggled.

"Pull hard," my father ordered.

I leaned back and pulled what felt like reeling in a large catfish—no struggle, just weight. Suddenly, my arm came out in a rush, the sow squealed, and my knees were sprayed with blood and backed-up fluid.

MY SON was born in a manner not much different from animals. His head had crowned; my wife's face was crusted with salt from a long night's labor. The machine beeped, signaling another contraction.

"Push, Katie, push hard," the doctor urged. "Let's get your baby into the world."

Katie's head was cradled in the crook of my arm, her teeth gritted, her eyes glazed with a look of determined fury that must have driven females in labor since primeval days. She pushed, I urged her to push harder, she gasped, and our boy bolted from her in a gush of water. The odor reminded me of turned fields, freshly mown hay, the sweat of animals.

DANGLING from my wrist, still impaled on the hook, was the pig. My father pulled it off and laid the infant on the straw. A three-inch gash had been sliced in the pig's belly, a string of intestines hanging from the wound. Incredibly, the pig was moving, opening and closing his mouth in search of breath. My father wiped mucus from the pig's mouth, then snipped the cord with his wire cutters.

"Think we can save it?" I asked.

"Might. We might."

The sow grunted again, then tried to stand, her protective instincts quickly returning. My father picked up the injured pig and cradled it in his palm.

"Let's go to the house and see if anything can be done for this one while she settles down," he said.

We retreated with the lamp. My knees were weak from a mixture of fatigue and exhilaration. My mother met us at the door. She had warmed chocolate milk for me, more coffee for my father. She stared at the injured pig, but in her years of marriage and motherhood had become accustomed to an assortment of wild and domestic animals passing through the house.

"What happened to him?" she asked, nodding toward the pig's slit belly.

"We had to pull it out with a coat hanger," I quickly answered.

My father was already at the kitchen table. "Darlene, I need some iodine and a needle and thread. Some newspaper to lay it on, too."

"You're not going to try and fix it, Reese? His guts are hanging out. You ought to just knock it in the head and end its suffering."

"I'm gonna damn try."

My mother was generally right when she chose to disagree with my father, but she also knew he was too hardheaded to ever be persuaded.

In the middle of the place where we sat down to eat supper, my mother set up an operating table. She put a towel down and covered it with newspaper. She got a bottle of iodine and a needle strung with two feet of fine white sewing thread. My father laid the pig on its side and studied the cut, the exposed entrails. The wound looked clean, the organs undamaged. He soaked the wound, the intestines, with iodine. The pig struggled. Using a pencil, he poked the intestines gently back inside, trying to arrange them in a manner that looked normal. He sewed up the gash, with tight sutures. My mother told him how to loop the end and knot it. Except for a line of bunched-together skin, the pig looked normal.

"Well, if it lives, you can thank the good Lord," my mother said.

We bundled the pig in a warm towel and carried it back to the barn. We found that in the thirty minutes we had been gone, the sow had given birth to eight more piglets. But in her excitement and confusion, she had lain down at the side of the birthing shed, her rump against the wire fence that separated her from the other hogs. A healthy sow gives birth much like a kid spitting out watermelon seeds. She had shot each piglet through the wire into the larger pen, where a boar hog was calming eating the newborn. We saved three and put them to the teats of the sow alongside their doctored-up sibling.

I BOUGHT my daughter a cockatiel a while back, and she was terribly excited when it began to lay sterile eggs. She is still too young to understand why we need a boy bird for the eggs to hatch. My son has a fascination with the cows my brother owns, but his interest in them is almost the same as seeing one in a picture book. They are objects too distant from his own life to seem real. If I walk out my front door and turn in a circle, I cannot see a single house occupied by a family native to North Carolina. I often wonder how I can plug my children into the heritage of this state where they will not see it as a series of interlocking streets and towns, a population of well-educated people who do not speak with my accent. I see no way to implant them in Dixie in the ways I came to understand and love her—no piglet to pull from the womb into night air while an owl hoots from the treetop.

So I continue to drag home snakes and other critters in

an attempt to teach them that although man is dominant, he is not removed from the animal kingdom, and underneath the perfumes and clothes, we are born and we die similarly to other creatures. My efforts will be rewarded if one day my son understands that seeing a cow in the pasture complete with manure, dirt, and flies is worth one hundred pictures in a book. Then he will have realized that beyond the lofty confines of Chapel Hill lies a rich, very different world called the South.

WE RAISED that sewed-up piglet to maturity, topped it out, and sold it at the market. Since that night, I've seen the birth of my two children, the death of my father, and the passage of many hundreds of farm animals over the home land. Life and death even up in the strangest ways. A sow's life saved by intervening with nature; in trade, several of her young eaten alive. The sin of murdering several fowl washed away in newborn piglet's blood.

WE BURIED the dead piglets in a quick grave at the edge of the woods and started for the house. Pink spokes of dawn streaked the eastern sky, Venus hung cold and silver like God's eye. My father spoke the only words as we walked home.

"You did all right, son."

JUNE 1984. The oak trees surrounding the homeplace rent themselves in mourning. Whole branches fell to earth on breathless summer afternoons—a *crack* as the wood splintered, a rustle of leaves, and a thud like a body had fallen. The trees were not diseased, the branches did not snap during high winds, they simply fell as if the spirit inside was relieved of a great weight. A cow was killed when a limb broke her back, the windshield of a car was shattered.

My father was dying. He lay in a bed in the VA hospital and stared through the window at the graveyard while cancer wasted his flesh. His weight rolled from him like rain. June passed while he wasted down, the robins nested, the kid goats from his milk herd quit nursing and nibbled fescue and clover. The season turned.

Finally, I heeded the letters and phone calls and came home from two years of living in Tunisia. I left my wife and infant daughter, fully intent on returning. I had only spoken to the doctor a few moments when I realized I would not return to Africa, but would do as any good Southern firstborn son and sit through the deathwatch. The doctor gave him a few weeks.

My father was sleeping when I caught my first glimpse of him. Many months had passed, and I was not prepared for the sight of the stranger lying in bed. His covers were down and his spine stood out against his skin like the ties on a railroad. He lay in a fetal position, arms drawn to his chest like one in prayer, his legs thin as a starved man. I could only remember the beer paunch he had carried, a body once bunched with muscles tanned by the sun. I wanted to weep, but blinked back the water; he sensed my presence and rolled to face me. His eyes reminded me of where animals burrow. I wanted to bolt from the room, go and walk the fields and pastures and emerge in the life and vigor of the young Carolina summer, but for the moment I could only stretch out my arm, grasp his thin hand, and say I was glad to be home.

JUNE 1989. By all expectations, the day should have been especially fine. June 7—our ninth wedding anniversary. We had planned to celebrate the occasion by boarding a 747 that morning for Paris to begin a two-week vacation. Instead, I lay in a hospital bed gazing out the window at the small patch of sky my window afforded.

I was nearing the end of my fourth day, after having undergone extensive tests to explore why my kidneys were failing. Although initially the doctors had expressed confidence that my problems were minor, each test discovered something new and strange going on in my body. Still, my spirits stayed high; I am young, with a strong history of health, and I figured the odds would eventually fall in my favor. We waited for the results of a bone marrow biopsy. The doctors had again expressed confidence the test would show no abnormalities, but could not rule out the threat of serious disease. I stared outside at a hawk floating on an air thermal and wished I was seeing him through the window of the jet. Katie sat beside me in a chair, trying to bury her fears in a book.

The doctor came through the door abruptly, walked quickly to the foot of my bed, and placed both his hands on the railing. He stared at his hands for a moment, then shifted his gaze and locked eyes with me.

"I'm afraid I've got some bad news for y'all," he began, real pain obvious in the lines in his face. "The test results came back and it looks like you've got a disease called multiple myeloma." He exhaled long and wearily. "I never would have expected it in a hundred years."

In stunned silence, I listened for the next ten minutes while he explained I had a rare form of bone marrow cancer that might kill me in as little as two to three years. Even with good response to drugs and a remission, my life expectancy was hard to predict. The possibility still existed that I might live to be an old man, but ten more years of life was probably pushing it.

"You're an unusual man, Tim, and you have an unusual

disease," the doctor said. "It's just not what we expected."

It damn sure wasn't what I expected. I had expected at that moment to be high over the Atlantic, drinking a whiskey and anticipating eating snails in a good French bistro. For a man who scoffed at flu season, to be told I might be dead in a little more than one hundred weeks sounded at best absurd.

"Well, I always liked a good fight," I replied, trying to ignore the ice in my belly.

"Well, you got a good one now," the doctor answered.

The doctor turned to Katie. She sat on the edge of my bed, one hand locked in my own, the other clenched so tightly her knuckles had turned white.

"It's all right to cry, Katie," he told her.

Her eyes were wide, only a hint of shininess in them. "I'll do plenty of that later," she answered.

I looked again at the window and found that the hawk had moved on to another patch of the heavens. I wished I sailed beside the bird, and was able to see the earth from an altitude where the whole picture loomed less subjective than the harsh facts before me. I calculated time quickly in my head and realized that even if I surprised the doctors and lived twenty more years, I would be but fifty-six when I departed—even younger than when my father died from lung cancer.

AFTERNOON

LAWRANCE WILLIAMS stood to himself toward the back of the crowd, a single, lean black man, dressed in a black suit and white shirt. I had not seen him in years, but recognized him immediately. I was walking at the front corner of my father's coffin, a brother holding to each of the other corners, two uncles grasping the brass handles on each side. We were laying the old man to rest. One of his last requests had been that his sons carry him to the earth.

The grave was cut clean into the lawn: a green tarp had been fitted perfectly to cover the raw dirt. I knew we must set the coffin on top of the pulley structure, that I must not let my leg go into the hole, or trip and tip my end. I tried to ignore all the faces. Probably two hundred friends and family were gathered on that bright July day, but as I planted my feet carefully, I thought of Lawrance, remembered his son and how in my youth we had been close friends. It struck me that little had changed. We share the South now publicly, eat together, even marry, but there is still a distance, a final separation that will never end.

I CALLED him LJ, for Lawrance Junior, a wiry black kid who lived a half mile down the road.

We were of the same age and grade. The Williamses lived in a rambling, wide-porched unpainted house that sat under a huge willow and several large oaks. Their seven kids rose in age like stair steps. Our fathers were both laborers by trade who worked farming on the side, our mothers about the same age, women who could wring a chicken's neck with a baby in one arm. Socially and economically, our families could not brag above each other, except for the fact that the Williamses were black. I called LJ's father Lawrence. LJ called my father Mr. Reese.

LJ lived just off the edge of civilized, white earth. The paved road stopped just beyond our house, and with the end of the tar stopped mail delivery, the telephone line, and school-bus service. In the mornings in winter when the weather was good, we often met on the road beyond my house to wait for separate buses to the segregated schools we attended. Our ages were similar, Mabel the oldest sister, Sheryl an older brother, LJ, Kareen, Jackie, a baby or two that stayed home. We usually carried bag lunches to school, mine filled with a bologna sandwich on white bread, maybe a banana and vanilla wafers with peanut butter, a nickle buried in my pocket for milk. LJ's sack smelled of home-cooked biscuits split with salt pork. We wore clothes that looked similar, a match and mismatch of originals and hand-me-downs. Both our noses tended to run during cold weather, our lips would chap from the wind. I sometimes used a tube of Chap Stick, making ceremony as I coated extra on the corners of my mouth. I never offered him any and he never asked. We would talk, skip rocks, or hug ourselves for warmth until our separate buses came. His bus, a fixed-up hand-me-down from the white school system, usually came first, for it had a greater circuit to cover. The windows would be slam full of dark faces all pressed toward me when his bus stopped, all ages because the black school went from first to twelfth grade. He'd wave goodbye and step inside, jostle for seating along with his brothers and sisters. Winters we were only roadside aquaintences, both of us too busy staying warm to really be friends.

The coming of summer vacation brought down the barriers of clothes and color. As the sun deepened, my own skin turned darker like LJ's, both our heads were cut close of hair. The distinction of what bus we rode to school or the quality of our clothes lessened until a parity was reached where we were basically just two kids with idle time. Maybe it related to our common age and grade, maybe similar interests, but for several years, LJ and I were close friends. The other members of our families played together, but they were of mostly opposite sex, a barrier not tampered with in that era in the rural South. LJ and I roamed the woods and fields like wild creatures.

Neither of us cared to play the role of Jungle Jim when we were "natives" hunting wild game in the pine-thicket jungle that bordered my house. LJ, myself, my younger brothers, we'd strip down to only our briefs, and for hours we'd hunt the imaginary lion and rhino that inhabited those brushy twenty acres. We spoke in grunts and hand sign except for when only words would do, and were content to be equal warriors. In my mind, Jungle Jim was a sissy for wearing boots and a hat and I wanted no part of him.

Our weapon of choice was a spear cut from a reed. Sliced off at the base and trimmed of the leaves, the long, thin stems whistled a straight path through the air, and if honed with a pocketknife or piece of broken bottle, would stick end first into the ground. They were quite capable of putting out an eye.

Occasionally when game was scarce, we'd ambush the traffic that used the road through the pine thicket. In those days a car came along seldom, more likely a tractor or someone on foot. We'd follow at the woods edge, make noise, flash our spears, and then retreat. We were being unusually bold the day we spied a pickup coming, the four of us massing at the edge of the ditch, spears raised.

We were in full war paint. I had acquired a dog-eared copy of *National Geographic,* and we had used natural resources at hand to mimic the garb of a real African tribe. Red clay mixed with water, purple poke salad berries, a tube of old lipstick I'd found lying behind our couch, fresh skullcap haircuts—we looked as if pulled from under a log in the deepest jungle of Zaire. As the truck approached, we lifted our spears and crouched, and as it was passing, slung our arms forward, pretending we had launched our spears. We grinned broadly at a white man driving the truck.

Our arms had hardly stopped moving forward when the man driving the truck locked brakes and slid sideways in his effort to stop. He opened his door and stood on the running board. I recognized him as a man who lived a few miles down on the dirt roads beyond our house, the father of several ragged children who seldom got on the school bus. He glared at us for a moment, his jaw swelled with a plug of tobacco.

"You throw at my truck again, nigger, I'll cut your goddam throat," he said.

We all stood in silence.

"You hear me, jig? I seen you sling that rock."

LJ gave me a sidelong glance. "We didn't throw nothing, mister," I answered.

"That little nigger did. Rock or something. If it had dented my truck, I'd be rolling his black ass in the dirt right now."

"He ain't no nigger," I heard my voice say.

"He's blacker than the inside of my asshole. What

y'all doing playing half-naked with a nigger, anyhow?"

For the life of me, I couldn't see a hair of difference between LJ and myself. Every exposed inch of skin was covered with either mud or berry juice. The man spit once on the road.

"You boys, I know your daddy. He wouldn't like you running around trying to act like a nigger. The nigger can't help it, but y'all can."

He slid back under the steering wheel and roared off. We never ambushed cars again.

At that early point in our lives, the end of the paved road between our houses seemed to divide our lives more than color. Not only did the mail service and telephone lines stop there, but so did the amenities that a few dollars a week difference in our fathers' salaries made possible. In the early years, I don't believe LJ envied my lighter shade of skin, but it was obvious he coveted my access to a bologna sandwich on white, store-bought bread with mayonnaise.

"It got to be on light bread," LJ stated emphatically. "Not no corn bread or biscuit."

"We got three loaves of white bread," I assured him.

"Mayonnaise too," he continued. "You sure y'all got mayonnaise?"

"There's a jar full."

LJ's eyes sparkled as he reconsidered the proposal. A whole bologna sandwich made with two slices of light bread and plenty of mayonnaise, in exchange for mowing the grass in our front lawn. Deal!

In a family blessed with an abundance of stale bread, sliced bologna was a staple of life. The exchange of a second-class sandwich for two hours of LJ's labor was an easy agreement for me. I wondered at his eagerness: his own lunches of smoked pork on homemade pan bread looked especially hot and crusty and good.

"You got to cut close to the fence too," I reminded him. "So the cows won't lean over the wire."

"I'll cut it. Let's go 'fore the sun gets any higher."

I studied the sun, and considered that my father didn't really care who mowed the grass as long as it was done. He wouldn't know, anyhow.

I'd stretch out in the shade of a tree while LJ labored behind the splay-wheeled lawn mower, his dark skin running with creeks of sweat. Occasionally I'd rise and direct him to a spot he'd missed. The air would fill with the good smell of clipped clover and fescue, toads and insects would flee the path of the steel tornado. In the shortened grass, my brothers and I would rediscover baseballs, dog-chewed Frisbees, a fork or spoon or top. At last, LJ would mow over the last spot, he'd pull the lever that shut off the gas, and again we'd hear birds, the whine of the radio from where my older sister danced inside. He'd brush off the grass that had clung to his sweaty legs, the crease of a grin turning up the corners of his mouth. He wouldn't mention the sandwich, and neither would I, but we'd start for the back door.

I think he enjoyed seeing the sandwich made almost half as much as eating it. He'd follow me as I took a loaf of bread from a shelf on the cabinet and laid it on the table, then to the refrigerator where a large jar of A&P mayonnaise sat cooling, the bologna one of those large economy packages, thick-sliced. He'd prop on his elbows and watch while I unscrewed the jar lid, laid out two slices of bread— never, never an end piece—took a spoon, and began lathering the mayonnaise on.

"Add little more to dat slice," he'd usually advise me.

When the proper amount of mayonnaise gleamed on each slice, I'd lift a piece of bologna from the package and peel off the casing around the edge. LJ savored the casing, would pull it between his teeth and scrape off the skim of bologna.

He would insist that I center the slice of meat between the bread, no edges hanging off, and place the top slice of bread on carefully, not mash the imprint of my hand. The result wouldn't have excited a hobo, but LJ found it exotic.

He drank his water before eating, two glassfuls straight out of the cold-water faucet in the kitchen. While I was the sandwich architect, drawing the water was his privilege. He was fascinated by the frothy water that gushed from the spigot. It tasted slightly of plastic pipe and had warmed in its long travel from the ground—in my opinion, it was a poor second to the pump water that gushed cold and clear in his backyard. He'd drink down two full glasses, never pausing while his throat pulsed. Then we'd go outside and sit in the shade, and he'd eat the sandwich slowly with small bites, rolling the sticky mass over his tongue, straining it well between his teeth and gums. The sweat would have dried now on his arms and legs like gullies cut through the film of dust. He'd chew slowly, thoughtfully. I'd feel guilty knowing that in an instant I would trade him two sandwiches for one of the fat, homemade biscuits filled with salt pork that he disdained.

AS the world moved into the sixties and our radio was replaced by a television, I became increasingly aware that a war was beginning between whites and blacks.

"You mark my words, somebody's gonna put a bullet through his head," my Uncle Jesse said. "People ain't gonna listen to such talk."

We were eating fried Virginia mullet, my dad and his older brother watching the television news as Martin Luther King paraded down a street backed by several hundred young blacks. The Porter Waggoner show had just ended, his twangy guitar and voice replaced by the oiled speech of a young Dan Rather. I was ten years old and stared uneasily at the television at signs and placards held aloft, demanding equal rights, blacks in clean, pressed clothes huddled together while surrounded by groups of angry white people.

"It ain't nothing but Communists," my father said. "Trying to stir up trouble. You look at Lawrance Williams right down the road there. Now, I respect that man. He works, looks after his family. You won't see him out there acting like that."

"The nigger needs a bullet," Jesse said, his eyes narrowing as King spoke into a microphone.

"Y'all hush that kind of talk in front of the children," my mother exclaimed.

"Well, it's the truth," my uncle continued. "Somebody'll get him."

After supper my brothers and cousins and I were herded outside while the adults enjoyed a cup of coffee. Twilight was settling, doves beginning to call, a few early bats swooped for insects. One of my older cousins thought of the game, and soon we were all lined up, marched in goose step, chanting "Equal rights" over and over. The parade wound through the yard, circling trees and moving along the edge of the road. Soon we were laughing so hard we could barely walk.

I spied LJ from the corner of my eye, and my laughter caught like a burr in my throat. He stood on the far side of the road, staring straight into my face, his arms straight by his side. I stopped, and the marchers passed me by and continued on, still goose-stepping, still shouting. LJ turned at that moment and began walking toward his house, but I ran to him and caught him by the arm.

"You want to cut the grass tomorrow?" I blurted. "The grass is getting high, and you can cut it if you want. We got plenty of bologna."

"Maybe I cut it," he said, staring at the line of marchers now rounding the corner of the house, their chant of "Equal rights" drowning out the animal calls of twilight.

"It needs cutting," I assured him. "My dad was complaining about it today. Mama brought home a new package of bologna just this afternoon."

We parted with goodbyes in the tepid air of that early evening, but a breach of trust had been committed and was the first crack in our union against time and change.

IN RURAL North Carolina, white was king, but being pure black was considered higher than the jumble of blood and genes that constituted the members of the Croatan Indian tribe.

"They all mixed up, ain't black, ain't white, might be anything," LJ told me the day a beat-up panel truck showed up at our farm to drill a new well. A rawboned brown man with matted hair, a wide nose, and pale green eyes began unloading his tools. He was helped by two boys about my and LJ's age, mongrel-looking kids, part black and part white, a little Indian thrown in, their features muddled together as if God hadn't given their mold much thought.

"What y'all be, anyway?" LJ asked one of the kids. Their father drove a pipe inch by inch into the ground.

"Indians," one said, picking at a scab at the corner of his mouth.

"Indians?" LJ said, disbelief rising in his voice. "I never knowed there was Indians around here."

"We Indians for sure."

The only Indians I was familiar with were the ones in western movies, lean, painted men with long narrow noses and shoulder-length straight black hair.

"I'm a black man," LJ said, sounding very boastful to be

only ten. "There ain't no doubt I black. But I never known there to be Indians round here."

The boy picked his scab, his eyes jerky and nervous. "We Croatan Indians."

LJ stared at me, his eyes saying that maybe he and I were different, but at least we were pure in our race. But here were two lowbrows, trying to pass as something they weren't.

"Well, we Indians. You ask my dad."

LJ stared at the kid, and in his black, glistening eyes I observed deep thought. "I always thought Indians, they run real fast and jump like deers."

The Croatan pushed out his bottom lip. "Yeah, we pretty fast."

"I bet I'm faster than you," LJ answered.

"Might be," the older kid answered. "But we pretty fast. Can jump too."

"I got a quarter in my pocket says I'm faster," LJ answered.

I was surprised at his bet. LJ did have a quarter, but I knew he was saving it for going into town. He was not the kind of person to challenge others unprovoked. LJ looked to see where the kids' father was, then pushed the matter further.

"What you say, Tonto? I bet ya a quarter I can beat you from that tall pine over there to that big gum tree."

I don't know if the Croatan kid really had a quarter, but his pride made him accept the bet. His father was busy driving the pump pipe, and paid us no attention when we started for the pine thicket. Within a couple of minutes, we had shed our sneakers and were lined up at a starting gate I had scratched in the soft dirt.

"We race all the way to that tree, now, ya hear?" LJ instructed. "Don't count 'less you pass that tree."

My legs trembled from excitement. We argued for a moment over who was going to say go, then finally decided that I would toss a stick into the air. When the stick hit earth, it was every man for himself.

I slung that stick high as I could. Four sets of eyes watched it tumble end over end, four sets of legs cocked, arms ready to pump forward. The stick struck ground with a thud and we came off that line, our toes snatching the dirt and throwing it backwards in a shower. We were pretty evenly matched, and for the first fifty yards were dead even. As the finish line grew closer, LJ and I held back and let the Croatans gain on us. The older boy glanced to his side and saw we were failing, grinned, and kicked his legs and arms even harder.

Months before, we had dug a hole in the edge of the pine thicket at the base of the gum tree. The hole was head-deep and big around as a bed. Just the day before, we had care-fully covered the hole with reeds, then a layer of pine straw in hopes of trapping a rabbit. The two Croatans hit the hole running wide open.

Both kids were swallowed whole by the earth. I heard the crisp snap of reeds as they fell through, then two solid thuds as their momentum slammed them against the far wall of the hole. I heard only silence for a second, then the wail of the younger kid. LJ and I peered into the trap. We laughed like hyenas. Both kids were on their knees at the bottom of the hole, pine straw clinging to their clothes. The oldest kid appeared to have had the wind knocked from his lungs, for he was moving his mouth in silence, his eyes squinted as if he too was trying to cry. His brother was wailing now, his hand held to his forehead. They looked pathetic, but we laughed and pointed. The older kid finally got his wind and began cussing a streak as talented as would a grown man. He squinted up at LJ and said, "I'll get you, you black son of a bastard."

As the two Croatans tried to climb out of the hole, LJ and

I stomped at their hands and kicked dirt down in their faces. The two kids scrambled and dived at us, but the hole was deep to the crown of their heads, the sides carved straight, the dirt slick from frequent summer rain. They cussed us as we ran around the edges of the hole stomping back their attempts at escape. LJ came up with the ultimate humiliation.

At a sudden, anguished cry from one of the Croatans, I looked up to see that LJ was peeing on him. Standing slightly spread-legged, penis in hand, he directed a stream of urine on the older boy's head. In my heart, I knew it a shameful act, one that God would write down, that my mother would take up switch for. I hesitated not one second, but directed my own urine on the head of the younger kid. Broken, both of them slumped in the bottom of the hole, their curses now rent with huge sobs. The dirt we had kicked in their faces ran in dirty brown rivers. When our bladders were empty, we forced out the last drops, then sprinted for the safety of the deep pine woods where we knew even Tarzan couldn't find us. When we emerged at early evening, the Indian man had set the pump, loaded his tools and sodden boys, and gone. My mother was not waiting for me with a stick. The two boys had had either too much pride or shame to tell on us. We didn't use the fort for several days afterwards. It smelled of urine and guilt.

BUT in a couple of days, I had forgotten my shame. I excused our actions as necessary to defend our home turf. But later that same summer, another incident happened, something private and unknown to anyone but myself, that proved my own heart was infected with the concept that other human beings might be inferior to me for the matter of their skin colors.

My parents had driven seventy miles down to South Carolina to a quick, cheap dental clinic to get a set of false
teeth made for my dad. We were left for the day in the care
of LJ's older sister, Mabel. She was an olive-skinned girl in
her mid-teens, quiet and studious, and was later to move
north and attend college.

Lunchtime came, and she fixed us banana sandwiches as
instructed by my mom. She laid on the table slices of light
bread and lathered each in turn with a coating of mayonnaise. I had to tell her how to cut the bananas—not in
slices like coins, for they slide out, but in lengths like
planks. She complied. I doubt she had ever made a banana
sandwich before, had ever wanted one. She finished each
sandwich and laid it on a plate, then poured glasses full of
cold, fresh cow milk. The buzz of talk and argument among
us ceased as arms moved to fill our mouths.

I had lifted my sandwich and taken my first bite when I
noticed the print of her fingers mashed in the soft bread.
No dirt, just a ghost left where her slender fingers had
closed the halves. I stared at the bread, chewed what was in
my mouth, and felt it grow larger and larger.

She had touched my food. Plain and simple. I had
watched her wash her hands with soap before starting to
make the sandwich, a hundred times I had eaten at LJ's
house—plates of collard greens, corn bread, side meat—
but she had physically touched my food, the evidence staring at me in the soft belly of bread.

I could not swallow. The wad of banana and bread grew
in my mouth until I thought I might gag. I bolted from the
table and hurried through the back door and went around
the corner of the house. I backed into the refuge of a fig
bush, squatted, and spit the food from my mouth. Joe, the
hound, had followed me from the porch. He sniffed the
white glob, then without hesitation bolted it down. I fed

him the rest of the sandwich. I heard Mabel calling me from the steps and returned.

"I had to go to the bathroom," I lied, hoping my embarrassment did not show in my face.

"Where your lunch?" she asked. "You already eat your lunch?"

"Yeah," I lied. "It was good."

She smiled, laugh lines creasing her pretty face. "You gonna get a tummyache. Bolt your food worse than a dog do. You want another sandwich?"

I vigorously shook my head. "I'm full."

The hunger I felt that afternoon was small compensation for the shame that gnawed me.

THE AUTUMN of 1969 when the completion of a new high school ended segregation, LJ discovered Black Power. Whether powered by the hormones of being fourteen, by daily confrontation with a majority of hostile whites, or simply by the appeal of belonging to a movement that was popular and exciting, he changed. I'd see him in the halls at school, but our hellos became increasingly brief. He wore his hair longer, Afro-style, took to dressing in red, black, and green, adopted the black soul shake. The following summer, we saw little of each other. He spent more and more time in Fayetteville, removed from the tobacco fields and outhouses of his youth, I had discovered girls and sports. The few times we did meet on the road or visited each other's house, our conversation was measured and forced, no thought given to roaming the fields and woods again.

In my junior year in high school, we had race riots. I had become a star athlete and the pack leader of a group of guys who drank beer and made grades just minimal enough to stay in school. I considered the riots great fun—classes were disrupted, police roamed the halls. LJ was among a core group of blacks demanding certain grievances be addressed. They wanted more blacks on the Student Council and a black to run for Homecoming Queen. Between classes I saw him in the hall and proposed that he and I keep both sides of the argument stirred-up, that with a little prompting we might even get the school closed down for a few days. His bewilderment made me realize then how totally different we had become. I considered the riots a joke—to him, they were a matter of basic right and wrong.

I was graduated from high school and discharged from the Marines when I heard of LJ being accused of raping a white woman. According to the paper, he and two other black men had picked up a woman downtown and carried her to an isolated gravel pit where he and I swam as kids. In court, the woman was proved to be a prostitute, the rape a business deal that had gone sour. LJ was acquitted. He went north to live. I hope his memory has been kind and that he has been able, as I, to recall that time early in our lives when for a brief few years, we ignored racial, cultural, or social differences and accepted each other simply as friends.

I THOUGHT of LJ and of those simple early summers while the preacher spoke of my father and of the rewards of the dead. I avoided looking at the flower-draped coffin by staring at Lawrance. He shifted his weight from leg to leg, his eyes trained on a space of ground as if his thoughts too were remembering a better time. I made up my mind that I would go to him following the prayer and tell him how I appreciated him coming, inquire about LJ and the rest of his family. But when the final prayer ended, we were hustled toward the big black car. I reached out my arm and shook Lawrance's hand and said I was glad to see him. But I did not tarry, people were watching and waiting. I got in the limousine and closed the door against the world.

———

THE WAIL of the siren pierced the air, and within a few minutes from our hiding spot in the edge of the woods we could hear the fire engine coming. By then, the barn was a goner, the sap-rich old timbers heated to the quick with flame. The barn had been abandoned, the lofty rafters that had once hung with tobacco now draped with bats and rat snakes. But the plume of smoke would bring out the volunteer fire department, farmers and storekeepers clinging to the sides of the big truck, or racing ahead of it in their pickups, and for an hour or so, the impossible boredom of being thirteen was punctuated with the thrill of sin. I had been "raised right," but for a few years while my hormones churned, I gambled dangerously close to becoming another of the fallen McLaurins.

I had taken to running with trouble. I didn't strike the matches that fired the barns, but I enjoyed the spectacle as one of the gang. My leaders in crime were the Jones and Davis brothers, military brats and older than me by a year or two. They smoked cigarettes and would slip a beer from their fathers' workroom stash. They had lived in Germany, knew cusswords in that strange language, had traveled on ships and planes. I was at an age where my fascination for the night sky was waning, my supply of testosterone was beginning to kick in, and life in Beard was just too slow. A lit match brought flashing light, the crackle of radios, and for a few minutes the delicious feeling that I held the power to start the world turning.

Burning down old barns is popular in the South, setting

fire to the woods or mowed fields just another means of
weed control. I believe the members of the volunteer fire
department enjoyed the fires as much as we did. It afforded
grown men a chance to drive fast and play once again.
Usually when the fire was burning furiously and the curious were beginning to arrive, we would come out of our
hiding place and move close to the fire, where we could
enjoy the full effects. If we were ever suspected of starting
the fires, all I ever saw was a narrowed eye, maybe a nod or
two in our direction. It was an open secret that members of
the deer hunting club set patches of deep woods on fire
every spring to clear underbrush for hunting. Some of the
old tobacco barns were insured, and that meant someone
got a windfall of money. As long as a person or his livestock
or machinery wasn't scorched, setting an occasional fire
was a safe start for a hooligan.

Twice we raided the black school and committed of-
fenses that might have sent us to a reformatory if we had
been caught—and if the school had been white. We slipped
in through a broken window and roamed the halls, collected baseballs and mitts, wrote vulgar words on black-
boards, and turned over trash cans. I took a fine microscope
with several powerful lenses, and soothed my conscience
by assuring myself I would hide the instrument in our fort
where LJ would have equal access to the wonders of the
small world. No justification exists for the theft, but in
reality, the microscope was used many times by me over
the next couple of years. I had seen the same instruments
collect dust on shelves in my own school. The second time
we raided the school, we got carried away throwing rocks at
the gym windows, and the event made the morning
paper—a tiny paragraph on a back page.

By heredity, I was prone to throw rocks at trains. My
father was caught shooting out railroad lights when he was

a teenager and avoided jail only by joining the service. I carried on his compulsion and got pretty good at timing a throw so a sizable rock would collide with the windshield of a brand-new market-bound car while the train passed at sixty miles an hour.

The fall line of the Piedmont stops on the west side of the Cape Fear River on the fancy side of Fayetteville, the high land where dogwoods and azaleas bloom. One has only to cross the old span bridge on Person Street to enter the working world. The land is damp there, holds the heat, and runs flat and wet toward the coast. East Fayetteville is a community of squat frame houses, pool halls, fish markets, auto parts stores and 7-Elevens, men who work with their hands, women who fret over their children and the bills. Laws are generally observed, but interpreted according to one's situation and opportunity. Eddie Brown, a schoolmate, was raised on Dunn Road, a stone's throw from the river bridge.

Once, my fifth-grade teacher told us to write a poem and bring it to class to read aloud. I can't remember what I wrote, but I'm sure it was of the sappy, rhymed lines the rest of the class scribed. I do remember what Eddie composed. He stood up in front of the class ramrod-straight and read from his paper.

> "My mama fucks.
> My daddy sucks.
> The younguns eat shit."

We giggled and snickered while the teacher turned pale, then sent Eddie to the principal's office for a paddling. He had written the only real poem in the room.

I saw Eddie often over the years. He was always in some form of trouble or another, either avoiding the law for a beating he had administered, or licking his wounds and waiting to even up with someone who had beaten him on the draw. I was bagging groceries at the old Cash Way market in Fayetteville one afternoon when Eddie stopped by. His eyes were swollen, his back and shoulder crossed with welts where someone had beat him with a rubber hose.

"Ahhh, ain't nothing," he told me, while buying a plug of Red Man chewing tobacco. "I'll get him. Just by and by. Say, you still playing with them snakes?"

"I got a few. Mostly just local stuff."

"Got one of them copperheads? Them are mean son of a bitches. Me, if I was mean as a copperhead, I wouldn't worry 'bout no one."

Eddie was bad for picking fights with most anyone who looked at him wrong, but between the two of us there had always remained a sort of peace. I think in my interest in snakes he saw a craziness he could identify with.

"If you want a copperhead, I could catch you one," I said. "You just have to be real careful how you hold it."

Eddie took a couple of steps backwards, one hand raised. "Noooo. You keep the snakes, I'll just look at them. 'Sides, I got a rattlesnake here in my pocket."

I watched as Eddie fished in his trouser pocket and pulled out a hawkbill knife. The catch had been filed to where it opened with a flick of his wrist, the curved blade honed to a razor edge. "This here rattlesnake will keep them off ole Eddie," he said and grinned.

I watched Eddie limp off down the street, flicking the knife blade out repeatedly and closing it until the move was a part of his reflex. A couple of nights later I heard how he had tangled with two soldiers at Steve's Drive-In, a popular night hangout. He cut the tip of one man's finger off, slit the other guy so deep in his chest that his lung collapsed. Eddie spent a few nights in jail, but was finally cleared for self-defense.

Children are as bad as pack wolves for attacking the

weak. I was raised on the edge of poverty and harbored various embarrassments and fears. For years I was ashamed to bring new friends home with me and let them see our cracker-box house minus a bathroom. The old pickup we owned was a rolling wreck that smelled strongly of hogs. On mornings when we missed the bus and had to be carried to school, I would make excuses for my mother to let me out on the far side of campus where none of my classmates could see the vehicle. But overall, I was accepted. My clothes were not the latest in fashion, but they were clean, I usually had an extra quarter to spend when a puppet show visited the school. But for Eddie Brown and a couple of others, the meanness in people and in life seemed to follow them and ride them like sores.

Plug tobacco didn't help Eddie's popularity. He chewed tobacco like other kids chewed gum and was always likely to have a wad stashed in the hollow of his cheek. He spit the juice out during recess and swallowed it during class. Eddie wore a certain type of dime-store tennis shoe that had a distinctive waffle tread. A game developed to always watch the sand for one of Eddie's footprints during recess, scream "Uhhhhh! Eddie Brown germs," and jump the treadmark. Usually the print would be circled with a line to warn others. Eddie usually just ignored the taunts. More often, he watched the ridicule from inside the classroom, where he was often restricted for some rule infraction. I remember seeing his face pressed to the glass, his expression sour and brooding, while he watched us team up for softball or basketball.

Eddie could not read. He stumbled over words, hesitated, paused, and stammered. As he fought the words, his face would redden, he would lower his face and mumble, then stop. Often the teacher passed to a better reader. I remember he was good at art, but his pictures were usually drawings of tanks and exploding aircraft and war-painted soldiers, and did not draw the praise of rainbow meadows and bouquets of flowers.

So Eddie developed his fists, learned how to knock the smirk off someone's face with one quick punch. We were only through the early grades of grammar school when most of the teasing directed at Eddie ceased. At least any he could see or hear. A bloody nose or swollen eye taught even the worst wise-mouth to direct his ridicule elsewhere. As we entered junior high, Eddie attended school less and less. Except for the poem he wrote, he never did home-work, refused to speak aloud or attempt to read in class. Teachers passed him up from grade to grade. He quit school at sixteen.

For all of Eddie's problems, he did have his fists and his hawkbilled knife. Some of the poorer girls who grew up on the east side were not allowed even this defense, but were trapped with the emotions and desires so intense in young females, while having to harden and withdraw into a shell that protected them from jokes and vicious tongues.

Kathy Maxwell was infamous from the first grade until the day she finally gave up and quit school as a high school sophmore. She was a big-boned girl, prone to chubbiness and further cursed with a very plain face, an abundance of early hormones, and a nonacademic mind. One of my earli-est memories of the first grade centered on Kathy.

The teacher was out of the room, and we kids were acting up, tossing paper and talking. Kathy climbed on top of her desk, lifted her frock, pulled down her panties, and turned slowly in a circle, all the while grinning ear to ear. I suspect that even at that tender age, she sensed there was one part of her body that could always draw attention regardless of what clothes she wore or how she fixed her hair. I remem-ber clapping for her. But as the months passed, the teach-

ers and classmates turned on her, and she rivaled Eddie
Brown as the source of jokes.

"Red rover, red rover, send Kathy right over," a kid
would shout, and Kathy would leave her place in line and
start toward the other side, her body jiggling in odd places.
She would slam against the opposite line, and the boys
would fall backwards with mock dismay, shouting that a
hippo had rammed into them, a freight train or elephant.
Kathy would only grin and try to cover whatever she felt
inside. She was forever talking out in class, chewing gum,
or getting caught cheating on tests and getting paddlings. I
particularly remember a licking she received in the fifth
grade from Miss Betty Bennett, a skinny, severe-faced little
spinster. Miss Bennett had Kathy bent over a table, one
hand on Kathy's collar while she blistered her with a
wooden paddle. Kathy was wearing a skirt that was a couple of sizes too small: it rode up her ample thighs to reveal
her broad behind clad in a pair of panties that were riddled
with holes. I remember Kathy weeping with shame as the
teacher thrashed her, one hand bent behind trying to tug
down her skirt, her dignity and fleshy buttocks exposed to
the world while the class watched in fascination and dis-
dain.

Puberty was especially cruel to Kathy, as if even God
and Nature enjoyed the joke too. In the sixth grade when
most girls developed a little curve to their hips, grew budding, small breasts, Kathy developed tits that would shame
an eighteen-year-old. Her already round hips grew rounder
and her face developed pimples that erupted like small
volcanoes.

Valentine Day was especially cruel to her. Each student
would labor half a day making a paper-and-lace pouch to
hang upon the wall, illustrated with our own versions of
cherubs, hearts, and archers. On Valentine Day, everyone

exchanged cards, filled the pouches with special messages of friendship or puppy love. Kathy's pouch, and Eddie Brown's if he even made one, remained empty except for a card from the teacher and one or two from a student like myself whose mother saw to it that no one in the class was omitted. Never once did she have a secret admirer write her a poem or leave candy hearts in her pouch. While the rest of the class buzzed with conversation, laughed, and flirted, she held the couple or three cards she had received and smiled.

In the seventh grade, our teacher tried to teach us about chivalry and manners. For a time, every Friday each boy drew a girl's name from a box, and at lunch he was required to sit with her after carrying her lunch tray to the table. Most of the fellows in class had "discovered" females, and for those fortunate enough to draw the name of a pretty girl, the meal was an event of heart pangs and triumph. Even if the girl was average, it allowed a budding young stud a chance to show off and experiment with new feelings and words. But for the unfortunate wretch who each week drew Kathy's name, the event was a humiliating experience worsened by teasing and catcalls.

"Oh God, I got Kathy Maxwell's name," a boy would cry, after reading the name, his face rent with exaggerated despair. Kathy would smile, maybe drop her chin an inch or two. The teacher would fuss at the boy for being rude. Depending on who had drawn the name, the meal shared by the two would be either eaten in total silence or punctuated with snide remarks and mean jokes.

I drew Kathy's name once. I was hoping to draw a shy, brown-eyed girl's name, but opened the folded scrap to see my fate. I didn't moan or shout, tried not to draw any attention. I folded the paper quickly and returned to my seat. Deep down, I had always felt sorry for her and others like Eddie Brown. I guess I realized how close most of us in the class were to their predicament, that with a larger nose on my face or a couple of weeks unemployment by my father, I could myself slide over the edge from being considered okay by the gang to being cast in the same league as Eddie or Kathy. I had actually talked with Kathy a couple of times when we happened to be cast together at school chores and no one else was listening. I found her voice quiet and smooth, an eagerness in her words that reminded me of a dog's attention after one snaps his fingers and extends a hand. I also remembered a time that I brought a snake to class for show and tell, and Kathy was the only classmate who would touch the reptile, as if she alone was able to find beauty in a creature that others saw with disgust.

I carried her tray to the table that day and sat with her and exchanged a few sentences, even gave her my peanut-butter-rice crispy crunch. Though I got some ridicule from some of the fellows later, I found their words forgettable, but the smile on Kathy's face was genuine and warm as a ray of sun.

As we continued through junior high, Kathy grew wider and bustier. Rumors sprang daily that she was pregnant, that she had taken on five guys at one time, that she had VD or some other social disease. I doubt seriously she had ever been kissed. I can imagine the thought of having children of her own was the furthest desire of her mind, for in many ways she had been a mother to her younger siblings all her life. Her mother worked the morning shift at a truck stop and left Kathy in charge of her three younger brothers each morning. The school bus came to her stop late on the route, and the sight was often comical as she attempted to herd her brothers on board. The family genes were apparent in all of them, wide bodies with fat, bulldoggy faces.

The brothers had usually been fighting, knees muddy, a shirt sleeve torn, a trail of snot on at least one's nose. Usually the smallest kid would bolt for the house at the sight of the bus and Kathy would haul him back by holding to his collar, the boy kicking and crying. She'd jam the three of them through the bus door, shoo them to the back to a seat. I often heard her question whether they still had their lunch money, and it was rare that each of them did. She'd take her own money from the small purse she carried and disperse it; she often skipped lunch, she rarely attended any of the puppet shows or magic acts that came for assembly, but sat in study hall with the other few unfortunates.

Kathy finally quit school early in her sophomore year soon after turning sixteen. I guess all the years of bearing the jokes and ridicule made even entering the adult world early seem the better choice. As I journeyed through high school, I would see her occasionally around town, usually working someplace like Hardee's or a 7-Eleven. She always had a smile for me, would ask how certain classmates were doing. One time when I ran into her during my senior year, I noticed she was wearing an especially loose dress and that her belly was large even by her standards. I didn't ask her who the father was or if she was married now, but hoped that finally she had met some fellow who was better than myself and my classmates, and was able to look beyond the plain shell of this woman and see the good heart inside.

Years later, following my divorce from my first wife, I was sitting in a bar in east Fayetteville, alone, nursing a pint of Wild Turkey, feeling drunk and sad. The bar was one of those honky-tonks where a man keeps his mouth shut and his eyes stationary if he's not one of the regulars. A couple of guys at another table kept eyeing me, and one made a wisecrack about my long sideburns. I was drunk enough not to know it was time to drink up and move on.

I felt a hand settle on my shoulder, soft and warm and firm, smelled perfume that smelled cheaply of flowers. I looked up to see Kathy. She was still round and large-breasted and plain, but she was a woman now, some of the weariness and harshness of her face masked with rouge and powder. She smiled down at me, kneaded my shoulder a moment.

"Why don't you walk outside with me a minute," she asked, already tugging at my shoulder. She frowned at the table of men who were harassing me. I slugged down the rest of my drink and stood, wondering what she wanted to talk about after all these years. She picked up my cap from the table, put it on my head, and led me to the front door like a child.

"Why don't you come on over to my place for a while," she said, moving close once we were outside the door. "I live next to here."

She looked halfway good through the alcohol, her hands were on my shoulder and were warm. If I'd had a couple more drinks in my gut, I might have gone.

"I would, sweetheart," I told her, "but I'm kinda drunk right now. I probably wouldn't be much good."

She smiled that same old knowing smile and leaned and kissed my cheek. "You always were a sweet one," she said. She narrowed one eye then, gripped my shoulder, then patted it hard with her hand. "Now I want you to go on home from here. This ain't no place for you to be sitting drunk."

I stared into her face and saw a determination that told me she would likely tote me to my car if necessary like she used to do with her little brothers. I nodded, she pecked my cheek, and I drove away from her and from a probable ass-whupping the guys inside had in mind for me. The last

I heard of Kathy, she'd had another chubby kid who looked just like her, was divorced for the second time, and was still hanging around the bars. I believe when a man undresses her and wraps his arms around her shoulders, if he will look in the hollow of her back he will notice she has tiny wings.

"FIRE UP ," Jasper cried, holding aloft a half-fifth of El Chico tequila, the nub of a cigarette between two fingers. He nursed at the bottle, then threw his head back and shouted again, "Fire up, y'all."

The day was warm under a clear springtime sky, the air scented with the contrasting odors of two hundred pounds of hog slowly cooking, honeysuckle blossoms, dime-store perfume, and marijuana smoke. Nearly a hundred men, women, and children were scattered in bunches across a pasture of fescue, all enjoying the festivities of the fifth annual May Day Melee held in Cumberland County. I was in my mid-twenties and had come to swap lies with friends, swill beer, and eat good, greasy barbecued pork.

While May Day in most places was celebrated with people joining hands and minds to wish for peace, prosperity, and growth, the May Day Melee was an orgy of Budweiser and pit-bull fighting. The gathering was held at Wayne's house, a double-wide that sat a quarter mile off the road and out of sight of the sheriff's patrol. Here many of the residents of Fayetteville's east side released a winter's tension accumulated from layoffs, high heating bills, sick younguns, and long days working outside in the cold.

The community of east Fayetteville for decades had been the poor side of town, a collection of squat frame houses in need of paint, boarded-up stores, and bars with names like Thelma's Place and Little Reno. Most of the residents of the east side were a no-nonsense lot, born to a life of laboring by hand—plumbers, route salesmen, waitresses, sales clerks, roofers—hard-living people who had seen life from all angles except the top. Many of the men were veterans of the military and worked fifty-hour weeks. The women juggled part-time jobs, cared for the children, and kept up with the bills. They paid their taxes, stayed barely ahead of their creditors, and generally lived within the law. The people of this community, and ten thousand similar ones across America, constituted the backbone of our culture. For their daily sacrifice, these people believed fiercely in their rights in private life. If someone wanted to take a drink of untaxed liquor or smoke a joint, he felt he had earned that privilege as long as the bills got paid. And if he wanted to fight a chicken, wanted to see a dogfight, he owned that animal, fed it, and watered it—by God, he felt it was his personal business and right.

Wayne was a mechanic, pushing forty, and had fought dogs most of his life. He admitted the practice was ugly and bloody. He also admitted that pit bulls were unpredictable and shouldn't be allowed unsupervised around children. Still, he defended fighting the dogs on several grounds.

"They love it. A pit bull would rather fight than eat," he explained. "We ain't making them fight. I've had dogs break their chain while I was working and tie up and fight till both couldn't stand up, with not a soul watching them or urging them on.

"As for the people who say it's cruel to fight dogs or chickens, that it should stay illegal," he continued, "I'll bet you a dollar that most of these same people defend abortion, say it's all right if they want to kill their own unborn babies."

Such was the logic of many dogfighters, tempered by a life of living hand to mouth, some dignity gained in the belief in a clear superiority of man over beast.

Jasper was in charge of cooking the hog. He took pride in that ability and had concocted his own sauce over the years, a potent blend of vinegar, hot peppers, and God knows what else.

Jasper pitched two no-hitters in his senior year in high school and was being scouted by the major leagues, but got busted with an ounce of pot a week before graduation. Things went downhill after that. He can still knock a bird out of a tree with a rock, and towards the bottom of a fifth he'll tell you what he could have done if it hadn't been for that rookie cop who nabbed him. He lifted the lid of the cooker, pierced the hog's skin with a knife, shook on a little more sauce, then slammed it shut.

"Getting there," he said. "'Bout another hour."

Powered by a drop cord, a stereo has been set up on the grass and tuned to the local country music channel. The air was filled with sounds of a good time: laughter, the clang of a horseshoe tournament, Emmylou Harris's melodic voice. Children shouted as they played tag between parked cars and pickup trucks.

Several of the trucks had pit bulls sitting in the cab or tied in the bed. The younger dogs yelped and pulled against their ropes; the older, experienced dogs saved their energy for later.

Pit-bull fighting at the Melee was not like the serious tournaments where thousands of dollars are bet, the dogs fought until one is dead or near dead. These dog owners were only out for local bragging rights—a little "roll," as they called it, a "scuff." Little or no money was bet. The dogs were only allowed to fight until one had clearly bettered the other—the owner called it when he thought his dog had had enough. Torn ears and facial cuts were usually the extent of the injuries, the pits good as new a couple of days later. The dogs were reflective of their masters, tough as nails for a few rounds, in for a quick knockout, but a little too soft in the belly to go the distance. As soon as the sun was lower, the crowd fed and well liquored, the fighting would begin.

A special buzz circulated among the dogfighters. Word was out that Tote Faircloth was coming to the Melee and bringing Roy Lee.

Years ago, Tote Faircloth sprang Roy Lee from the dog pound the day he got out of jail after tearing up the insides of a bar. The two had been inseparable ever since. Tote was an east-side legend. He was born Franklin Faircloth in the mountains of North Carolina and came to Fayetteville via the 82nd Airborne. In France during World War Two he won the Silver Star. After being discharged, Tote stayed in Fayetteville, married, sired a child, and settled into ordinary life as a welder.

His boy was three years old when he fell into a septic tank and drowned. The tragedy drove Tote and his wife to divorce, the war hero slowly turning to a life of hard drinking, fistfighting in bars, and catching canebreak rattlers that he sold to Special Forces at Fort Bragg.

Two theories circulated as to how his nickname began: one, that he often toted rattlesnakes around in a bucket in his truck; two, the more favored version, that he was christened by a lady friend who was impressed with what he toted around in his trousers.

Tote was a tall, barrel-chested man with big arms and lots of body hair. He wore licensed twin military .45s. Tote described Roy Lee as one-third pit bull, one-third crocodile, and one-third retarded. Roy Lee had one blue eye and one brown eye, a face full of scars, and yellow teeth, and might have been the fightingest creature on dry land. He had only one gear—forward. He let children ride his back, and hated all other dogs, from poodles to St. Bernards.

Several years before, I was riding one afternoon with Tote, searching the dirt roads of Cumberland County for snakes. Tote drove barely ten miles an hour, Roy Lee tied on a rope in back, yapping fiercely whenever we passed another dog. We were drinking Kessler's blended whiskey and iced tea, a Tote specialty. The sun was low, mourning doves calling from fields of cut hay, the air fragrant with overripe melons. "Where the hell is Roy Lee?" Tote asked suddenly, his eyes glued to the rearview mirror. "I thought he was tied in."

I craned my head around to see an empty truck bed. Tote jammed on the brakes.

Roy Lee was lying in the dirt behind the truck, the rope stretched tight between the spare tire and his collar. He wagged his tail but was slow getting up. The best we could figure out was that about three miles back, the harassment of two roadside dogs had got the best of Roy Lee. He had decided to "damn the rope" and jumped. The rope didn't snap and he had been dragged behind for a few miles while we exchanged small talk and sipped whiskey. Roy Lee had a bad collar burn around his neck and most of the hair on one flank was scraped off, but otherwise he was fine. Tote lifted the dog into the truck and shortened the rope, and within a mile, Roy Lee was barking again. Similar antics slowly magnified his reputation.

Jasper fussed over his hog, a second keg was tapped. Several melons were split for the youngsters, little hands grabbing gobs of sweet red flesh. The grumble of a low-geared motor sounded and another truck came into view— Tote, with Roy Lee riding shotgun. A murmur rolled through the ranks, and all the young bad-asses of east Fayetteville chewed their lips as the master arrived.

"Ain't it a goddam sight," Tote hollered through his

window, easing his truck forward until he was parked close
to the cooker. Roy Lee spied another dog, a tremor rolled
up his spine, his ears perked forward. "Hide the pretty
gals," Tote shouted. "Ole Tote likes them young and lean."

I hadn't seen Tote in nearly a year, but I had heard about
his greatest battle—cancer of the lungs. The doctor had to
cut out one to save him. When he swung out of his truck
and took two steps, I understood why he had driven so
close. Tote walked as if he balanced a crystal vase on his
head, putting each foot down carefully, swinging his shoulders to balance each step. He was still a big man, but the
operation, the chemotherapy, and the drugs had robbed
him of his balance, stripped away his speed and muscle
tone. Roy Lee followed at his heels, as if he sensed the old
man might need to put his hand down and rest. They came
slowly toward the cluster of people near the cooker.

"Lord, it's every hoodlum and sweetheart in Fayetteville," Tote said, calling names and shaking hands as he
passed clusters of men and women.

"Roy Lee is looking tough," a man said.

"Tough as two alligators and twice as mean," Tote answered. "I fed him nails and gunpowder for breakfast."

"You gonna fight him today?" another asked.

Tote hesitated for a second. "I doubt there's anything
here that would make him break sweat."

"Hey, you ain't got a rattlesnake in your pocket, have
you?" one of the women called.

Tote continued until he was close to the cooker. Jasper
grinned and lifted the lid and let him have a look, the steam
rising in a cloud around both of their heads. The skin was
starting to split on the hog's flanks, the fat bubbling.

"I ain't smelled it that good in a while," Tote said.

"You won't either," Jasper bragged. "This here is east
Fayetteville gourmet hog."

Everyone formed a sort of semicircle around Tote, those who had never seen him awed by his presence, those of us who knew him pained at the sight of what cancer had done. One of the men sitting in a chair offered it to Tote. The old warrior thanked him, then sat slowly, grimacing like his knees ached. He turned down the offer of a beer, and it was then I noticed he held no cigarette in his hand; I had never before seen him when he wasn't chain-smoking. Roy Lee sat at the arm of his chair, the white hair around his muzzle obvious in the bright sunshine.

Tote folded his hands over his gut, clasped his fingers together, and looked as fragile and wounded sitting there as he had looked the time I went to see him in the hospital. I'd heard the story recounted many times over the past few years, but never like the first time as he lay there propped up in the bed, his words slow and pained, his eyes flat like a lazy sky in August.

"Bad blood had been between me and Earl Cooper for some time. I don't even remember how it started, but we had a few fights, me coming out the better each time. We started keeping out of each other's way, and I thought the trouble had ended. Then one afternoon I was driving into town and saw a car approaching. It swerved into my lane for a second, then out, and when it passed, the driver had his arm out the window, shooting me the bird. I looked in my rearview and saw his brake lights flare, thought for a second maybe it was one of my buddies kidding with me. Then I recognized the car as belonging to Earl's son, a smart-mouthed twenty-two-year-old who had started hanging around the bars. We'd already had some words.

"If I had just kept on going, God I've wished a many times I did, but I'd had a few drinks. If I just hadn't turned around.

"The car pulled to the shoulder of the road, so I turned

around and drove up behind it. There was traffic on the road, so I got out on the passenger side and walked up to the car. Inside were four young men, beer cans in their hands. I could smell dope. They were all staring at me, the front window rolled down. I was leaning to look inside the window, to ask what their problem was, when I saw the glint of the barrel, and threw myself backwards a split second before the boy fired. He would have hit me square in the chest, but instead the slug ripped into my right shoulder.

" 'You hit him,' I heard one of the boys holler, then I could hear them scrambling and ducking like they were afraid I'd shoot back. I rolled up close to the car where he couldn't hit me again, blood spurting from the big hole in my shoulder. After a second, the driver's door opened and the boy's tennis shoe appeared, then the second. He was coming to finish me off. I already had one of my .45s out, so I cocked the hammer and rolled to my belly, watching the steps under the car.

"I was praying he'd stop. All I wanted was for him to get back in the car and leave. I even hollered for him to stop. Told him to go from there. But he wouldn't stop; he was coming to kill me.

"I watched the boy's steps until they paused at the rear of the car. My finger was tight on the trigger, sweat trickling down the furrow between my eyes. I heard him take a deep breath, then he came in a rush.

"I was ready, had my arms locked. He jumped out cowboy-style, feet wide, had his gun held in both hands, raised over his head. He brought it down, had it almost leveled on me when I shot, hit him right between his eyes. Where the bullet went in, it made just a little round hole, but it blew out the back of his skull and slung blood and brains all over my truck windshield. He was dead before he hit the ground.

"Something died inside me that same day," Tote said slowly, "but if I hadn't killed him, he would have killed me. It drove me kinda crazy for a while."

Tote was cleared in a self-defense plea. For two years after the killing, he drove around with an inch-thick steel plate bolted to the rear window on the driver's side to prevent someone from shooting him from behind. I've read that some doctors think people let cancers start in their bodies when they allow stress and heartache to get the better of them, and I believe on that hot afternoon when Tote squeezed off that round, the first cell turned on him, starting growing strangely and multiplying into what was killing him today.

"Whoever eats the fastest, eats the most," Jasper finally yelled, waving aloft a steaming rib he had pulled from the hog.

Most of the men stood back and waited for the women and the children to fill their plates, some out of politeness, most out of reluctance to pile food on top of a good high. For the next half hour, the shouts and fits of laughter were muffled as people stuffed their bellies full of hot barbecue, coleslaw, and hushpuppies. Tote fixed himself a generous plate, but didn't eat much of it, instead shoveled bites off to Roy Lee, who thumped his tail in gratitude.

The first dogs were faced off when the trees were throwing shadows across the field. The pits were brother and sister, but family matters little to this breed once past adolescence. Mothers will fight sons, fathers their own daughters just as readily. Both dogs were brindle in color, both veterans, their ears notched and ragged, scars showing on their lips and snouts. They sat with ten feet of grass between them, heads lowered and eyes intent while their owners loosened their collars. The crowd had formed a wide circle, giving the animals plenty of room to turn, tumble, or run if inclined. Few ever ran.

On cue, the collars were slipped, and the dogs leaped forward on bunched muscles. When they were a yard apart, the male dog leaped, the bitch rose to her haunches to meet him head up in midair. They locked, jaw to jaw, a chorus of snarls coming from deep in their throats. The male's momentum knocked the bitch to her back, but she held her grip, her better leverage making him lose his hold. The male snapped at air, trying to twist his head enough to get another bite. Blood showed on his teeth.

"Eat that nose up," the bitch's owner encouraged her. "Tear that nose off."

"Skit 'er," the male dog's owner encouraged. "Pull loose, Demon. Skit 'er, boy."

The bitch held her bite for half a minute until the male was able to twist loose, his lip tearing as they came apart. Both dogs scrambled to their feet, the bitch grabbing the male by one front leg, the male nailing her on the ear. Both dogs had good holds; they stood on splayed legs and shook and growled and shook some more, tails wagging as if being caressed. After they held for two minutes with neither losing grip, the owners moved and pried the dogs' mouths open with wedged-shaped sticks. They were allowed to rest a minute, their breath flinging slobber flecked with drops of blood. The bitch's ear was cut again, the male's jaw bloody, one leg swelled at midjoint. When the dogs were released, they slammed together without hesitation.

The siblings fought through two more breaks, each time the bitch going for a leg hold, the male chewing into the loose skin covering her head and ears. Most people shouted for the bitch. When the dogs were broken apart a fourth time, although the bitch was bleeding worse, her wounds were only skin cuts. The male had fared worse, his sister having bit into muscle backed by bone, puncture wounds that were swelling rapidly. The male's owner studied the dog, a ring of observers gave advice. Finally, the man straightened.

"Let's face 'em for a second," he said. They turned the dogs, held them a couple of feet apart, both animals lunging to fight.

"Y'all see him now," the male's owner shouted. "He's game. He's got heart."

People in the crowd agreed, helping the man ease his pride. "Come on, Demon," the man said, leading the dog toward his truck. "You'll get her next time." In a lowered, scolding voice, "You can't slack off them ladies, boy."

Three more sets of dogs fought, all the fights ending the same way, a lot of blood but nothing that couldn't be cured with a shot of penicillin, a night's rest with food and water. The beer flowed, joints were rolled and passed. Jasper, who had passed out a half an hour ago in his garden chair, struggled to his feet and stood there on wavering legs, his eyes still closed, while urine darkened the front of his trousers. He sat back down, heavily, returning to whatever inning he was pitching, the cheers he deserved, oblivious to the guffaws and catcalls.

"Hey Tote," a man in his late twenties shouted. "My dog wants Roy Lee. He's calling him out."

He was a big guy, rawboned, with black hair greased back like Elvis. He had drunk heavily since noon, and his mean streak was starting to surface.

Tote eyed the young man from where he stood on the far side of the circle. "Buddy, I've done put Roy Lee in the cab. He's so full of barbecue he wouldn't fight a rabbit."

"Tote, nowwww, Tote, I don't want to hear it," the man said, walking into the open circle. "I been hearing half my life about Roy Lee. You brought him. Let him fight my dog."

"Let Roy Lee scuff," several other men joined in.

"Let him go, Tote," another said. "Roy Lee could fart and knock his dog down."

I could tell that Tote was against it the way he chewed at his lip, but there were just too many bright eyes turned on him, too many half-cocked smiles. Finally, he nodded once, turned, and started for his truck. A chorus of cheers erupted.

The younger man started for his own vehicle. He was back in less than a minute with his dog, a short-legged animal with a big head and massive jaws. His name was Repete—the son of Pete, a dog that had once fought Roy Lee to a standoff. Pete was dead from heartworms. Repete was fighting for the first time, barely past puppy stage, but he had good blood, looked fit and hard as a hickory knot.

Tote was gone a full five minutes, but he returned with Roy Lee walking beside him on a short length of chain, the dog acting different now, his head high and his eyes shiny as quarters. He knew damn well what was about to take place. Roy Lee searched the crowd, looking for his opponent, and when he spied him, his ears went back, his nostrils flared, a ridge of hair stood up on his back. The black dog was more interested in wagging his tail and looking at the crowd, but when his owner turned his head toward Roy Lee, he momentarily lunged against his chain and barked—the sign of a rookie.

Tote kneeled slowly beside Roy Lee, talked into his ear, and unhooked his collar. Across the circle, the other man was joined by his son, a seven-year-old who had played with the black dog since he was a weaned puppy. The man assured the boy that his dog would be all right, the kid's eyes shifting from his pet to Roy Lee and back again.

The dogs were faced off. "Roy Lee gonna put war on his ass," someone called. Roy Lee stared intently at his opponent, the black dog still interested in the excitement around him, licking the kid's hand when he reached to pat him one last time. Tote looked into the younger man's eyes, then nodded his head. Both dogs were released at the same time. Roy Lee hit the black dog while he was still gawking, slamming him to his back and grabbing a mouthful of throat.

The black dog learned quickly what closed fangs felt like, his world suddenly reduced to one fight. A guttural growl came from deep inside, all thoughts of the boy, of afternoons lying in the sun, erased. Using the strength in his big shoulders, the dog pivoted and got to his feet, twisted Roy Lee's neck until he lost his hold. Both dogs reared up on their hind legs and locked up jaw to jaw, gristle popping and slobber flying. Encouragement was shouted from the crowd on both sides. The dogs broke hold, backed off a foot, the slammed together again, the natural styles of fighting starting to emerge.

The black dog was by build and nature a "leg dog," using his shorter stature to bulldoze under Roy Lee to get at his legs or belly. Roy Lee was a "throat dog," instinctively going for his opponent's windpipe. The dogs feinted and parried, the younger dog using superior speed and strength, Roy Lee relying on his experience, leaning on his opponent, tucking his front legs far back to keep them out of his jaws. When both dogs got strong holds and kept them for a couple of minutes, they were broken apart. Roy Lee breathed hard, but was unhurt, just a small gash opened on his lower jaw. The black dog bled from his mouth and ear.

"Let's don't fight him no more," the kid said to his daddy, eyes wide at the sight of his bleeding pet. The man ignored him. A woman came up behind the boy and laid her hands on his shoulders.

Roy Lee hit the black dog again, slammed him to his

back and got a good hold on his throat. The black dog gasped for breath and struggled to free himself. Roy Lee fought only with his mouth, lying limp while the other dog wasted energy trying to get loose. He choked and sucked at the air, unable even to growl. The boy whimpered and asked again for his father to stop them. Finally, the black dog broke Roy Lee's hold, but was behind on breath and short on energy. Roy Lee hit him again, this time bit into his soft belly. The black dog turned and snapped Roy Lee's leg, but he jerked it from his jaws and out of reach before he bit down. Roy Lee chewed at his belly, shook his head violently back and forth. Suddenly, the black dog yelped a shrill cry of pain and frustration.

"Stop them, Daddy," the boy cried, tears suddenly in his eyes. "He's getting hurt."

"Stop them, Larry," the man's wife said, a big-hipped woman in jeans. "You're scaring him."

"Y'all shut the hell up," the man said, his eyes still intent on his dog. "Damn dog was born to fight." An embarrassed murmur rolled through the crowd.

When the black dog squealed, Roy Lee fought harder, bit deeper into his belly and shook, then released his hold and sprang for his throat again. The black dog met him with open jaws, but Roy Lee feinted, let the dog's inexperience carry him by, then nailed him from the rear. He soon had his opponent on his back again in a throat hold. The black dog gasped.

"We ought to stop this," Tote said to the man. "Your dog's game. He's just young."

"He's gotta fight to learn," the man snapped.

Roy Lee's tail twitched back and forth as he choked the younger dog. The black dog got weaker, unable to break the hold, his breath now coming in short gasps. He tried to squeal again, the sound high-pitched like a dying rabbit.

The boy sobbed. His mother pushed him toward the rear of the crowd and took a step toward her husband. "You don't stop them, I will, Larry," she shouted shrilly. "The dog's gonna die!"

The man whirled about and lashed out with one arm, slapped the woman hard across her face, caused her to pitch backwards to the ground. She put her hand to her mouth, her eyes stunned as she stared at her husband.

Tote stepped forward. He shouted, "Roy Lee!" and touched his dog's back. "Off now, off, Roy Lee," he said. "Ease off now."

Roy Lee broke his hold immediately, and Tote pulled him backwards by the tail. The black dog tried to get up once and attack, but his legs buckled. He rolled to the side and panted for air.

"Fight's over," Tote said to the other man, buckling the collar around Roy Lee.

"Let the damn dogs fight," the man said loudly. "My dog ain't finished."

"Mine's finished," Tote answered.

"You scared?" the man said. "I thought you were supposed to be so tough." His fist curled slowly at his side. "You look chicken to me."

A hush fell over the crowd, the only sound the boy crying. Tote stared deep into the man's eyes. "I ain't scared, son," Tote said. "But I ain't letting my dog kill yours."

The man pointed his finger at Tote. "I still say you're chickenshit."

I saw that same look enter Tote's eyes, the sheen I noticed when he was lying in the hospital bed, as if he was tallying up a life spent fighting and boozing, with only a fading reputation to show for it, a cancer in his chest that would eventually kill him. Any one of a dozen would have stepped in for Tote if it came to blows, but I feel Tote could probably still have taken the guy, fighting like Roy Lee had, on experience and guts and the grace God seems to give some people. I suspect as Tote stared across the ring, as the man's insult still rang in his ears, he saw the resemblance of another would-be warrior, one who'd still be living today if he'd had the sense to keep driving.

"I ain't scared of you, son," Tote finally said. "Not of a man who would slap his own wife."

The man's gaze faltered, his eyes flicked to the ground, then to his wife and son. Tote turned and led Roy Lee to the truck, the old dog limping slightly. Tote placed his feet carefully, like walking a beam. The two shuffled away from us, brushing together occasionally as if they leaned inward to one another for support.

I HAVE always carried a certain fascination for the likes of Eddie Brown, Tote, and Kathy and the other characters of Fayetteville who live the hard life. I mingle with them, drink with them, even enjoy a certain reputation of my own as a man unafraid of handling rattlesnakes, but know inside I don't have their grit. I would walk away from a man before I would cut his lung in half, hope I am never faced with having to shoot another before he kills me. My mother taught me boundaries that so far I have refused to cross. But I harbor a certain amount of shame for not defending those children I grew up with who did not have the strong ties of love to tug them through the hard job of growing up. "My mama fucks, My daddy sucks, The younguns eat shit" is a pretty loud cry for a fifth-grader. Back last winter, he was walking home late at night from a bar when he was jumped by a carload of men. They beat him, then drove the point of a hunting knife through his forehead and into his brain. By the trail of blood, Eddie's grit made him get up and walk another hundred yards to the middle of the span bridge that dropped to the east side. In the middle of the bridge, ironically, juxtaposed between the split-level brick homes and manicured lawns of west Fayetteville and the bowels of real life on the east side, he gave it all up and collapsed. They say a man's life passes before him when he is dying. I hope for Eddie, when he was bleeding to death in the middle of that bridge, suspended between the two worlds of Fayetteville, he didn't have to live all that hurt again.

A COCK crowed somewhere beyond the tobacco field. He sang of freedom, not long rows of backbreaking labor curving slightly for a quarter mile. The sun still huddled behind a thick stand of pine as six croppers, aged fourteen to forty-nine, stood in silence at the edge of the field. Johnson was President, the Beatles were doing drugs. The cool July morning was socked in with fog. The rooster crowed again, and I would have gladly wrung his head off for a couple more hours in the warm bed.

From the barn we heard the chug-chug of the Farmall tractor that would soon be bringing us the first trailer to fill. Bandy Williams, a short, thick black man who had pulled time for manslaughter, began pissing on top of a nest of fire ants. He scraped his tongue with his teeth, then spit in an arc that carried twelve feet. I glanced at Roy Chavis, who was studying the wet tobacco stalks with similar dread. His pale blue eyes still had sleep cracklings in the corners. He held a blade of grass between his thick lips, and tufts of curly black hair spilled from under his toboggan cap. He claimed to be a Lumbee Indian and would fight you if you doubted him. The chug of the tractor grew closer as I checked the buttons on my flannel shirt, hitched up my jeans, and adjusted the rim of my baseball cap. Bandy finished flooding the ants, then pulled a pint bottle of Richards wine, better known as "the blood," from his back pocket. He unscrewed the cap, winked at me, then made the wine boil, a *gluk, gluk* sound escaping from his mouth between swallows. "Fire up, boys," he shouted as the tractor was pulling between rows. "Bet every one of you is toting the monkey by ten o'clock."

We all knew our rows. Today was the second time we had cropped this field. Although we would be walking bent double all day, at least the heavy, gritty bottom leaves known as sand lugs were gone. Frankie Smith, whose dad owned the field, stopped the tractor and trailer a hundred feet down the rows. He was eighteen and loud-mouthed and due to report to the Army in two weeks. He stood up and turned around and smirked. "Y'all might as well dive on in. Barn help will be arriving in a minute."

Diving in was a good description of the shock that came from butting headfirst into the tangle of dew-dripping leaves, my right hand curling around the stalk and snapping off the bottom three or four yellowing leaves, tucking them under my armpit. After only a few yards, my clothes were as soaked as if I had dived into the creek. Any last memories of sleep were snatched away and the reality set in—today is Wednesday, the middle of a week of working sunup to twilight in the tobacco fields of eastern North Carolina.

A thick-bodied water snake lay curled at the base of one of my stalks, enjoying the moist shade. I saw it at the last second and instinctively jumped backwards, stopping my shout just behind my teeth. The snake flattened his body against the sand. I saw that Roy was at the trailer, placing his armload of leaves down carefully, stems to the outside. I nudged the snake with the toe of my shoe until it slipped over into his row, then bent and resumed cropping, biting my tongue to keep from laughing.

Roy and I were racing to the end of our rows, and only seconds passed before I heard the expected gasp, then the crackle of leaves breaking. He broke down two stalks in his backwards flight.

"Asshole. You saw that snake," he swore at me. "Damn thing like to bit my hand."

I was laughing at Roy now, peering over the top of the stalks to see where the other croppers were. Bandy was across the tractor lane, bringing his row along steadily as always. The two McNatt brothers were a stalk or two behind Bandy. Preston Watts was bringing up the rear, a pimply-faced gangly boy who was working his first year in the fields. "Kick it over there in Bandy's row," I told Roy.

"Yeah, I know I will. And get myself killed," he said.

The stalks were drying, the sun hanging red and swollen above the treetops. Now that the dew was gone, tobacco gum was beginning to collect on my hands and wrists, and would eventually coat them like a second skin. I beat Roy to the end of the field by a few stalks. We laid down our leaves and flopped down to rest while the tractor and other croppers caught up. Bandy's forehead was gleaming with sweat when he finished. "The monkey gonna get y'all soon enough," he said, chuckling at the young boy just finishing his row. The tractor had already turned down the next row, Frankie standing up and shouting for us to get started.

"I'll snatch his young ass off that tractor," Bandy swore under his breath.

The rows slipped by, each full trailer hooked behind Mr. Smith's pickup to be hauled to the barn, an empty one left so we could continue cropping. My back was all aching above my belt when we heard a shout from the end of the field and knew break time was here.

I have seen little in life that could compete with that cold Pepsi-Cola and a pack of cheese nabs. The barn help had to pay for their snack, but the croppers—the elite—got theirs free. I rubbed dirt over my hands to cover the stickiness, then settled back against the stump to enjoy a ten-minute feast of sugar and caffeine.

Bandy had unfolded his pocketknife and was stabbing it repeatedly into the sand. Each time the blade emerged, it gleamed a little brighter. "Ole Preston wishing right now he was back at the barn," Bandy kidded. We laughed with him as Preston mumbled under his breath and turned away. Last year I had endured the same hazing. Too soon, Frankie was cranking the tractor and shouting that it was time for us to get back to work.

"I'll be glad when your butt is in the Army," Roy told him, "and some big-ass sergeant is yelling in your face."

"There ain't nobody yelling in my face," Frankie answered, lifting his chin and bowing out his chest.

Row after row after row, standing to stretch, to look and see how far still to the end of the field, the gum on my hands growing thick like a black callus, sweat funneling down the lines of my brow and stinging my eyes, gazing into a sun that was high and silver and hot—there was always an empty trailer waiting for us. I could have danced when we heard the long blast of the truck horn coming from the barn, finally calling us to lunch.

I was a fourteen-year-old whose world consisted of an area about twelve miles in radius, and I found great ceremony and pride in coming to the barn from the field, a cur dog barking at the tractor as it approached, Roy and I standing on the rear of the trailer, backs straight and heads up, the women and children and men too old to crop looking up and watching as Frankie gunned the throttle, dust boiling up from the wheels.

"Y'all quit looking at the men and hand me that 'bac-cer," snapped Charlotte, a heavy-breasted black woman. "Y'all want to eat, we got to finish this trailer."

She was one of three loopers, whose job was to tie the tobacco to sticks before it was carried to the barn. The handers were mostly young women, grabbing handfuls of the leaves by their stems and holding them out for the looper. "Stick," Charlotte cried, snapping the end of the string, glaring at an eight-year-old boy whose job it was to carry the finished bundles of tobacco to the barn, where two men were hanging it. "You better get that stick, youngun," she fussed when the boy was slow.

"You heard her. Move," Roy said as he hurried by. Several children too small to work were playing in the dirt with sticks and toy trucks, the tracks of snot under their noses coated with dust.

I had my eye on one of the handers, a girl my age from town who was visiting her cousin for the summer. Her name was Melody. I knew she had never worked in tobacco before by the way she took twice as long as other handers to bunch the leaves together. Mary Elliot was her looper, and I could tell she was impatient with Melody's slow work by the way she snatched the leaves from her hand. Still, Mabel said nothing. Melody was white and from the city. I leaned against the trailer and studied the girl, her skin pale, her white shorts and pink polo shirt forever ruined by smears of tobacco gum. Although her hands had a generous coat-ing of tobacco gum, I could see that her fingernails were painted red. She stood out like a bluebird among crows beside the other women dressed in drab work clothes that could be washed and worn again and again.

Charlotte shouted, "Stick," and this time the boy was quicker to get the forty-pound bundle out of the way. "Girl, I wish you'd get your eyes off them boys and look at that 'baccer," she fussed at one of the handers who was smiling at Roy. "Tired as my legs are, this ain't no time to be courting." The girl hung her head in embarrassment. Once I caught Melody's eye, but immediately looked down and began dusting off my trousers.

The trailer was finished and everyone began loading into the beds of pickups to be driven to Jake Carter's country store for lunch. Jake kept a card where he scribbled down the cost of what you ate, and Smith took the sum out of your pay.

Carter's store was a squat wooden building with a big front glass window and one gas pump advertising regular at thirty-one cents a gallon. Inside were shelves stacked high with tin goods, a chest cooler filled with sodas, a small meat counter containing lengths of liver pudding, hot dogs, and hoop cheese. I finally decided on a lunch of canned cold spaghetti, graham crackers topped with slices of sharp cheddar, and a quart of chocolate milk. Roy chose to splurge and buy a short loaf of white bread, a half pound of bologna, a can of Vienna sausages, and two Mountain Dews. We walked outside to sit under the shade of a big willow tree on upturned Pepsi crates, the croppers sticking together, the women bunched in another group. Charlotte had brought her lunch, taking two homemade biscuits filled with salt pork and molasses from a paper sack. She ate slowly, pulling the tough meat through gums that had been minus teeth for years. Melody had gone home with her cousin to eat, so it was easy for me to gobble the food, then slip into a half hour of light sleep.

BY TWO O'CLOCK, the temperature was in the nineties, and the humidity made the sweat coat my skin like another layer of clothes. The sky was clouding up, the west beginning to darken with thunderheads so common during the summer. Everyone had slowed up—Roy and I deciding to call the racing a draw, Bandy nipping from a second pint he bought at lunch, Preston lagging further and further behind. "Monkey's got your ass for sure," Bandy told Preston when he finally staggered from his row, while the rest of us took a few minutes' break in the shade of a cottonwood. Preston looked bad, his face pale, the skin around his eyes pulled tight and shiny. Our peace was spoiled by the booming of Smith's voice as he emerged from the field with a full load of ripe leaves under one arm.

"Shit, y'all quitting on me?" he grumbled. "Damn 'baccer is burning up in the field." Frankie hurried to his seat on the tractor while his dad laid his load of leaves in the trailer. "Who's cropping this third row?" he asked, pointing at a stalk. After hesitating a moment, Preston raised his hand. Smith glared at him. "Well, son, you're leaving way too much. See what I got off just one row?"

Preston said he was sorry and hung his head. Frankie pulled the tractor into the next row, and the rest of us dove under the leaves again to escape Smith's quick temper. The clouds in the west had grown darker and heavier, the wind picking up, occasionally a low growl of thunder sounding. We were finishing the row when Preston fainted.

He walked out from between the last stalks, stood for a moment tottering on his feet, then stumbled backwards and went down like someone had clipped him solidly on his chin. He rolled his head to one side and puked up what looked like a couple of chewed hot dogs.

"Jesus Christ," Smith swore as he emerged from the field where he had been cropping behind Preston. "Get that water jug over here," he shouted at Frankie. We clustered over him, none of us laughing, for we all had had our bouts with the monkey. Smith poured water on his handkerchief, then mopped the boy's forehead. Preston mumbled something, then tried to sit up, but Smith kept him down. The wind was rising, the thunder was louder and closer. Smith scanned the clouds, his face bunched under the creases of a frown. "Y'all go ahead and carry five rows," he said. "We need another trailer to finish the barn. I'll take him home."

We raced down the rows then, but not in competition, with the lightning getting sharp and none of us liking to be in the middle of a field.

"You ain't laughing at us now, are you," Bandy shouted to Frankie, who was hunkered down atop the tractor. "Your ass liable to get zapped up there."

We chugged out of the rows when the trailer was barely full, with the wind roaring in the treetops and the rain moving toward us across the field. The flashes of lightning and blasts of thunder came simultaneously, and the noise hit my ears like the roar of shotguns. Ahead, people at the barn were scurrying to get everything under the big shelter. The rain caught us, falling in huge drops that splatted against the ground, throwing up puffs of dust. I could see Melody's pink blouse like a beacon, now that the day had changed to twilight.

HARVESTING tobacco was never the same in the seasons that followed. Frankie got gutted by a mine in his second month in Vietnam, and Bandy was found floating in an irrigation pond the following spring, a half-drained wine bottle stuck in the mud, a six-pound catfish on his line. Smith bought one of the new tobacco harvesters and we all were demoted to barn help. But I have forever carried in my memory the image of that afternoon—Frankie standing up lean and tall, his hand jammed against the throttle, Roy and I holding on to the end of the trailer like soldiers on a wild chariot ride, racing away from the old days, into the future.

———

DONNIE JERNIGAN fished in his jeans pocket and pulled out a dollar bill. He rubbed it between his index finger and thumb.

"You boys go get ya a drink and a hot dog," he said, reaching into the back seat to where Bruce and I sat behind him and my sister, Karen. Karen peeped at us and smiled shyly.

I took the dollar and nodded for Bruce to get out. I knew the game well by now; Karen was not allowed to go to the drive-in alone. The trade-off for the food was that we were not to return for at least thirty minutes so they could get some smooching in without two little brothers' eyes burning the backs of their heads.

Late sixties, the heyday of drive-in theaters. I was thirteen and Karen sixteen, and already dating the boy she would eventually marry. Donnie was from Broadslab, North Carolina, a farming community known best for making good moonshine, and was the son of hardscrabble farming people. But he was hardworking and smart and already in his first year at Fayetteville Technical Institute, where he was studying business management.

A western played on the big screen of the Fox Theater. Bruce and I peered over our shoulders at the enlarged gunfight taking place while we maneuvered through cars to the snack bar in the center of the parking lot. A dollar would buy two boxes of popcorn, two Pepsis, and a couple of those plastic-tasting hot dogs that were so good. A person could add as much mayonnaise, mustard, and relish as he liked.

We carried our food to an empty speaker a row in front of Donnie's car, brushed off the hard-packed dirt, and sat down. I clicked on the loudspeaker. The autumn was still warm, and we could see the screen even better outside. I wasn't too worried about Karen, anyway. I knew she could handle Donnie.

One night only weeks into Karen's relationship with Donnie, I had spied on her as she defended her virginity. The hour was late, my parents asleep, I had gotten up to pee. The door to the living room was cracked open, and from the dark hallway I could see light flooding from the room. No noise. I crept closer.

Karen and Donnie lay on the sofa kissing, my sister on top where she knew she could spring away at the slightest sound from Mama's door. I watched them kiss for a moment, slightly disgusted at the smoochy sounds they made. As I watched, Donnie slowly slid his hand from the small of Karen's back to her behind, kneading the flesh under her jeans as he worked his way down. I felt a flash of anger at him fondling my sister, mixed with fascination. After several seconds, Karen reached with one hand and grasped his, and placed it back upon her spine. Seconds passed, Donnie made his move again. She moved his hand. He tried again. This time Karen held on to his hand and locked fingers. After a couple of minutes, his other hand began trailing down from her shoulder toward her armpit. I felt the urge to laugh.

I crept away from the door and went into the bathroom. We'd had conveniences like hot and cold running water, a washing machine, and an indoor toilet for a few months now in the new house, but the toilets flush could still surprise us in the middle of the night. I made a little extra noise and flushed the commode in case Karen had grown tired of the wrestling match, then got back in bed.

Bruce and I stayed outside under the speaker until we had crunched the last ice in our cups. The ground had gotten hard and we were getting cold. I peered over my shoulder and could see Karen and Donnie's heads, so I knew a time-out had been called in the struggle.

"Come on," I said to Bruce, and we started for the car. I knew that twenty minutes into the second feature, Donnie would hand us each a quarter and say, "Y'all boys go get you some candy."

MY GRANDMA McLaurin has fought the domestic wars with husbands, sons, brothers, and fathers for ninety years. Her mind is still clear, her wizened hands as tough as leather. She has lived these years with her mind directed toward heaven and her feet firmly entrenched in North Carolina soil.

Grandma and her brothers were raised in an orphanage. She was studious as a child, the orphanage was backed by several churches, and following high school, Grandma was sent to a two-year woman's college. Romance intervened; she met my grandpa, a young, handsome dirt farmer, quit college, and married him. Afterwards, she lived a hard but honorable life, birthed seven children, worked the fields, taught Sunday school, buried her three sons, and outlived her husband by now twenty-some years. She is a natural storyteller, and I can listen to her talk of the old days for hours.

"We were farming a lot of cotton back then when Reese and the other younguns were being born," she said. "I'd go to the field with the children. The oldest would work and those too little would play in the shade of a tree. Whoever was a baby then I'd let sleep under the tree and assign one of the older girls to keep the gnats chased away. For lunch, we'd eat whatever was coming out of the garden. You didn't see baby food back then. I'd chew up food in my mouth and spit it in a spoon and feed the baby that way."

Granny Baggett, my mother's mom, was a woman torn between her religion and her attraction to big-shouldered men. She was a devout Primitive Baptist, wrote essays and poems based on her beliefs, worked a career as a practical nurse, and loved and divorced three husbands. She lived inside Fayetteville, bought the first color television I ever watched, and fished for hours, regardless if she got a nibble.

My own mother seems a mixture of the two grandmothers. Granny pushed her in high school to attend nursing school, but she opted to marry my father at sixteen. Their first home was in the upstairs of a large farmhouse where Dad worked as hired help on a dairy farm. Three years later she began having babies, the last, my baby sister Kelli, born when she was forty-one. She is strong in her belief in God, but not so fundamentalist she cannot accept the possibility of evolution or even reincarnation.

Mama has always hated alcohol and its effect on the men she loves. Too many times she helped my father into bed after worrying late into the night if he would make it home. She has seen me and my brothers try to slip by her on wobbly legs, our breath perfumed with Certs. Ironically, she enjoys a very occasional half-glass of wine, but she prefers sweet, fortified wines like Mogen David or Richards, the choice of winos, and known locally as Mad Dog and the Blood. She will turn her nose up at a good, dry California or French wine. Since my youth, I have always been able to talk freely with her of subjects ranging from drugs and sex to religion.

Today, I often feel guilty when I complain of the pressure and trials in raising two children. Mama raised five of us at one time in a house without an indoor bathroom, on limited income, and without such escape as Mother's Morning Out social programs, movies, or vacations.

"I remember good as yesterday staying up after midnight with a sick baby in my lap," she tells me. "Reese would be working, the baby crying, and I'd be so tired I could hardly sit up. But what was I going to do? I couldn't throw you out the door. I would tell myself, 'It'll be better tomorrow. Just hold on till tomorrow.' "

I WAS not unique coming of age in the days of the early seventies. Sex and drugs among teenagers were still uncommon. Today, I have nephews who are more experienced at these things at fourteen than I was when I went off to Marine boot camp. Times were simpler then, we moved slower into new areas. At fourteen I was more interested in perfecting my game of basketball than getting laid. I did receive my first kiss at fourteen, however, and the brief duet hinted strongly that there were more interesting ways to break a sweat than just bouncing a basketball against hot asphalt.

She was my second cousin, a year younger, raven-haired and blue-eyed with the full pouty lips of a baby and the body of an eighteen-year-old. She was visiting my aunt for a few days from the city of Goldsboro. We sat together in a swing in the side yard and she kept staring deep into my eyes.

I ran out of ridiculous small talk. I was not so naive as to think she only wanted to talk. I was simply scared and without the least knowledge of how to make a first move. She had sprayed herself with mosquito repellent, and the sweet odor was like perfume. I finally reached out and touched her hair; she moved closer to me, lifted her face; I told her her hair was nice. When I finally did press my face to hers, we bumped noses. I rotated my head and pressed against her lips and discovered a new use for my tongue. It all suddenly seemed as natural as candy. We held the kiss like we were stuck together until my aunt hollered blindly through the back door for her to come inside. She was leaving that night to return home. We exchanged addresses. I floated down the road home, totally awash in infatuation. The hand I had clasped behind her neck still smelled of bug spray, and I refused to wash it for a couple of days; the scent churned my stomach with love pangs. But within a week, I was back on the basketball court; she was miles away. The kiss was buried under dreams of playing first-string guard.

I remember distinctly the day that basketball took second place forever to females. I was a sophomore starter on the junior varsity team. We were playing Seventy-first High School. She was a cheerleader for the opposite team.

We crossed paths in the lobby of the gym after the game. I remembered her face. She had attended my grammar school for a year way back in the fifth grade. Her dad had taken a job over town and they had moved. She had evolved into a strawberry-haired, green-eyed beauty with deep dimples. Somehow in the awkward conversation we had, I managed to come away with her phone number.

I would have liked to call Vickie Gurdy as soon as I arrived home that night, but I had to play it cool. I *was* the leading player on the team. Instead, I daydreamed of her eyes a full three days until the weekend. There was another reason for my reluctance. I had never called a girl on the phone. I knew my brothers would razz me to death. I also feared where the conversation might lead. I had never actually been on a date; our only vehicles were my dad's dilapidated pickup and an old, sprung-door Mercury handed down from my Granny Baggett. I had had my license only a couple of months, wondered if my dad would allow me a night with the car, and then worried if the car would start, roll, and stop on cue without embarrassing me. The growing ache in my heart urged me to tempt the odds.

"Hello, hello," she cooed into the phone, waiting for a reply.

"Hello, Vickie," I answered. "This is Tim McLaurin. I'm the basketball player you met after the game last Tuesday."

"Oh, hiiii, Tim. I'm glad you called. But I can barely hear you. Are you at a pay phone?"

"No, I'm home. Must be a bad connection."

I had stretched the phone cord through the door into the bedroom, closed the door, closed the closet, then burrowed under a solid layer of dirty linen. My entire family was in the next room, and even through the clothes and walls I could hear their muffled speech. I was close to suffocating, but that was better than letting my brothers and father know I was phoning a girl. I managed to carry on a decent conversation for a couple of minutes, then ask whether she was interested in going out on a date, even though the air reeked of dirty socks and sweat was dripping in my face. Once I dropped the phone and lost it in the dark when our twelve-year-old female Chihuahua surprised me and came clawing from out of the clothes where she had been sleeping. I found the receiver and told Vickie the line must have temporarily gone dead. A minute later we said goodbye and I surfaced to breathable air, the proud owner of a bona fide first date. I slipped back into the hallway and spoke several lines of fake dialogue into the receiver to make everyone think I had been talking to a pal, then hung up.

I had five days to come up with the courage to ask my dad for use of the car. I dreaded it like a whipping. The date was set for Saturday night, and finally I gathered my courage Friday afternoon. To my astonishment, he gave me no grief.

The genuine humiliation and dread etched in my face must have told him that asking for that car was an extremely serious matter to me, and he possibly recalled his horseback dates from his own youth. He only asked her name and nodded his head.

"She ain't that big-titty girl, is she?" he asked, referring to Kathy Maxwell. I shook my head.

The moment I surveyed the condition of our old Mercury and contemplated what elbow grease would be required to clean her, I lamented I hadn't made the date for the following month. The car was ten years old, at least nine of those years without a new wax job. The fenders had rusted through in spots, and the vinyl top had cracked and peeled and blistered. The engine was a big, gas-guzzling 350 that burned oil and failed to start about half the time. But all that was minor compared to the interior.

A small cash crop grew inside the car. My dad sometimes drove the car to the feed store on rainy days. Anyone that has ever lugged a fifty-pound burlap sack of horse feed knows how there is always a hole in one corner that spills out a few grains of oat, wheat, or corn. The carpet in the car had probably never been vacuumed since it rolled from the factory, and the dirt and crud had accumulated over the years until the very piles of fabric had disintegrated into a fertile mulch. The mulch was kept moist by a leak in the roof and various spilled soda pops. A seed kernel barely had time to cease rolling before it germinated in a burst of growth. From the open door of the car, I counted tufts of hard wheat, alflafa, oaks, hybrid corn, and various weeds and wildflowers. I needed a scythe more than a vacuum cleaner.

I worked on that car for several hours, stripped away the layers of plant life, raked the crust of dirt, swept and dusted and polished and sweated and cussed, only to discover that scraped rust, chipped paint, and threadbare carpet looked worse than the car had as a rolling terrarium. The early-February twilight was settling, the day cooling, and I was actually contemplating standing her up when a simple but profound thought came to me.

I removed the interior light. I didn't plan on driving under any floodlights to begin with, so with no interior light to come on when I opened the door, she wouldn't be able to tell if she was sitting on hand-rubbed leather or canvas. I could always lie and say the bulb had just burned out.

The good-night kiss was the next hurdle. Sure, I had kissed my cousin, but that had been a year before, and I had practically cracked her nose in the process. Vickie was a bonafide cheerleading city girl who already wore makeup and probably had kissed a dozen boys. I was a bit in awe that she would even go out with me to begin with, and hoped she didn't balk at the silhouette of our Mercury and tell me she rode in nothing that did not sport mag wheels. I figured the good-night kiss would either herald my emergence as a basketball-shooting, face-sucking young stud from the east side or would send me packing back to the tobacco fields and cucumber rows on the wrong side of the tracks.

I countered by practicing kissing in the bathroom mirror. With the door securely bolted, I gazed into my reflection, replacing my image with Vickie's. Slowly puckering my lips as I bent toward her, I finally meshed skin against steamy glass and rolled my mouth from side to side. I cracked open my eyes and graded each performance.

I arrived at her house a fashionable two minutes late, clad in a stiff new pair of Levi's I had washed several times with a little Clorox. My hair was long to my neck and I wore fuzzy muttonchop sideburns. She opened the door when I knocked—an angel in a pink knit dress that came halfway up her thighs, her curly hair held in a matching bow. I didn't know what to say, she didn't so we just stood and stared at each other and smiled until her little sister barged between us.

Vickie's sister was two years younger, and mightily interested in what was going on. She stood there cracking gum and looking me up and down until Vickie came out of her trance and invited me to sit down.

Soon it was obvious to me that maybe Vickie was a cheerleading city girl, but from the looks of her living room, she didn't live so different from me. The room was simple, could have used a fresh paint job, the furniture comfortable but worn in places, the air smelling of people and supper and maybe even a dog. Vickie hustled her sister from the room, but the kid remained just outside the closed door, her toes visible jammed in the little space at the bottom. From the giggles I heard, I realized little sister was not the only sibling.

In a way, I was relieved to discover Vickie was not of the fancy Haymont Hills/Vanstory crowd. She was still just as pretty as I had remembered her, and might, just might, be fond of riding in an ancient Mercury with tail fins. At least I knew she suffered the humility that comes with coping with smaller siblings. At that second the living-room door sprang open and a chorus of laughter erupted before a red-faced Vickie slammed it shut. There must have been a half-dozen of them grinning at me.

I suggested we go ahead and go. Vickie excused herself, saying she needed to tell her mother we were leaving. She returned in a moment, her face long with shame.

"Mama wants you to stay and eat supper with us."

I would never have expected that. Not on this side of town. I could have expected to be invited to dinner some night with proper advance notice, but not asked to "supper" on the spot. "Supper" around our place was a boiled chicken cooked with rice and served to whoever was standing around when the burner was turned off.

"I thought we might just get a pizza or something," I volunteered.

Vickie shook her head. "Mama would be disappointed. She's already set another plate." Her embarrassment showed clearly through her makeup.

Now, the last thing I wanted was to have to sit down to a full meal in front of Vickie's family. I had already heard a muffled, grumpy voice through the wall and imagined her father to be either a trial lawyer or Army brass. I didn't know a salad fork from a dinner fork and was leery of meat that had to be cut with a knife. But I knew my own older sister never got away from home with a new date without him sitting down to eat with the family, and realized the custom must be universal, even west of the river. About that time, Vickie's mother stuck her head through the door, smiled at me, then walked forward, her hand extended.

She was Vickie's mother, no doubt. They shared the same almond eyes, the same hair. The mother was maybe fifteen pounds plump, but had once been a beauty. She smelled like fried chicken.

"I'm so happy to meet you," she said. "Vickie has told me so much about you."

Vickie rolled her eyes and tried to draw smaller. The children were openly clustered around the door. They giggled.

I was seated beside Vickie at one end of the table. At the far end of the table sat her father. He was a smallish man wearing some type of blue coverall. I quickly realized he did not defend criminals or plan military strategy. He fixed his eyes on me once, stared long and hard as if he was looking for something below my skin, then swilled the ice in the glass he was drinking and turned it up. He drank a clear liquid, and I doubted it was 7-Up.

The forks were no problem. Each of us had one by our plate. The fried chicken was eaten with fingers. The meal could have been one from my mom's table except that Mrs. Gurdy put too much lemon in her tea, and left lumps in the mashed potatoes. I relaxed somewhat, chewed my food carefully, and answered small questions directed my way. I thought I had it made.

I saved the peas for last. I've never been real keen on peas and especially don't like how they mix with other food. I figured by not breathing between bites, I could shovel the small helping down my throat and chase the taste with a gulp of tea.

I choked, tried to hold it down with a deep breath, then spewed a mouthful of peas that littered the table. Most bounced harmlessly between the plates and forks. One fell into Vickie's brother's tea glass. One final pea sailed the length of the table and lodged in the corner of Vickie's father's eye. He squinted his eye, as if trying to train his vision inward on the object, then slowly reached and plucked it like a small burr. I was mortified.

"You all right, honey?" Vickie's mother exclaimed, leaping to her feet and grabbing a napkin.

"There's a pea in my tea," the brother grumbled. Vickie's mother flashed him a withering stare. With deft fingers, she soon had corralled the peas from where they had rolled under the edges of plates and saucers. Mr. Gurdy held his pea between two of his fingers as if he held a pearl. He dropped it in his wife's hand.

I wished I could slide under the table, but before I could

act, Mrs. Gurdy was spooning a fresh helping of peas onto my plate. "Eat 'em up. I'm pleased to death to see someone who will eat peas around here. Lord, these younguns just roll them around in their plates." I wished I could roll on out the door.

I had made it back to the living room and was waiting on Vickie to freshen up when she stuck her head in the door and, with a pained expression, said her dad wished to speak to me on the front porch. A jolt shot through my belly. I expected him to hand me the pea and tell me to carry it across the river.

He was not a large man, but wiry and tightly built, like he was strung together with wire. He still had his glass in his hand.

"Hey, buddy," he began in a friendly tone I had not heard through the walls. "Wonder if you could do me a favor?"

"Sure. Yes, sir."

"See, my car ain't working real good. Battery is low. I was wondering if you might run me over to a buddy's house down the road so I can pick something up."

"Yeah, sure." I glanced back at the front door to see if Vickie was watching.

"She'll wait on you. Hell, she'll fuss over her face another damn hour."

From the odor on his breath, I reasoned we were going after more liquor. He began talking as we drove over, telling me how he had run away and joined the Marines at age fourteen and had fought through three major campaigns in the Pacific before he was eighteen. He reminded me of my uncles, and I began to like him. His buddy did live only a few blocks away, and he was back outside soon with a paper sack. He had me stop at a soda machine where he mixed himself another drink. He didn't offer me any, and I was glad for that. When we were getting out of the car he said, "I've never liked damn peas, either."

I ended up taking Vickie to the nine-o'clock showing of *A Man Called Horse.* I felt embarrassed when Richard Harris was being led naked through the forest by the Indians. Afterwards, we stopped at the Pizza Palace, but both of us were too nervous to feel hungry. I made sure I parked the car on a hill so if the battery proved dead, I could roll-start it. I stayed away from the lights, although I was less self-conscious about the car now. Finally, eleven-thirty arrived and I was slowing down in front of her house. The porch light was on, but the house was dark except for a back room. I felt the old panic returning. In a moment, I was standing close in front of Vickie on her steps, our hands clasped. I was trying to think of that right line that would lead into "the kiss," the one I had so practiced for. I cracked a small joke, cocked my head slightly to one side so I wouldn't smash her nose, and waited for that moment of cosmic intervention that would draw our lips together.

A light switched on through the window closest behind us. The glow illuminated Vickie's head. I heard her father clear his throat and spit, then a tinkle of water as he urinated into the toilet. He broke wind once. Before I knew what was happening, Vickie kissed me, virtually sucking my face into hers, as if she hoped to block out the sounds of her father's toilet habits. All I could do was hang on and try to move my mouth as I had practiced on the mirror. The commode had flushed and filled again when she drew back from me, smiled shyly, and said she needed to go in. My lips burned. I asked her about coming over the next weekend, and she said sure, to call her. I walked on air to my car, and stood beside it and waved until she had gone inside. The car battery was stone dead, but I was on enough of a hill that I pushed it rolling and got her started

without Vickie ever knowing. Driving home, I sang along
with the radio.

VICKIE became my first steady. A few dates later I gave
her my Future Farmers of America ring. We dated for five
months, went to dances together, movies, shared many
pizza pies. I perfected my kissing. With her I also learned
that living east or west of the river did not necessarily affect
the affluence or luck of one's life. Her dad was a construc-
tion worker, prone to drink, her mom a fleshy, good-
hearted woman who doted over her five children. I learned
her care was tempered by the fact that a daughter had died
from a massive brain tumor only a year before Vickie and I
met. I had never been close to a family that had lost a child,
and I found the picture of the lost daughter haunting in its
place over the mantel, like a chilled spot above the room.
Vickie's father told me he had killed a Jap soldier with a
ceremonial sword he ripped from the man's hands, and I
wondered sometimes if a curse had not been focused on the
family. A dead daughter—someone was forever sick—
Vickie's father fell from scaffolding and was hospitalized
for a week. Sometimes when I drove him on his liquor
runs, he would be lacking a quarter or two and I would give
him some change. Vickie was fervent with her kissing, but
made sure my lips never made it lower than her jawline. I
suspect now that the thoughts of small babies, of being
thrust into motherhood as her mother had been at age sixteen, was a real fear in her life.

Finally, after six months, we broke up. She was the one
to end the affair, citing her fear of becoming too attached to
one boy. I ached for a couple of days, then found my heart
drifting toward a new love.

I didn't see Vickie over my high school years except

when we played her school in basketball. I usually played my best against them, and she strutted and cheered her loudest. We never talked. Mostly, we smiled at each other during time-outs and went different ways at the buzzer. Before we both graduated, another of her sisters choked to death in the chains of a swing set. Her mother and father separated during the throes of their grief.

I ran into her at a mall in Fayetteville about ten years later. I recognized her immediately. She looked more like her mom, fleshy, toting a child on one hip, another hanging on to her arm. She smoked while she talked, the ends of her fingers stained brown. She told me she had sung rock and roll with a band for several years, but smoking had gotten the best of her voice, and then the babies started. I wanted to ask her how her dad was doing, but in the way she avoided speaking of him, I was afraid to ask. I was making an excuse to leave when she grasped my hand and looked me in the eye.

"You never did come back," she said. "I always thought you would come back. I didn't mean I never wanted to see you again."

I made some excuse about us being young, about kids never knowing what they want. I did not say that even at sixteen her family scared me. In her mother and father I had seen the image of my parents, that same relentless belief found so often in the working class. If you loved hard enough and worked hard enough and filtered each failure through either God or whiskey, you just had to come out ahead in the end. I couldn't tell her how that scared me, and how since childhood I had doubted I would ever be able to hold my end of the bargain. I feared whatever misfortune followed her family—it smelled on her even now—might rub off on me. Everyone I loved seemed to go on forever wishing and wanting and waiting and waiting. They lived their lives waiting to win the great lottery, the Reader's Digest Sweepstakes. At the ends of their lives, they held on to two or three items of pride and dismissed every other ambition as wishful thinking, nothing more than a dream. I felt an increasing need to elevate myself by going amongst people I felt challenged by, even inferior to, who would prompt me to push myself into new realms. I did not want to wait on that million-to-one chance of being chosen, but wanted to be the one pointing his finger and calling the names. I *wanted* a girlfriend from a nice home in Vanstory, one who would force me to cut chicken with a knife and liked live theater better than the drive-in. I wanted to be with people who longed to travel to India more than to own a Camaro to circle McDonald's in on weekend nights. I didn't want to wait for "God's will" but wanted action now. I was quickly seeing how eager people were to believe and be led. At school I was finding I had a talent at stringing words together to sound elegant and informed. I made A's on term papers I wrote on unusual subjects, making up my facts, statistics, and bibliography as I went along. I also found myself attracted to writing short fiction, but would admit it to no one. There, I found a world where I was God, the one in control, where actions and results occurred on my timetable and with my results.

I remember Vickie today in the same vision as that dilapidated Mercury and her willingness to accept it, as if that car was an omen of her life to come, gutted of all frills, the light switched off, best seen in the twilight of shadows.

MATTIE and I were again parked on a dark road. No snake was in the car this time. "Stick it in deep," Mattie urged in a throaty whisper. I thought for a moment I might faint.

She meant my finger. What a shock at age sixteen to feel the smooth, jumpy inner muscles of a female.

We had been dating for several months, and in the beginning I had been the perfect gentleman, stopping in the midst of fevered kissing at her first request. As time rolled on, the knot I carried home in my jeans became more insistent. I first trespassed her bra line, but that ended after a few minutes with tears and pleas that I "never do that again." I would make it a few nights on my oath, then resort again to animal passion, only to restart the cycle. Then I learned an important first lesson concerning how women use their bodies to manipulate men, and how men in different ways are just as deceptive.

Getting drunk started the lesson. I was supposed to meet Mattie at the McDonald's where my crowd hung out, after bagging groceries half of Friday night at my part-time job. I was rosy-cheeked from scrubbing with a washrag and reeked of English Leather, ten dollars burning my pocket and ready for a night of the intense infatuation that can only churn the stomach of a teenager. She was nowhere to be found. After circulating through town for an hour, I ran into a group of guys my age who tempted me to have a beer. No Mattie, my thoughts full of the torment that she was kissing another guy, one brew led to another, and soon we were all parked at a deserted house on a country road where we got gut-heaving drunk.

Mattie called me the next morning, her voice heavy with emotion. She and the girlfriends she rode with had arrived late, and she had searched for my car half the night while circling the various fast-food joints. She swore the night had been miserable, that she had finally been let off at home in tears. I believed her totally; she was the most honest person I knew; but I let an edge remain in my voice that hinted that maybe I suspected she had gotten up with another guy and not even tried to look for me. Besides, I knew I needed to play all the cards in my deck. I was nursing a terrible hangover and knew that in the small, gossipy circle of friends I was acquainted with, the story of how I had puked all over my shoes and hung out the car door most of the night was sure to get back to her by Monday. To Mattie, drinking was an absolute, terrible sin, that fact drilled into her by her strict parents and her up-bringing under the direction of a Southern Baptist church.

I made it through a long Saturday of work by gulping aspirins. The alcohol slowly leached from my cells, and by quitting time at nine o'clock I had nearly convinced myself that I had been the worse wronged. After all, I would never have sipped that first beer had she been on time. I scrubbed up again and drove across town, but tarried just long enough before arriving so that she might suspect I was still hurt and angry.

She was wearing that dress I liked so good. The dress was short and made of a slinky material that felt good rubbed against her skin. She was not wearing panty hose. The blouse to the dress was peasant-style, with a large elastic neckband that could be easily pulled down. She wore an extra dab or two of Chanel No. 5, and her full bottom lip was dabbed heavily with strawberry lip gloss. The way she met me outside the door and kissed me deeply made me realize I held the high ground.

We made small talk on the couch for a few moments, spliced with more kisses. She fished for hints of what I had done with my night after we didn't meet, and finally I volunteered that I had only stopped briefly to talk with a couple of the fellows. Again, she poured out her sorrow over letting me down; I said it didn't matter, that I had needed a good night's sleep. We left her house with me intending to drive us to a movie.

"Turn here," she said as we neared a crossroad. She pointed in the direction away from the lights of Fayetteville. "I want you to take me to that little road."

My heart skipped a beat. "That little road" was a two-wheel path cut into a forest near my home leading back to a hidden cornfield. Parked there in the deep night, we had already been through several arguments over the placement of my hands. But I wasn't going to question her now, certainly not smelling as good as she did with her skirt riding high on her thighs. I backed into the small road until we were well hidden from any passing headlights, cut the engine, and rolled down the window enough to listen to the call of locust and whippoorwills.

We had hardly begun smooching before she clasped my hand and placed it directly upon one of her breasts. I decided to play the game further and immediately removed my hand to her ribs. After a few moments of kissing, she took my hand again, placed it back on her breast, and held it there, moving it in small circular motions. My attempt at playing hard to get quickly dissolved.

Only a couple of minutes passed before her peasant blouse was down to her navel and I was kissing skin that hadn't seen the sun since she was a baby. When my hand wandered south, it met no resistance.

My finger deep inside her, she began wiggling, breathed like she was running a mile; I knew my time had arrived and was trying to figure how to get my pair of tight Levi's unzipped and down with one hand. All of a sudden she began breathing even heavier, rose toward me and squeezed very tight, then relaxed into her seat like the air was let out. She promptly removed my hand from her privates, as my other hand still fumbled at my zipper. I reasoned that her Southern Baptist senses had returned to her just on the brink of the point of no return and she had willed her virginity another night's existence. I tried to ignore my lust and just be glad for what she had allowed. She dressed and we clung together and vowed our love, her neck smelling nicely of perfume and sweat.

Monday morning I had to fess up. Mattie knew of my drunkenness only moments after she arrived at school. She confronted me, eyes brimming with tears, at first class break. I couldn't even attempt to lie; she knew all the facts, dry heaves and all. Actual tears flowed when she admitted she had given so much of herself on that dark country road to show how sorry she had been, only to find I had spent little or no time in remorse. I could only hang my head.

But the storm passed, as many others did over the coming months. Our petting sessions routinely became heavy, although until Mattie and I married she was "technically" a virgin. It took me months to realize that in the midst of heavy petting when Mattie stiffened and squeezed me, then suddenly faded away, she had not simply received fresh strength from God, but had climaxed, leaving me far behind and temporarily useless. Eventually we worked out forms of parity. Throughout our relationship she used her good looks to appease or persuade me. In times of conflict I told her what she wanted to hear, then did what I wanted to do. In our minds, we each held the upper hands.

BUT even in those idealistic, troubled days of Woodstock and Vietnam veterans, a curious young man did not have to look far to find a girl who was also looking for more than just kisses. In Fayetteville, a city that had for years catered to the primeval urges of a large military population, one had only to know the right streets to drive to find girls willing to go all the way. They demanded, though, more than a hamburger and milk shake and a trip to the drive-in.

Hillsborough Street constituted the center of the red-light district in Fayetteville. The street lay beside the railroad station just off of famed Hay Street, where soldiers jammed neon-lit topless bars. Hillsborough Street was on the edge of the black side of town, was run-down and dotted with taxi stands, pool halls, all-night diners, and a couple of seedy hotels. At night, the corners of the street were sprinkled with women wearing short skirts, fishnet hose, and high heels. They waved to people driving by in cars and approached men walking on the street. Their standard line—"Wanna date?"

A "date" was fifteen dollars on up, depending on what services were bought and how close the night was to military payday. Stopping your car on the street and letting one of those billowy-haired painted women stick her head through the window and talk a little trash was free.

I'd heard all the trash since Gary Ivy got his driving license and a remodeled '57 Chevy. He and I and Mike Spake would cruise the street slowly, occasionally stopping at the curb to listen to what some prostitute had to say about what she could do with her mouth. Our jaws would drop open at her description, but we were never really close to taking up an offer. A full roll, "fuckie-suckie," was twenty dollars, and even if we'd had the courage, none of us had the cash. We'd nod our heads and blush at the woman's words and tell her we would have to give it some thought. We'd usually leave and buy a large soda to cool our jets, then do something stupid like circle the Market House roundabout in the center of town repeatedly until we felt drunk. At last count, Gary's record stood at seventy-five continuous revolutions. We'd usually swear how next time we were going with her inside.

My bluff was called in the fall of 1971, in the early season of my junior year on the varsity. I was a rising star player. We were scheduled to play Terry Sanford High School for the first time, a highfalutin city school whose students had already put out the word they considered us to be a bunch of river rats from the bad side of town. We wanted desperately to humble them.

I don't remember whose idea it was, but a promise was made that if we beat Terry Sanford, a collection would be raised to buy me the choice of prostitutes on Hillsborough Street. Of course, I agreed. I secretly doubted we could beat the much larger school, and besides, we had been swearing to get laid by one of those whores for months without ever coming through.

We beat Terry Sanford by four baskets. I scored fourteen points. The home floor erupted in a party at the game-ending buzzer. Mattie and I were steadies, but the game had lasted late, it was a school night, and after a round of smackie kisses, she rode home with a girlfriend. I was going to the dressing room to shower and change when Mike and Gary headed me off at the door.

Some of the guys were loading into cars to drive uptown and continue the celebration. The November night was still warm, and before I knew it, I was sitting in the front seat of Gary's Chevy still clad in my full basketball uniform, a cold Colt 45 malt liquor clenched in one hand. The beer immediately went to my brain and magnified even more the immensity of our victory. Of course, we ended up talking to the whores.

"Twenty dollar get you the finest thing since your mama's tit," the prostitute told me through the car window. She was black as strong coffee, a gold tooth glinting in the top of her smile. A couple other prostitutes stood behind her, hands cocked on ample hips.

"Get on out of that car," one of them taunted. "There's enough love here for all you white boys."

I thought I was safe. I remembered the victory promise, but knew that talk was cheap. I didn't count on the fact that with three other guys riding in the backseat, between them they had just enough cash. Suddenly I had three fives and five one-dollar bills in my hand, a black prostitute smiling at me like the rising sun.

"Come on, honey," she whispered. "I'll show you where you came from."

Male pride is a beast. I did not want to go with that prostitute. My first thought was of Mattie, my second of how I might get a disease, third I imagined getting my throat cut in a dank motel room. But the whore beckoned, the boys grinned at me, and from across the street, I heard the cheers of another carload of guys who knew what was going on. I could not back out now and wear trousers again.

Actually, I wished mightily I was in my trousers. I was halfway across Hillborough Street, walking a step behind the long-legged lady, when I realized I was still wearing only my basketball uniform. A skinny white boy decked out in blue and gold, Cape Fear Colts lettered in large letters across my chest, I was a spectacle to passing cars. A couple of women leaning against the doorway to the hotel eyed me up and down, their faces breaking into smiles.

"Ohhhh, he ready, ain't he," one taunted. "Look at them legs. He readdddy, Freddy."

I was mortified. I was also horrified to find myself climbing a long dark flight of steps. The stairway opened into a musty-smelling room where a couple of large black men stared up at us from chairs. One peered over his shades at me, then took my money and handed the woman a key. We went down a hallway to a room I knew I would never leave alive. Inside, there were only a bed with one white sheet and a scarred table.

"You get them clothes off, hon," she instructed me. "I'll be right back."

I stared at the wavy surface of the bed. The mattress was sunk in the middle. I got my jersey off and laid it on the table, but balked at removing my trunks. I wished I had taken a shower. If I was fixing to be murdered, I wanted to be found clean.

The door creaked and she entered the room—no pimp with razor—carrying only a pan of water and a rag. She glanced at me, saw my thumbs under the elastic band of my trunks.

"Better pull them on off," she said. "It hard to do through nylon."

She stripped quickly, laying her clothes in layers as they came off. When she turned to me, she was naked as the day she was born and looked years younger without her finery. Her breasts were high and small, her stomach smooth, with none of the flab of carrying babies. I guessed she probably wasn't too many years older than me, at most, mid-twenties, but she'd had an education of the world that could have spanned decades. I guessed she was from somewhere north from her accent. She had a small scar on one cheek, moon-shaped, like maybe someone had flicked her face with the tip of a blade. She shivered once.

"Come on over here," she said. "I ain't gonna bite."

She grasped the top of my trunks and pulled them down to my feet, then my underwear, and told me to step out. She used the warm soapy water to wash my member, carefully but discreetly checking for disease. She led me by my hand to the bed, lay down first, then pulled me on top of her.

"You do your thing, honey," she whispered. "I'll never tell."

I knew what to do. I had practiced it in my mind a thousand plus times in intricate detail; Mattie and I had reached the point where we faked it in the backseat. But there was nothing between me and this naked black woman but a skim of sweat, and my mind went blank like switching off a light bulb. I reclined against her, my legs crossing one of hers scissor-style. She wrapped her arms around me and tugged at my buttocks, urging me over between her thighs. I lay there like a log, my heart pounding. Finally she whispered in my ear, "Throw the other leg over, honey."

I did throw my other leg over, but it was the wrong leg, and I found myself sitting a straddle her, not at all unlike the many times I had climbed on a bareback pony. She stared up at me with a quizzical frown, as if she was debating whether I was wanting something kinky, but then her frown changed to a sad smile.

"This the first time for you, white boy?" she whispered. I nodded.

She took matters in hand. In a second we were properly positioned, she guided me inside, and within less than a minute it was all over. She faked passion, but even then I realized it was an act. Afterwards, she washed me up with the same wet rag. My crimson face showed shame over my rookie showing. She must have sensed it, had probably seen it before a hundred times.

"You a quick learner there, hon. Didn't take you no time to learn the game."

"I'm sorry I was so fast. Maybe I'll come back again when I can do something for you."

She leaned then and kissed my forehead. "You got a girlfriend?"

I nodded again. "I did."

"She be there tomorrow. You save it for her. Lord, I get plenty coming around. You save it for her, it always be better."

I was out of the room in another minute, scooted down the stairwell, and burst into the busy street. I heard a round of applause from the two cars parked beside the curb. I was

suddenly a hero, the man who had handled the Terry Sanford basketball team and a prostitute all in one night, and
for the rest of the evening I was true to male form and
didn't downplay a thing. But when I arrived home that
night, I spent a good half hour washing myself with soap
and alcohol and imagining what rare disease I had brought
home. I went to sleep with my thoughts on Mattie and my
trust that the guys would not betray me.

They didn't. I did not contract disease. But that first real
copulation with a woman taught me a lesson that has
stayed. I am no Casanova, was never cut out to be one
interested in only meshing parts. A young prostitute knew
that truth and tried to warn me early, and it would take a
foolish man not to follow what he knows in his heart.

THE virtue of most women who have touched my life lies
somewhere between that of Mattie and the prostitute. The
women of the fallen camp gave up on tomorrows. They
stopped waiting on better times coming if they just kept
faith and somewhere along the way elected to take opportunities as they came.

Connie Lewis is my third cousin through marriage and a
member of a branch of McLaurins that has fueled much
bad gossip. I attended school with Connie; she was a cute,
quiet girl who cooked and cleaned the house for her
younger brothers while her mother worked nights in a
country music bar. Her dad, once a running mate with my
father, was long gone. A few of my friends in high school
took her on dates, but they complained she would go no
further than kissing and often had to be home early to get
her siblings in bed.

I swung by her house one night after midnight when I
was between marriages. I had a couple of six-packs in my

gut. She was still living at home and tending to a conglomeration of kid brothers, sisters, and cousins. She asked me for a beer and had hardly finished it before she asked me in for the night. Her face had lost its softness, lines creased the corners of her eyes. She smoked one cigarette after another.

"I'll cook you a good breakfast in the morning," she said, nuzzling my neck. "I got some good country ham in there." She winked. "A little 'down-home' would do you good after all them college girls you been hanging around with."

She had me nearly convinced. I *was* hanging around with coeds or college-educated women and had grown a bit tired of discussing Socrates and politics. Connie was pulling at my arm and I was about to follow, when I got to thinking about how I was pretty drunk and how the last time I saw her she wouldn't have even smelled a beer. Besides, a couple of tiny faces were crowded against one of the windows, and inside I could see her oldest brother. He was on parole for breaking and entering.

"Look, it's nearly one A.M.," I begged off. "What you say I come over tomorrow morning. We can spend the day together."

I finally convinced her I was sincere and left with a lipstick-smudged face. The next day at noon when I crawled from bed at Mama's, I found out she had already called twice.

"You ain't going to see her, pray tell," Mama scolded me. "I thought I had raised you boys better than that."

I didn't go see her. Connie has a few children of her own today and no husband. Her little girl looks just like her and baby-sits when her mom is gone nights.

JULY 1984. From his high hospital window he could see the rolling, forested land slope to the river. The brown water snaked through the trees, catching the sun here and there and shining with a flat, broad sheen. Beyond the river lay flat, fertile farm soil that grew good tobacco, corn, and beans. On clear days the boundary of his own seventy-seven acres was visible as a dark line between the curve of terra and heavens.

He looked from his bed, propped up by pillow, one thin arm jacked under his neck to thrust his neck higher. His eyes were bright as if he waited to see a certain person walking on one of the far roads that sliced the land, hoped for the flight of a hawk across the sky, maybe the glimpse of a boat of fishermen on the river. When he did turn toward the center of the room, his eyes would lose their fire like the light slowly drawing from a television tube, the reality of where he was and what was happening would seep in, and he would slump against his mattress and curve to it like sediment settling on the river's bottom. I could read his thoughts.

Fifty-nine—lung cancer—what'd they say, maybe three more weeks at best—shit in the bed and lay here in it—can't eat, don't want to eat when eating will only make me lay here a little longer in this damned room—can't sleep at night, toss and turn all the time, legs hurt like hell—everyone comes in and sits here and stares at the wall and don't know what to say—can't even get up and go piss—only thing to do is smoke, and they say smoking is what did this to me.

When he did sleep he dreamed the torment of one skewered by disease and drugs. I awoke one night in my recliner to find him fighting the tubes that ran into his arms, penis, and nose. I laid my hands against his thin shoulders and held until he ceased struggling.

"How the hell did we get out of there?" he asked, one eye cocked wide, the other squinted.

"You were just dreaming, Dad."

"How in the *hell* did we ever get out?" he asked again, grasped once more the tube in his arm, reared his head back and stared in my face. If he recognized me, it didn't show.

"Just lie back," I told him. "You were having a bad dream. It's me, Tim. It's Tim, Dad."

Light rolled back into his eyes, slowly, like the sun warming in the east. His neck went limp against the pillow. "Yeah, oh yeah," he said softly. "Yeah, I remember now. I got cancer. Yeah, I remember."

His hand went to his pajama pocket, where his cigarettes stayed. He patted the cloth. "How 'bout lighting me one, son."

I took the pack from his shirt and pulled out a cigarette, then snapped off the filter, lit the beast, and held it to his lips. He sucked long and hard.

"I thought you were a dead man," he said.

I didn't answer, just stared back and waited. He blew out smoke and sucked again.

"I thought I was in the truck and it was wrecked, and you were a dead man. I was trying to get out."

"Those drugs make you dream crazy. I thought for a minute you were going to tear up from there."

"I was going somewhere. I thought the truck was wrecked and you were dead and we were fixing to burn up."

The smoke burned his eyes, and he coughed once. He blinked and swallowed and I could see in his face that he wished he was still in the dream, wrecked on some curve where he had been drinking and driving too fast, with nothing between him and life but some broken glass and fire and a dead man. At least he would have a fighting chance.

He sucked his cigarette till the fire heated my fingers. Dawn had begun as a thin red shimmer on the horizon. He stared at the window again, his memory trained on some fragment of better time when he had watched that glow. . . .

A boy eating a link of fried sausage and dreading a long day in the fields—stirring sugar into a cup of coffee before a campfire, fixing to check catfish lines—rising early to bale and gather fescue hay before a summer rainburst spoiled it—the good slosh of flooded boots trodding home after a night of going to where the hounds had treed—driving slowly getting the story right on one of those nights when everything got carried away, whiskey still good and strong in his blood, the smell of that small place in her neck sharp in his mind like the odor of an animal. . . .

"When's she coming home?" he asked, jerking his eyes back my way. "When is Katie coming?"

"About ten more days. They're training a replacement for her."

"I want to see her, but I hate she has to come. I hate you had to come home like this."

"This is where I wanted to be."

His mouth opened and closed, he swallowed. "You got a good one. I like Katie. You don't need more than one woman."

"I'm planning on sticking with her. You don't need to worry about that."

"Yeah, but you got to remember that. A man, he, he does things, son, he wishes he'd never done. You can't change them then. I did some. I did some things and I can't change them."

His mouth flapped, no words came, he flicked his eyes back toward the land and hushed. I knew what he wanted to say—he knew it, but I doubted he would ever find the strength to unearth the words.

THE days had rolled into the throat of summer, July, the season of dust, horseflies, summer storms, and tobacco priming. I watched many of the days through the hospital window as my father inched toward death while trying to find peace in the record of fifty-nine years.

I was still separated from my wife and daughter by the span of half a globe. I felt even more detached from Dixie, caught in a struggle of reverse culture shock. The slow life of living in a small town in North Africa seemed more distant than miles, as if I had been jolted forward in time to a place where people lived at a frantic pace. The hot bread and grilled mutton I had grown to love had been replaced by McDonald's hamburgers snatched and wolfed down en route to the hospital. I found myself wanting to speak to strangers in Arabic. I took solace in alcohol, sipped vodka so the doctors would not smell it as I sat with my father over long nights while he endured coughing spells, shit in his bed, and thrashed in his sleep from drug-induced nightmares. During days, he swung between moods. We had some of the best talks of our life, as if the barriers between father and son had been removed, or at least lowered so we were able to talk as two friends. But more often, he turned his face to the window and looked toward a place I could not see. I wondered if his vision of heaven had been revealed and he watched it lower through the clouds, or if he was looking back into time, into pockets of his life that still needed explanation before the memory died. Probably both—he spoke of heaven, said he wasn't afraid of dying, just sad to have to leave us early. No fight was left in him.

But he also choked on words he was unable to say, rolled the syllables inside his mouth and tried to verbalize them, worked them over his tongue until slobber glinted in the corners of his mouth. He ungorged the thought one morning when the sun was just breaking through the treeline, as if he had discovered in one of his tossing, troubled dreams an answer to his torment.

"I got some people over in town," he said, looking me in the eyes. "I got me—got a couple."

His chest rose, the wind caught in his throat, and whatever truth he had decided to reveal caught too, he swallowed harshly, rolled his face back toward the window and was silent. I didn't push him to explain. I didn't need now to hear his confessions—what he had given me through the years far outweighed any neglect.

I turned up the paper cup I drank from and downed the last of my vodka and Mountain Dew. My sister would be coming soon after sunrise to relieve me. I wanted greatly to spit, clear my throat and sinuses of the smell of medicine and diseased flesh.

IN THE final days of his disease, my father suffered a stroke. One side of his face lost its definition, his eyes bludged, and his speech was slurred. One afternoon he beckoned for my mother to lean close, and through gritted teeth he hissed, "I'm ready to get the *hell* on out of here."

Two days later he was released from his prison. His breaths simply got slower and slower until finally one did not come. As was his request, my three brothers and I and two uncles carried him in his coffin to the earth on a sunny summer day with all the South in leaf.

NIGHTTIME

WE JUMPED over Dad, back and forth, running and leaping across his back and rolling in the grass beyond. He was out cold, his breath whistling softly through his nostrils. His pickup was parked crooked in the driveway where he had rolled to a stop, the door still wide open. A new goat bleated from the truck bed, tied with a rope to the spare tire.

Just minutes before he had been wrestling and playing with me and my young brothers, grabbing us and lifting us in bear hugs and swinging us around. We ignored Mama as she told us to go into the house, we resented her worried face, her pleas for Dad to stop. Why did she want to stop the fun? He never played with us like this, and now she wanted us to quit. Dad swung us around and around, until he bent and gagged and heaved up a bellyful of sour-smelling brown liquid. He sank to the grass on his belly and closed his eyes. Mama went into the house to call my uncle. We began the jumping game, hoping he would wake up and want to play again.

THE first time I ever drank beer, at fourteen, I had lifted a couple of cans of hot Falstaff from the bottom of the clothes hamper where Mama had hid them from Dad. Our house was seeded with the leftovers from his binges—the last two cans in a six-pack, a couple of fingers of bourbon left in a pint bottle—the evidence stuffed in the bottom of drawers, behind the washing machine, and other places out of sight. I shoved the cans under my shirt and crept outside and through the woods to my best buddy's house a half mile away by the crow's flight. Mike's father was a career soldier, a spit-and-polish man who had fought in three wars. Now Sergeant Spake was losing his final battle with alcohol.

Mike and I retreated to a favorite hiding spot hacked out in some brush behind his house. We popped the two cans and turned them up, both expecting the taste of something divine.

Only pride kept me from spewing that first mouthful of beer. I looked at Mike's contorted face.

"Good, ain't it?" I lied.

"Yeah," he answered. "Better than Kool-Aid."

We sipped at the beers. When Mike's mother called for him from the back door, we used that excuse to heave the cans far into the woods.

Another year passed before I discovered the magic in those cans. Mike already had his driver's license. He had the family car for a few hours on Friday night, and we were cruising the boulevard in Fayetteville. We ran into an older fellow from Beard who suggested we meet him at the Rendezvous Lounge for a couple of cold ones.

This was in the old days in Fayetteville when anyone who stood more than five feet tall and had a dollar in his pocket could get into the topless bars. We walked into a cool, dark room lighted with fluorescent bulbs that caused our shirts to glow. I gawked at a young woman gyrating on the stage wearing only a strip of sequined cloth threaded around her pelvis. Mike and I pooled our money and in a moment were staring at a pitcher of beer so cold the sides dripped with condensation. The beer still tasted like piss, but it was cold, our friends were watching, and a pair of bare, flapping tits challenged us. The first mug went down, then another, and a delightful tingling began to spread across my forehead. The music got better, the jokes funnier, the dancer more and more beautiful. And the beer— nothing ever tasted so good. By the time we ran out of money two hours later, the world had blurred under a warm, fuzzy cloud. I did not worry that I was drinking underage and the police might come in and arrest me or that I had spent all my money on an amber-colored liquid that I pissed out almost as quickly as I drank it in. Of no concern was the fact that midnight had passed and I was late coming home and was supposed to be back at my grocery-store job at nine the next morning. Those worries were miles and hours distant, and for now I was full and warm and happy. I suspected then that I might be included in that group I heard referred to in whispers by teachers and church people as "those drinking McLaurins."

———— ■ ————

CLINK. We heard the sound of the cell door closing as it echoed against the bare walls of the drunk tank. "Sleep tight and don't let the cooties bite," the jailer said, then grinned meanly. "Up yours," I mumbled as he turned. I looked at Mike Spake, who stood beside me in the dark of the cell. He was smiling, but his smile was tight; crow's-feet pulled at the corners of his eyes. There was no true mirth in the lines crossing his face.

"Just like old times," he said.

I grunted, then peered into the dark at figures slowly forming—a couple dozen bodies huddled under blankets, some sitting on the narrow metal bench that ran along the wall, others sleeping in fetal positions on the cold concrete floor. One man sobbed quietly, cradling his head against his palms. The air smelled of cigarettes and sweat and beer puke.

"When you reckon they'll let us out?" I asked Mike.

He chewed his bottom lip. "Not before morning. Not after all the shit we talked."

After standing for half an hour, we found our own spots on the nasty floor, hugged our knees, and burped up ghosts of tequila and beer. I fought back feelings of claustrophobia by thinking of what had happened earlier that day.

Everything had started out fine that morning on our odyssey to relive Parris Island. We arrived in Beaufort, the small town outside the base, at midday. We rented a motel room, then spent the afternoon visiting the sites where we had trained. All the memories flooded back—of our barracks in 2nd Battalion, the PT field where we thought our lungs would burst, the mess hall where we ate every morsel on our plates, the parade field where each misplaced step or dropped rifle tattled as loud as thunder. We returned to the rifle range, the confidence course where we had climbed rope ladders, walked narrow beams and rode pulleys down steel cables above pits of water, the small chapel where every denomination flocked together on Sundays to sit through an hour of peace. We chuckled at the stories we exchanged, long removed from the fear that had gripped our bellies then.

As we toured the base, I found that not much had changed at Parris Island, except that everything looked smaller and a bit less awesome than it had to eighteen-year-olds fresh out of the tobacco fields of eastern North Carolina. I guess that should have been the first hint that we were bound to get into trouble before we left—the taut, disciplined young Marines who last stood on the base softened now and eroded by college, careers, marriage, divorce, and kids. When the police pulled us over later that night, it was second nature to question their authority, to tell them we were not drunk, curse a little, let them know our taxes paid their salaries. Private McLaurin would have answered their questions with polite "yes sirs" and "no sirs," and probably have been allowed to go. Not many minutes of debate passed before we were spread-eagled against the squad car, searched, and on our way to the slammer. As the minutes dragged by on that cold floor, I had plenty of time to compare myself then and now.

As the drunks in the cell snored, I thought my way through two years of service, only to drift finally into fitful sleep. I awoke lying on my back early in the morning. The air spilling through the high, barred window was chilly and damp. My mouth tasted like bile and my head ached. I looked over at Mike, and we began laughing over and over. I hadn't been locked up since the Marines. We laughed at ourselves, for being such fools. Getting locked up for fighting was one thing. But getting locked up for running our mouths at the law when we knew we were guilty was simple stupidity.

Our laughter dropped off as several other inmates stirred and cast baleful eyes, streaked red with hangover, in our direction. The man who had been crying when we came in was still huddled under his blanket. Cigarettes were lit, muffled conversations began. My back was stiff and I regretted that the fifty-dollar motel room we'd rented didn't have a wrinkle in the bedspread. A raw-looking fellow with bad teeth got up from his place on the bench and walked slowly toward the exposed stainless-steel commode in the corner of the cell.

"I hate to do this to you fellows," he apologized, unbuckling his trousers, "but I got to."

Those sitting closest to the commode stood and moved away as the poor fellow sat down to relieve himself.

"Reckon I'm going to the work farm this time," he said, shaking his head and mumbling. "Yeah, reckon I'll be going."

Machinist, soldier, carpenter, writer, or street bum, we were all equal that morning. We averted our eyes to lessen his humiliation and wished for a cup of coffee, or the hair of the dog that bit us.

One by one, men were bailed out. Breakfast was powdered eggs, something glutinous that resembled grits, and two lengths of greasy pork sausage. I gave mine to the man with bad teeth, who wolfed down both plates. Finally, around nine in the morning, the jailer opened the door again, grinned at Mike and me, and said, "Feeling better, boys? Come on, y'all are history."

I said "Yes sir" without hesitation, paid my forty-dollar fine, and walked outside to sunlight.

GRANDPA McLaurin was a mean drunk. He was a large, coarse farmer, honest and hardworking, but tended to forget his strength and temper when drinking. He sometimes teased me and my brothers until we either cried or ran away. But Grandma was every bit as tough, and would stand up to him toe to toe. While she and my mother canned peas or shelled butter beans, Grandma sometimes coached Mama on how to deal with drunks. I listened to her stories as I shelled my own pan of beans, my fingernails sore to the quick and stained green.

"I could sometimes hear him coming a mile down the road," she began, her voice blending with the drone of Japanese beetles. "He would be drunk and beating his two mules to hurry them and cussing at the top of his lungs. I

hated it worse when Reese was older, because they'd argue
and I was always afraid they'd get in a fight. Reese
wouldn't stand to hear him talk ugly to me or to see him
mistreat the mules."

She paused, the bugs hummed from the tree branches, I
strained my ears waiting for her to continue. Mama glanced
into my pan to see if I needed another few handfuls of
work.

"I'd make Reese go to the barn and hide. He'd grumble,
but I'd make him. In a minute, I'd see Huey coming down
that dirt road, the dust a-flying, standing up in his wagon,
swaying from leg to leg. I don't know how he kept from
falling out. He'd roar into the yard, looking from side to
side, just itching for something to fight about. But by then
Reese would be behind some bales of hay and the girls
would be in the house. He wouldn't mess with me. He knew
I wouldn't stand for none of his drunk mess. I'd stare him
down and get him in the house and before long he'd be
asleep."

Mama listened to her advice; I wished I had never seen a
butter bean. The Japanese beetles flew from tree to tree.

Mama had a harder time dealing with Dad's drinking,
because we were beyond mule-drawn wagons and into the
age of automobiles. Occasionally when drinking, he would
run out of beer and decide he needed more. Then the
stashed-away cans came into play.

"Reese, you don't need any more beer," Mama said
from where I listened in bed. "Why don't you just stay here
and go to sleep?"

"I just want one more," he argued. "There's one in the
truck."

Mama knew if he got in the truck he would leave and
cruise the roads and not return for hours. She sighed heavily.

"Wait a minute," she urged. "I think you left a can in the bedroom."

Mama pushed back from the table and walked to the back of the house. She fetched a can or two from one of the hiding places. Dad still wanted to ride the roads, but for the moment was outwitted. He opened one of the hot cans and guzzled it, and soon passed out. I did not sleep until I heard his voice cease and change into long breaths.

Next morning, I stood in the shadows of the hallway watching my father sit at the kitchen table, a cigarette burning in the ashtray, a cup of black coffee steaming under his face. He rubbed his forehead with his fingers in small circles, his bloodshot eyes set deep in his skull. The room still smelled of puke where he had spent the night passed out on the floor, his vomit still dried on the linoleum rug. The clock ticked the minutes away. He lifted his cigarette, grimaced as he sucked down the hot, harsh smoke, closed his eyes as if longing for just one more half hour to lie down and comfort his head. He dumped the contents of two headache powders down his throat, washed it down with the rest of his coffee, and at the second in which he had to leave his chair either to go to work or to stagger into the bedroom and sleep, pushed himself standing and went to a ten-hour shift. Never did he turn toward the bed.

My father was neither a sophisticated nor a complicated man; he drank when he needed to get drunk, enjoyed his high, paid for it dearly the next day with a hangover, and went on with life. He dealt with life's situations as they came to him, was not a great planner, but more relied on his ability to act on impulse and provocation. These instincts and a patient God and wife pulled him through various outrageous drunken episodes. I worried about him when he drank and spent many nights lying awake listening for the sound of his truck in the driveway, but neither then nor now felt abused by his bouts with alcohol. I had witnessed real abuse in some other families—fathers who did not come home late that night, nor the next day nor the next, electricity and jobs lost, money needed for food spent on a bottle of wine. Their children constantly scratched and clawed at head lice and missed school lunch for lack of a quarter. When puppet shows or magic shows came to school, these same children lacked the few coins needed for admission and were herded into a classroom to stare at their desk tops while listening to our rounds of laughter.

DAD was driving one night with his older brother, Dewey, passed out cold in the backseat. Somewhere in the city limits of Fayetteville, my father looked in the rearview mirror and saw a blue light flashing on his tail. He kicked the gas, slid around a few corners, and gained about a block on the police car. He swerved into a deserted parking lot, jammed the car into park, switched off the engine, and dived over the driver's seat into the back with his stupefied brother. The officer jerked the car door open, gun in hand, to find both men pretending to be deep in dreamland. He roused them both to their feet, but could get neither to confess to driving. The case went to court, where a judge threw it out for lack of evidence.

Another night, Dad was indeed passed out and sleeping it off on the seat of his pickup when a state patrolman jerked him upright and demanded to see some identification. My father, torn from his stupor and fearing for his safety, proceeded to cold-cock the trooper up beside his head. He was promptly arrested, handcuffed, and carried downtown and charged with assault on an officer, a serious charge.

In court, the guardian angel came through again. The

judge sided with Dad and told the arresting officer that he would have done the same thing if someone had jerked him awake late at night while he was trying to sleep. My father walked free.

Another time, Dad didn't quite make it around the sharp curve a mile from our house and rolled his truck a couple of times in the road ditch. He climbed out the window, finished off the beer he still held, got his bearings, then staggered up the ditch to the pavement and headed for the lights of a house. In the middle of the road, the alcohol crossed up his feet, and he sprawled face-first and skinned his chin on the pavement. He pushed himself standing, cussed, and staggered on. At the house, my father was able to call for help, and a friend arrived with a tractor in time to pull his truck from the ditch before a patrol car happened to drive past. The old pickup was only dented a bit more, was even driveable after a jump start. My father drove home and slept it off.

He discovered the next morning that his bottom false teeth were missing. Cradling his swollen head in his hands, Dad asked Mama to drive him to the accident site. Where he had nose-dived into the pavement, his teeth had been jolted from his mouth. Cars had driven over them during the night, and plastic teeth were scattered up and down the pavement. On his day off, he and my mother had to drive to South Carolina to a cheap one-day denture clinic for another set of teeth.

Occasionally, God seemed to brush Dad with disaster, as if warning him that his patience should never be tested.

Dad was late coming home again, nearly midnight; I had lain awake listening for the sound of his truck. I was nine years old, my parents in their mid-thirties. I listened to Dad and Mama argue in muffled tones from the kitchen.

"Reese, don't go out there now," Mama begged. "It's pitch-dark. The horse is all right."

"I just want to give him this bread," Dad said. "Damn horse would starve if I didn't look after him."

"You can feed him first thing in the morning. You need to get to sleep."

The screen door opened, seconds later the gate to the horse corral squealed. Dad was especially hardheaded when drinking and would usually insist on doing the opposite of what he was advised to do. I crawled from the bed and watched through the screen. The moon shone bright. Dad held out a handful of bread and coaxed the horse to him. The young stallion nibbled the bread, his ears perked forward. Dad rubbed the horse's neck. Springing off his left leg, he mounted the two-year-old Appaloosa. He kicked the horse's flanks, holding to the mane without even the control of a bridle. My mother stood silent in the glow of the large summer moon, her arms at her sides. Dad urged the frightened horse into a canter, then a full gallop around and around the circular pen. The weather was dry, the tempo of hooves spaced and loud above the night chorus of frogs and whippoorwill.

Dad and the horse faded into the night air. Suddenly, the hoofbeats stopped. A few seconds later the stallion flashed into view, this time riderless. I saw my mother stalk a few slow steps toward the corral, then hurry to where my father was getting up from the dust. She fussed over him as she brushed the dirt from his clothes and half-supported him as they walked inside.

The next morning he was seeing double. Reluctantly, he reported to the VA hospital, where an X-ray showed his skull had been cracked. He spent nine weeks in the hospital.

Another time, he stopped at a bootlegger's house to get more whiskey. As he talked with the man, the bootlegger's pit bulldog walked out from his dustbath under the edge of the trailer. My father commented on how fine an animal the dog was, then leaned to pet him. The bulldog leaped and bit into his face. By the time my father sobered up the next day and let my mother attend to the wound, infection was setting in. He spent another three weeks in the hospital.

Despite my father's antics and injuries when under the influence, his behavior paled when compared to that of his older brother, Dewey. Dewey drove a bread delivery truck for the Merita Bakery and worked the downtown route for twenty-odd years. Because his stops included the hamburger and hot-plate joints where the city's lawyers and judges ate lunch, and because of his jovial, joking manner, he grew to know on a first-name basis some of the most powerful men and women in town. He was always good for a joke, would hand the biggest bum a loaf of fresh bread on credit from his truck knowing he'd never get paid. Dewey lived a charmed life and seemed destined forever to slip through the fingers of the law.

Dewey drank Popov vodka and grape soda. He always had fixings handy in the pocket of his car, and many times when I was a teenager or young adult, he'd wave me over and fix me a snort if we crossed paths. He mixed the vodka and soda half and half, a volatile fuel I would sip, swear was good, then either toss it when he left or buy more soda to dilute it with. Dewey finished his bread delivery route each day by midafternoon, when he loaded up with a fresh fifth of booze, enough soda pop to wash it all down, and a buddy or two collected from the bar stools of Phil and Jerry's, his favorite watering hole. Then they all headed for the country, where Dewey liked to drive the unpaved roads he had walked barefoot as a kid. He and his pals would cruise about fifteen miles an hour, sipping from their paper cups, listening to the radio and waving at people they knew. Everyone recognized Dewey and liked him. Anytime a car was held back by the parade, Dewey would pull to the

shoulder and wave it on by. By the time the sun was dropping into the trees, the fifth would be nearly gone, and he
would turn toward home. The local deputies were accustomed to his slow-rolling car and knew he was of little
menace to the road. They also realized that a ticket written
to him seemed to vanish into thin air. But once, only the
grace God gives to drunks and the judgment of a veteran
lawman saved him from disaster.

A new state trooper was in town and on patrol on the east
side of Fayetteville. He was parked watching traffic at a
country intersection when he spied Dewey's battered old
Ford station wagon rolling along at turtle speed. Koot
McLaurin, Dewey's cousin, rode shotgun, and Ray Lewis
manned the backseat and mixed drinks. The three bleary-
eyed men threw up their hands in salute. The state patrolman fell in behind them, and after a mile of tailgating,
flipped on his blue light.

State patrolmen in North Carolina have never been ones
to discuss life and the weather, and when Dewey stepped
from his car, his breath sweet with liquor, legs wobbly, the
lawman promptly spun him around, frisked him, and
began reading him his rights. The two other drunks stumbled from the car and came to defend their buddy. The
patrolman was not impressed with the breadman's driving
record, nor with his high-placed friends in the court system. He took out his handcuffs and grabbed Dewey's arm,
preparing to cuff him and take him downtown. The day was
sunny, the fifth not even half gone. Koot took action.

Koot slid the trooper's .38 from his belt holster while the
young man was wrestling Dewey's arms behind his back.
He pointed the oversized pistol at the surprised lawman
and told him to leave his buddy alone. The trooper backed
against the side of his car and raised his arms when told to.
Dewey reached into the car and took out his fifth, and they

all took another drink while discussing the matter.

Koot hadn't the slightest intention of shooting the trooper. All he wanted was the day to go right. But now he had a state patrolman at gunpoint, his radio crackling and blue light flashing for the world to see. What to do?

Dewey reasoned that the light had to go off first so as not to attract more attention. He fumbled inside the cruiser, looking for the cutoff switch, but managed only to start up the siren for a moment. The blue light continued to flash. Dewey then ordered the state trooper to climb on top of his cruiser and hug the light with his long body to blot out its infernal glow. The state trooper objected until Koot jiggled the pistol.

The trooper did a good job of blotting out the light, but he looked extremely odd lying there on top of his car in a fetal position. Cars slowed, the drivers gawked. The drunks put their heads together and discussed the matter. They could hand the trooper his weapon and let him take over, but Koot was afraid he might start shooting. They could shoot out the car tires and take off in their own vehicle, but in minutes flat the trooper would have every law enforcement officer in the county looking for them. Finally, Dewey decided to get on the radio and call for help.

The radio was busy with the usual traffic on the police band. Dewey picked up the handset and began talking to anyone in general, saying they needed some assistance and where they were located. The dispatcher heard his broadcast and asked to speak to the officer, but Dewey put the handset up, lit a cigarette, and waited. In less than a minute a Cumberland County Sheriff's Department car drove up.

The deputy had been less than a mile from the location when Dewey's call came over the air. He was an older deputy who knew Dewey and Koot from years back, had shared a snort with them on days off. He pulled off the road

behind the trooper's car and radioed that no more assistance was needed. Koot met him at his car and handed him
the gun. The trooper came off the car top in one fluid moment and grabbed his shotgun from inside the car. In less
than ten seconds, the situation had reversed; Dewey and
Koot and the other drunk were spread-eagled against the
side of the trooper's car.

The trooper had every right to be angry. If another state
trooper had arrived before the deputy, he would have had
good reason to come out of his car shooting. Dewey and his
buddies were facing serious charges. The trooper took deep
breaths while frisking each man, trying to regain his com-
posure. The deputy stood back and assessed the situation.

Regardless of the laws that Koot and Dewey had broken,
the young trooper had an image problem to consider. While
he got out his handcuffs, the deputy asked what his superi-
ors were going to think of a six-foot plus, hefty young state
trooper letting an intoxicated fifty-year-old man take his
weapon away without a struggle. The trooper balked as he
pictured in his mind how the story would circulate among
the other troopers.

"Why don't you consider letting me take these fellows
on home," the deputy suggested. "I promise you they'll
stay off the road, and we'll let this little matter stay right
between the two of us."

The trooper sucked on his bottom lip, nodded, and got
out of there as fast as he could. Dewey promised to stay off
the road for a few days until things cooled. Drunks seem to
have extra lives like cats, and Dewey used several of his
that day in averting a tragedy.

He was about out of lives the last time I saw him. I was
twenty-one and due to be married the next day, was driving
around with Bruce when we happened upon Dewey at a
filling station. He was well into his vodka and grape soda

and gassing up for his evening glide. I noticed he had lost weight, his eyes hollow like gun-shot holes. He pulled a twenty-dollar bill from his wallet and handed it to my brother and told him how happy he was about the wedding. Dewey thought he was talking to me. He stumbled back to his car and left to pilot the back roads. He entered the hospital a couple of months later with lung cancer, wasted down to a near skeleton, and never came out. He was fifty-four when he died. His driving record showed eleven arrests for drinking and driving, none of which had ever been tried.

THE Kingfish drank bourbon and chased it with liver pudding. He was a large man, with meat-slab hands and a puffy face streaked with broken veins. His real name was Carson Autry. I often heard him say he had ten cancers in his body but he kept them all pickled with alcohol. He was married to my mother's aunt and worked at the Merita Bakery with my father until he was eventually let go for coming to work drunk too often.

Kingfish had a habit of setting out to kill himself. Occasionally when in the depths of a drunken jag, his family down on him to sober up, he would fetch his shotgun from the closet, slowly insert a shell into the chamber, and announce to his wife and children that he was going out behind the barn to blow his brains out. The first few times he started the journey, his wife clawed at his back and begged him not to do it, and the oldest boy was sent across the field to fetch my grandfather to come and help. As the years dragged on, Kingfish's threats were taken less seriously, until he was allowed to go to the barn unescorted. The first time he fired his shotgun into the air, his family bolted from the house and came screaming across the backyard, only to find him standing erect, the hot barrel smoking. They never came again. He would fire the heavy gun, sit down and wait, sip a little more from his bottle, wait some more, then finally return home, even more devout in his conviction he was unloved and unmourned.

I usually only saw Kingfish on Wednesday nights when his wife was at prayer meeting. After I had reached a height sufficient to see over the steering wheel and mash the brake at the same time, he'd call and ask me to meet him out of sight of my house. Kingfish was as well known as my Uncle Dewey by the local law enforcement, but had never been allowed the same grace. He had been stripped of his driving privilege for life and never ventured over the city line while at the controls of a motor vehicle. The liquor store lay a good half mile inside the forbidden zone. I'd usually meet him beyond the first curve and for a dollar bill, take over driving, risking persecution by the law and the wrath of my mother.

He always had me stop first at the Red Apple Supermarket in East Fayetteville, where from the meat counter he purchased a foot-long length of liver pudding, ground together from hog liver and parts unknown, then stuffed in a casing of intestines.

"Have a snort, boy, damn," he'd always say when we were halfway back home and the alcohol was kicking in. "Your daddy was drinking at your age."

I could barely stomach beer at fourteen, and a slug of cheap bourbon followed by a bite of cold liver pudding, the end shiny with Kingfish's spit, was not appealing. But I usually managed a small swallow, the slightest bite. I loved driving his truck while earning a dollar and figured I needed to be good company.

Years later in my early twenties, I ended up living with my first wife in a small house just across a field from Kingfish. I was his closest neighbor, and from my front porch could often hear the roaring verbal fights he and my aunt waged. Mattie and I were having our own fights, and I discovered more and more in our discontent how the haze of alcohol muted what I feared in the world and enhanced my resolve to live differently. The bills would still roll in, roll call at work had to be met every morning, Monday through Friday, the realities of life often proved different from what a man had dreamed of as a boy. But for a couple of bucks, a six-pack or pint of whiskey could stay those feelings or ignite my imagination again until I believed my job as a Pepsi salesman was only temporary, and I would still one day explore the world as the leader of expeditions or view the far galaxies through the lens of a giant telescope.

Mattie finally left me, as I have said, when on a five-hundred-dollar loan from Dial Finance I had bought a six-month-old lion cub to add to my menagerie of snakes, monkeys, and other exotic beasts. She did not like the menagerie, liked even less the payments she discovered I would be making over the next two years. The lion acted like a hundred-pound kitten, loved to pounce from behind doors, wrap her claws around a person, and bite. Mattie liked that even less. The third night I had the lion, my wife went to visit a girlfriend, probably to be consoled and reassured that matrimony was worth the bumps. I got into a bottle while she was gone, my round buddy trying to assure me the same thing. When Mattie returned, I was passed out in bed, the lion comfortably positioned on her pillow. Against my protests, she left the next day and moved home with her folks.

In hindsight, I liken my collection of animals to Noah's Ark. I was a good Pepsi salesman, hustled and sold my quota. But each week that passed, I became more and more fearful of being forever sucked into a life of working five-day weeks, scraping to make payments on a house, a car, a new living-room suite, pulling down overtime whenever possible to lay a few bucks aside. I had seen the glimmer slowly fade in my father's eyes, in the eyes of other men, as they gave up long-harbored dreams in the face of adult reality. We were Southern, working-class men, expected to hammer out a paycheck, produce children, and hold our liquor. Anything less was failure.

My animals made me different. I was a Pepsi salesman, but I was also the owner of a lion and a snake handler. I might look the part of a laborer in my pinstriped uniform, but I was a man who milked rattlesnakes and rode monkeys on his shoulder. Such a man I imagined could never become permanently mired. I refused to envision myself as a reflection of my father—and feared I might not have his grit.

So I added a lion, a new snake, a parrot as the storm inside me grew, surrounded myself with the exotic to shield myself from the average world. Add a few beers and this strange boat I captained could float out of Beard and across mountaintops.

Kingfish was over the next evening after Mattie left to comfort me. The week had ended, payday, I was tired and ready to forget my sore hands and sorer heart in a bottle of Wild Turkey. Kingfish was ready to help me drink that fifth while assuring me that no woman in the world was really worth a damn, but you had to put up with some of their shit for pussy and cooking.

"Hellfire, boy," I remember him telling me. "You ought to be down on Water Street right now, getting up with some of them Injun gals. That damn Reese has got younguns all over town."

A tale of my father's infidelity was not what I was in the mood to hear right then.

"I don't need this talk," I told Kingfish, and raised one hand for him to stop.

"Well, you can't sit around and drink by yourself and mourn a woman." He squinted one eye while lifting his bottle. "You don't know where *she* is right now, do ya?"

I cold-cocked Kingfish under his eye and sent his bottle flying. Kingfish pulled out his pocketknife and told me he was going to cut me. He wouldn't have really cut me, but I slapped the knife from his hand, then proceeded to bang his head against the wall. Afterwards, he sat on the floor, blood drying on his lip, squinting one eye and saying to me between draws on his bottle, "Boy, you've gone crazy as damn hell. What's wrong with you? You've gone crazy as damn hell."

The heat of morning awakened me. I lay in the front yard rolled up in a blanket. My lion was still in the house and had chewed the armrest off the couch. I staggered inside and surveyed the wreckage from drunks and lion while downing a quantity of water.

Kingfish showed up that afternoon. If he remembered any more of our fracas than I did, he didn't tell it. But he obviously was concerned for me, because he brought me some fried chicken left over from lunch. He chain-smoked Camel nonfilters and sipped whiskey from a pint bottle. He offered me a snort, but my belly heaved at the thought. While viewing the wreckage of my living room, I wondered how seriously angry my wife was this time and who in the world might be interested in buying a lion.

I ended up selling the lion at a small loss to a fellow who owned a roadside zoo. Actually, I cannot call the deal a loss, for I had owned a lion for one month, a claim few people can boast. I also gained new insight, if not understanding, into how Kingfish behaved. For all Kingfish's sorriness through the years, he possessed some merit. He brought me fried chicken and concern only hours after saying he would cut my throat, and that made me doubt even more he ever would have pressed his knife blade to my throat.

A couple of months later, Mattie and I temporarily patched up our marriage. I returned from work one afternoon to find her standing in the backyard peering across the field at Kingfish's house. Several cars were in his yard, one a long, black late-model limousine. I stood several minutes at the phone before I lifted the receiver and dialed my mother. She confirmed my fear that Kingfish had passed on.

For a man who had hurtled and raged through life, Kingfish slipped into death as easily as sliding into a bath of water. His wife came into the house carrying a bag of groceries. She saw Kingfish sitting in an armchair with his eyes closed, a half-glass of whiskey held in his hand. The television was on. He was supposed to be chopping the garden. She called harshly to him. She set her load down, then went to awaken him. Something about how his jaw hung made her pause. She called softer this time, then stepped close and shook his arm.

He had died from a massive heart attack at sixty-six. He was well into another drunk when his trumpet sounded, all physical cancers well pickled. A cigarette was held between two fingers. The tobacco had burned down to his skin and gone out. I wished that on one of those occasions when he had fired his shotgun into the air and waited alone for his mourners who never came I had walked behind that barn and asked him to put the shotgun down. But he wouldn't have stopped drinking or threatening to shoot himself. The round neck of a whiskey bottle fit his temple as snugly as a gun barrel, and by pulling his arm down I would only have made myself feel better.

LAUGHING at another man's weakness is easier than to cry for him. To chuckle at the humor in Uncle Dewey's or Kingfish's escapades allowed me to lighten the tragedy behind a husband and father holding a patrolman at gunpoint or threatening to kill himself. Right or wrong, working-class America admires hard-drinking men. If known for nothing else admirable, a man can boast a reputation as a good boozer. Once I gave a dollar to a man who approached me while I was pulling cases of soda from my Pepsi truck. He reeked of alcohol and sweat, and I asked him why he wanted a drink so early in the day. As if to challenge me, he held my stare while pulling a bottle from his pocket and drinking.

"You don't even know me, yet you just gave me a dollar. If I had a suit on, you wouldn't a give me a nickel."

He sucked again from his bottle.

"Hell, I walk in any restaurant on this street, they hand me a sandwich, just so I'll leave. You don't get shit, buddy, in this world for free if you're clean and hardworking."

He patted his bottle. "This here bottle of wine is a ticket to ride."

ROGER SPAKE was a brave and good man who never asked for anything free, but in the end wasted himself on vodka. He was too fine a man for me to ever laugh at the damages he did to himself and his family while under the influence of alcohol.

Roger was a lean, rawboned man of average height with the courage of a gamecock. He grew up on a hardscrabble farm in Oklahoma and left home at eighteen to lessen the load on the family table. He joined the Army and was soon a member of the 82nd Airborne Division. During a military career that spanned more than twenty-five years, he fought in three wars, stayed married to one woman, helped raise three sons and a daughter, and built a reputation as a no-nonsense man who could be counted on to pull more than his weight in the community. In the starched lines in his uniform and his seven acres of garden, trimmed yard, shrubbery, and neatly painted house, I found a sense of order and dependability I sometimes longed for in my own life.

"Lock it up there, soldiers," Roger barked, stepping from his pickup truck to where a bunch of us waited for the school bus. He wore his military greens, buttons and boots as shiny as the sun glinting through the trees. We drew our bodies erect, thrust out our small chests, and tried to copy Roger as he snapped his heels together and threw us a salute. "Now, I want to see each of your lunch-money quarters," he growled again, in his honed drill-instructor voice. "Pockets inside out, now."

He stopped often for surprise inspections. On the days one of us was unable to show lunch money, he dug in his own pocket and provided it.

Roger also lined his sons up at inspection, usually at midnight when he came home late after stopping off to drink. His boys would stand locked at attention while he raved about the grass that hadn't been properly cut, the calf that had not been watered. Roger was accustomed to a military world where he carried out his superior's orders at the snap of a finger, and in turn, passed orders down. He could not bear the incompetence and lackadaisical work ethics of young boys who had not suffered the Depression and gone to bed hungry. His drinking was mostly restricted to Falstaff beer back then, his sons too young to challenge his iron rule. Usually by the next day his anger would have passed and he would find some simple but sincere way to make up—praise their work, shell out a few dollars from his pocket, challenge his boys to a little horseplay on the basketball court. His drinking really only became a problem when he retired from active duty, found his sons rapidly becoming grown men with ideas of their own, and felt the control of taking and giving orders slipping from his grasp. He then turned to vodka.

"Goddammit, Tim, people don't use their noodles no more today," Roger said between sips from a large glass of iced vodka and Mountain Dew. "I could go in one of John Smith's tobacco fields and pull someone off a row and he'd do better than most people in Washington."

Roger was an intelligent man who read the papers daily and stayed tuned in to world affairs. He could carry on a reasonable argument concerning any matter you confronted him with and could name the capitals of every state in the union. After working his way out of a youth of poverty, then excelling in a career that took constant decision, preparation, and action, he grew more and more intolerant of schoolchildren who could not find the United States on a map and a world in general that seemed to be settling more and more into the comforts he had suffered through three wars to guarantee. He became increasingly confrontational and critical of his sons.

The Spake boys inherited their father's quick temper and independent mind, but as most of my generation, had not been tempered by poverty or war. Roger had worked hard, suffered in battle, learned what he needed to survive, and discarded the bullshit. Now at the time in his life when he felt his sons needed his guidance and knowledge most, he was discovering them to be men of a different age and priorities who were determined to discover their own paths through life. Mike, his middle son and my best friend, often talked to me about his dad.

"You can't please him," Mike said. "Always, anything I

do is too much or too little. Give him a shirt for his birthday, he raves about spending too much money. Don't give him anything, he gets mad and says I don't give a damn. He'll pick a fight with Mom over how much she pays for a pound of hamburger."

When grown I stopped by often on afternoons to share a drink and listen to his stories. He told me a tale once when he was well into his bottle, and the story helped me understand better what the man had been through.

"We jumped into France ahead of the Normandy invasion, a night jump, couldn't see a damn thing out the door of the plane. We came in at low altitude with full combat equipment, and pop, we were out the door and praying to feel that chute open. Weren't in the air but a few seconds before we were busting the ground open. I was squad leader, and when I rounded up most of my men I saw we had landed in the courtyard of a bombed-out church. The Germans popped some flares on us and started hitting us with small-arms fire. I rolled up behind a tombstone and tried to see where the shooting was coming from. We returned fire, but mostly just fired into the dark."

Roger paused in his story and mixed himself and me another drink. He measured out the liquor and soda slowly and carefully as if he dreaded telling the rest of the story.

"Finally the shooting stopped and we just hunkered down and waited. Then something started crying, sounded almost like a cat yawling, but after a while I knew it was a man. I had everyone count off and found we were one fellow short. I saw him when the Germans lit more flares. He came down like the rest of us in pitch black, but his luck had been bad. He had landed on top of a splintered telegraph pole, and the end had rammed up through his backside and stopped somewhere up in his gut. He knew he was done for but couldn't help crying out from all his pain. The

Germans heard him and started shooting again, and for another ten minutes both sides just wasted lead.

"I knew what I had to do even before the shooting stopped. The boy was done for. Even if we could have sawed him down, half his blood was already dripping down that pole. The Germans would have picked off anyone who got halfway to him. I was squad leader, and by God, it was up to me to act. I didn't have to use but one bullet, but it hushed him and stopped his pain. I think the snipers understood too, 'cause they stopped firing and moved on. We sent a party back later to cut him down."

Some of the stories Roger told me when he was drinking were repeats, he might mix up the facts, forget a thing or two. But he only told me the above story once, told it in a clear, cold voice, as if he still saw that soldier impaled on that splintered telegraph pole on dark sleepless nights when he tried to add up the balance of his life. It helped me to understand and admire him even more.

His vodka drinking increased to a fifth a day. For a few more years he managed to produce a fine garden and tend to a crop of hay, some cows, but eventually the booze became the center of his life. For a few months his wife moved out to an apartment in town, and the added grief and loneliness aged the old battler. I would still stop by often and talk with him, share a drink, maybe drive to the liquor store for him. Occasionally I would come in and find him doing push-ups, still stronger than many men in their late fifties. But more often, I would find him nearing the end of a bottle, his eyes glassy and ready to wage verbal battle against a world he believed more and more was going to the dogs.

He fell one day and busted some ribs, but refused to go to the hospital. He knew in a hospital bed he would be forced to confront the reality of his drinking. His wife moved back home to care for him; her love was still stronger than their problems. Talk circulated among the family of having him committed against his will to a clinic, but such matters are difficult by law and heart. Mike lived closest to his father and was more tolerant of his forceful nature. He talked to me of ways to save his father.

"I gotta do something. He just sits there day after day killing himself. If we could have him committed? Maybe if he dried out some, then the doctors could help him."

"You mean commit him against his will?" I asked. "Ain't that pretty hard to do?"

Mike pulled a long draw from a can of beer. Pain shone dully in his eyes.

"Not if he's a threat to himself. Suicidal."

Mike sat his can down and looked me in the eye. "I been thinking. What if we were to wrestle him down? You could hold him and I could cut his wrist a little. Just enough to bleed, but then I could call the law and swear he tried to kill himself. A judge would sign a paper then. Mom and the rest of the family would back me up."

I told him I would help, but the plan stayed only talk. Secretly I was glad. The two of us could have manhandled him, but instead of a withered drunk, I still saw most the squared-away sergeant in dress greens. I was afraid he had only to shout "Lock it up, soldier" and I would spring to attention and show him my lunch quarter.

Not long afterwards, Roger was diagnosed as having cancer of the lungs. The disease spread to his brain. He died quickly of the disease and was buried with military honors to the roar of a rifle salute.

SINCE childhood, I have studied men who drink hard and tried to understand their need, and why I harbor that same thirst. I still do not understand. No real manliness is found in losing one's physical and mental control through gulping alcohol. Some men find the same escape in religion, others in extreme devotion to their families and community. I cannot explain why one man seeks refuge in a church while another seeks his sanctuary in a bottle of Jim Beam. Each looks for something to fill his mind and senses, a presence that is greater than he. Whiskey, the Bible—both are dope.

All the men I've seen defeated by drinking have not deterred me from loving a cold beer, a shot of tequila, but even more from loving the peace that begins after guzzling two or three beers or shots. I have inherited my Uncle Dewey's love of riding the back roads and sipping beer. I love to drive slowly with the radio tuned to a favorite station, the window rolled down so I can feel the air and smell the fields and woods. The effect is hypnotizing. I rarely drive faster than twenty miles per hour, and to pass another vehicle is unusual. My mind rambles, I watch the road for crawling snakes, think of my family, judge past events, contemplate the future, and think of stories I'd like to write. In fifteen miles, I might down four or five beers. I am breaking the law by driving and drinking, and in the eyes of many people I am wasting time. But for me the time is well spent, therapeutic, and so far, harmless. Chug that first beer, down another nearly as fast, settle back in the seat, and enjoy the soft, warm cloud as it settles over me. For the next hour I know I have no need to defend myself; I am Tim McLaurin, handler of poisonous snakes, world traveler, stargazer, and one-day Nobel laureate. Of little concern is the fact that as a man in my mid-thirties, I have no retirement plan and little in savings and in the eyes of most of my working-class peers do not even have a legitimate job.

Sometimes toward the bottom of a beer I can admit to a

great truth. It is far easier to chase the stars than to hunker
down on a piece of solid land and love it and hate it. With
acreage comes commitment—sticking to one woman, your
children, working a job that pays the bills and keeps you
fed and clothed. I fear I am not the same man as my brothers or father, could not continue to punch that clock every
day. I noted early in childhood the hope in my father's eyes
when he looked across his fields and imagined cash crops
and large herds of cows. I saw how his eyes had dimmed
later on early mornings when he blew steam off his coffee
and waited those last minutes before leaving to pull his
shift. His eyes shone flat as glass late in his life, reflective
of land still under mortgage, his plans unchanged to next
week clear that back field for pasture land.

I walked easily from my first marriage, from a woman
who loved me and wanted only a husband devoted to her, a
community, and church. I am married now ten years to
Katie and find my greatest love in my children, but still
daydream of tramping off alone to some corner of the earth.
I've surrounded myself with snakes and own a telescope
that lets me search way beyond my property. I may very
well end up like a mirror reflection of my father, my own
head cradled in my hands, dwelling on what I did not ac-
complish in my life. But I will know I tried, dammit.

YEARS ago I was serving as a Peace Corps volunteer when
my back began hurting after an especially long run through
the Tunisian countryside outside our town of Siliana.

"You'll have to come in and get checked out," the Peace
Corps nurse told me over the office phone. "There's a
chance it could be your appendix."

I argued that it was probably only a pulled muscle, but
she prevailed. That meant Katie and me getting on a

packed bus and riding three hours into Tunis. An American doctor looked me over, poked my belly, then announced he thought I was right, only a muscle pull. He asked for safety's sake that I wait until a Tunisian clinic opened the next day and have a blood test done on my white corpuscle count. Since the Peace Corps director had an overnight trip planned, he invited us to stay at his house, a mansion by the standards we had acquired, complete with television and videos, western bath, refrigerator filled with food, and a bar fully stocked with American whiskey.

I thought I had found paradise when I entered that house and opened the liquor locker. Jack Daniel's, Johnny Walker, George Dickle, the whole damn gang was there. I hadn't had whiskey in nearly six months, and I proceeded to get knee-walking, fish-eyed drunk while watching *Star Wars* on the video.

At five to eight in the morning, Katie roused me and said I had five minutes before the nurse arrived to carry me for my blood test. I staggered into the bathroom with the most god-awful hangover I had ever had and pray never to have again. I gagged and tried to throw up and splashed water on my face. When I opened the bathroom door, the nurse was standing there. She stared at my pale skin and bloodshot eyes and exclaimed, "Gracious, Tim, you look terrible. You must *really* have appendicitis!"

I was too ashamed to tell her I was only stinking drunk, so all the way to the clinic, I lay with my head on the back of the seat, trying to keep from gagging. Katie and the nurse stared at me with great concern. When I walked into the clinic, the Tunisian doctor approached me with American dollar signs reflecting in his eyes. He poked my stomach once and said, "We'll operate at two o'clock."

Now, I knew I didn't have appendicitis, and there was no

way in hell I was going to let him cut on me. I did want mightily to lie down somewhere, so I let them lead me to a room where I was instructed to put on a white robe and lie in bed. A nurse took a blood sample. I knew I had four hours before they would operate. I'd lie in the bed a couple of hours till my head wasn't splitting open, then head back to Siliana, hell or high water. I drifted into light sleep.

I awakened to the prick of a needle in my arm. I don't know what they shot me with, but it beat the dog out of any Valiums or Quaaludes I've ever abused. In thirty seconds I was so high they could have been discussing castration and I'd just have lain there and floated and grinned.

They wheeled me into that operating room and cut out my appendix. My blood test came back normal, and I still get that pain sometimes in my lower back when I overexert. But I got a free appendectomy and don't have to worry about appendicitis hitting me in the middle of the Everglades or on some mountain range.

I lost that piece of myself to liquor. In years of associating with drinkers, I have seen whole chunks of men disappear, usually the will first, then the mind, and finally some important part of the body. But there is a lesson in a person's problems and how we cope in ways that seem to fit. A drunk washes all his life away, but the drinkers cling to a core of respect that in the end is what we chisel on their tombstone.

DURING the early summer prior to marrying my second wife, Katie, I spent a couple of weeks working alongside my father. I was finishing up my first year of college and soon to marry a fine woman who would travel a large portion of the world with me and would birth my two children. My father had recently retired on total disability for heart and back problems after twenty-odd years at the bakery and for the first time in his life was forced to slow down and watch his pace. I was in my mid-twenties, he was fifty. Our project was tearing down the old McLaurin family house, a rambling, wide-porched dwelling of aged oak. It had been home to my great-grandfather and great-grandmother, then passed on to several of my great-uncles who, besides fathering a few mulatto children, lived bachelor lives.

The house had been deserted for a few years since the last of my great-uncles was found dead in his farm truck. But the house was well roofed with tin sheeting, and stood tight and dry despite new inhabitants of mice, wasps, and dirt daubers. I wanted lumber to construct the floor and ceiling of a log cabin I was building by hand from cypress logs. The cabin was to stand on some of our back land, far from the nearest road or neighbor on the edge of the field where as kids we had ridden our ponies and hunted arrowheads. The cabin was simple in design, one large room with a sleeping loft and a front porch. It would be a fitting new home for the hundred-year-old fat pine lumber. With another good tin roof overhead, the mixture of cured lumber and tough new cypress would marry well for another century.

My father wanted the tin sheeting off the old roof. The metal was still good and would serve well on top of the crude goat and cow sheds he liked to build to shelter his growing herds. But actually, he needed something to fill his idle days, wanted to feel a good smooth hammer handle in his palm, the heat of sunlight on his neck, to spend some time with me where work buffered our relationship and allowed us to talk like friends.

His back did not allow him to do much of the harder labor. Loosed from the confines of a desk and invigorated by love and lust for a new woman, I felt strength for the two of us and aided by crowbar and hammer wrenched nails loose that had slept since long before either of us were born. The nails groaned but yielded their anchor in aged, sap-cured wood; we disassembled in hours what had taken days to construct.

My father still did most of the directing, but he spoke with tolerance, seeming to notice for the first time that no boy worked beside him on that steep pitch, but a man larger than himself in body, if not in experience. Many of his words were spent on caution, fearing I might topple backwards off the roof or bring a heavy timber down on my head, a reverse from younger days when he fussed at me for being too cautious and afraid of diving into hard work. I mostly ignored his warnings, maybe boldened by the increasing knowledge that now I was the stronger. The boy who had grown up fearing and loving his silent, violable father now realized that in work, play, or fight, he had become dominant. I felt the victory, but also a delicate sadness.

The house came down layer by layer, revealing the stains and odors of ages long buried and forgotten. Under a layer of old linoleum, we read yellowed newspapers fragile as a butterfly wing, the headlines filled with reports of World War One. In a hole covered over with wallpaper were dozens of unused rubbers, the sheaths of sheepskin still moist in tinfoil packets. Another smaller hole in one wall yielded a large-caliber bullet. The oak floor in the living room was spotted with my Great-Uncle Hersey's blood where it flowed the day they brought him from the grain field where his arm had been ripped off in a thresher.

In the late afternoon of the last day we spent tearing down the old place, we loaded our stacks of lumber and tin and put our tools away, then sat on the tailgate of the truck parked in the cool shade of a hickory nut tree and opened a can of beer. My father preferred Schlitz, tall ones, hot or cold, it didn't matter. I liked my beer cold, but after a day's labor was not prone to be choosy. We talked of minor things, a problem with safely pulling down the chimney, what we would do with the bricks in the foundation. Our bellies were empty, we were tired, and the alcohol easily and quickly kicked into the blood and eased any remaining tension.

"You know," my father said, "I remember coming here when I was a little boy and this house seemed like the biggest place in the world. Granny would sit on the porch and rock and tell stories and I felt that if the whole world changed, this place would stay the same."

He drank loudly from his beer. "Now look at it. Ain't nothing here but some bricks, and they'll be gone soon. People ten years from now won't even know this house existed."

On a small hill overlooking where we sat was located an ancient graveyard. Many of my ancestors are buried there. I studied the gray stones, looking like mushrooms popped from the earth. My father tapped his nearly empty can. I saw in his eyes he wanted another.

"Beer's mighty good after a hard day," he cautioned, "but it can get ahold of you too. You let it, it'll be just one more thing you got to answer to. It'll be like a job you hate, but you got to keep at it in order to live."

I nodded and remembered the afternoon I had hopped over him in game when he was passed out, the nights I lay in bed and worried and wished to hear the sounds of his truck tires in the drive, the times I had gone to get him from his cousin's home when he was too drunk to start his truck and attempt to drive. But I remembered more the mornings I peeped around the corner and watched him doze while sitting at the table, his face cradled in his palms, fighting a blinding hangover while listening to the clock tick away the few minutes before he had to rise and go pay his dues.

———

"OUT there flapping that ball up and down. All he ever does is flap that ball." My father stood at the window, watching me dribble a basketball on the hard-packed dirt court.

"Well, he loves it so much, Reese," mama defended me. "I'd rather him play basketball than run around getting in trouble."

My father had never been one who enjoyed sports. He had trouble justifying time spent not earning a paycheck or growing food. But he spent good money buying me a ball and hoop, then hammered together a backboard and nailed it to a length of telephone pole, and though he grumbled. I think he was secretly proud I was on the basketball team.

North Carolinians are by nature crazy over basketball. With four major universities in the state and four national championships to brag over, fascination with the game comes easy. Early in grammar school, I became interested in the game, would hurry to the court at recess, where we would choose sides. I was always tall for my age, and with dogged determination, dribbled and shot and practiced until I was usually one of the first chosen. Keith Culbreth, a friend of mine, and I would often on Saturdays walk four miles to our school playground, where we would play one-on-one for hours.

Making the school team became an obsession with me. For a country kid whose world was measured in a few square miles, to wear one of those shiny uniforms and run out on the court in front of hundreds of screaming fans, to maybe connect on a twenty-foot shot just before the buzzer sounded, was the stuff of heaven. Every night in my prayers, I asked that when I was old enough, I might make the team. To be cut from the squad was unthinkable.

For years and years, I have been a fanatic of University of North Carolina basketball. To a good portion of the Tarheel State, Coach Dean Smith ranks above mortal man and one day will sit up front with God. He runs a clean program that wins, graduates players, and is an example of quality in the increasingly troubled world of college ball.

I used to become almost physically sick when Carolina lost a game. I would walk the street late at night, my mind filled with images of foul shots, referees, and screaming fans. For a couple of days the loss would nag the back of my mind. I am better now concerning losses—when a man has seen his children born, buried his father, and been told his own days might be limited, the loss of a ball game loses some of its sting. Still, I sit there on the edge of my chair, shout, cuss and cheer, and urge them on. Little in the world of art can top a Carolina fast break, a lithe guard sailing down the middle of the court and dishing off to the likes of James Worthy or Michael Jordan, who then takes flight and soars above the rim to slam the ball home.

FINALLY, my freshman year arrived and I was a student at Central High, a small school with only a couple hundred students. I tried out for the jayvee team, along with about thirty other hopeful freshmen and sophomores. The first afternoon, a few of the kids were asked not to come back. I turned from them, could not bear to witness their pain, afraid their bad luck might rub off. By the end of the week, fifteen of us were left. The team would have only ten players. Every lay-up or jump shot I concentrated on as if my life depended on it, every loose ball was reason to dive without regard for bruises or floor burns.

I drew uniform number 31, a faded, slightly tattered jersey and pair of shorts. Spun gold would not have pleased me more. With my feet clad in a pair of Converse high-tops with white athletic socks, I could have stared at myself in the mirror for an hour.

I didn't start that year, but I played more than most of the other freshmen, hit a shot every now and then, snagged a few rebounds. We played schools from across town that were larger than us, beat all of them, and won the conference championship.

My sophomore year saw the opening of the new consolidated high school named Cape Fear. Instead of the tiny school I was accustomed to, with its cracker-box gym, I would be attending a school with nearly a thousand students. The gymnasium seemed as large as my former school, boasted glass backboards and bleachers that would seat several thousand spectators. The basketball uniforms were glorious—a rearing colt adorned the chest, the jerseys and trunks were trimmed in blue and gold. Thick warmups, stirrup socks, and new shoes were included. I needed to wear that uniform like I needed air and food. But to make the jayvee team, I would be competing with fellows from the two other schools, many of whom had played for their respective teams. My prayers intensified. Every spare second my hands cradled a basketball.

All those hours spent "flapping" a ball paid off. I had grown to my full height of six feet and could dunk the ball with both hands. My shooting eye had improved to the point that I could burn a jump shot from twenty feet. When the week of tryouts ended and the final list was posted, I had earned a position as starting forward.

Our first game was against a school in the nearby town of Clinton. I scored thirty-one points, including a foul shot at the end of the game that put us ahead. The performance caught the eye of Leon Brock, the varsity coach.

Coach Brock had quite a reputation around Fayetteville. He had a fire-and-brimstone personality, was as quick to chew out a player as praise him. Several very good players had quit his teams over the years after being ridiculed for mistakes by Brock in front of a crowd. Brock had actually struck players before, once nearly prompting a fistfight with an irate father. But Brock was a winner who year after year turned out teams that competed for the crown. When he approached me the next day and said he wanted to bring me up to the varsity, I walked on clouds.

I rode the varsity bench for the rest of the year. The few games I did get in were usually in the last minute when we were way ahead. In retrospect, I cannot understand why I was pulled off the jayvee where I was burning the net and gaining considerable experience and confidence, only to ride the pine and make spot appearances on the varsity. But we did win the conference title, and I knew another two years lay ahead.

In my junior year, I saw considerably more action, even started several games. I particularly remember the big game against Terry Sanford, the game that brought me my encounter with the whore. Our students responded to the Sanford students' dismissal of us as country bumpkins by decorating the gym with bales of hay and shocks of corn. The snack bar menu was changed to advertise moon pies and possumburgers. Many of our students showed up wearing overalls and straw hats.

I started the game, in fact, was chosen to jump the opening tip-off against their star player, Calvin Riddle, who was six feet five inches tall. When the ball was thrown into the air, unintentionally I made one of the most important plays of the game. Calvin and I jumped our highest, arms stretched to the limit. We slapped the ball at the same instant, caught it between our palms; gravity yanked us toward the floor. As we landed, I heard a noise like a sheet tearing. Calvin fell to his back, his face twisted in a mask of agony. Already his badly sprained ankle was swelling and turning blue; he writhed and cried out in pain.

We took the game from there and beat Terry Sanford by eight points. I banged in seven baskets; we sent those city boys back to their split-levels and apartment buildings and claimed bragging rights for the year.

Coach Brock continued to be his fiery self. One of our best guards quit after a dispute with the coach. Brock hit me in the head once with a ball during practice for not following a play correctly. I slowly learned that a Leon Brock player put out his best during a game, but that energy was often motivated more by fear than by commitment and pride.

Finally my senior year rolled around and it was my time to lead. I was well into my image as a young rebel, my hair long, muttonchop sideburns fuzzing the side of my head. I hung out with the fellows who drank beer and smoked a little pot and slid by with minimal grades. But I had a jump shot that was good for about sixteen points a game, and to most girls the swish of the net held much more appeal than membership in the scholarly Beta Club.

And as with snakes and astronomy, I used basketball to separate myself from the average guy and my fear of being entrenched in the working class. I was probably the first in my family to ever have my picture in the paper, and it appeared there regularly. Having to practice every afternoon took me off the farm and away from feeding hogs. I would arrive home after dark, tired and salt-crusted, my supper kept warm in the oven. My brothers complained my parents were cutting me too much slack. I bagged groceries on weekends and summers most of my high school years, but the boss always bent my schedule around practice. And as a star player, I could run safer with the "bad boys." When I knew it was time to turn down another beer and go home, explaining I had to keep in shape was far easier than saying I knew Mama was awake and worried.

True art existed in our entrances on game nights in the gym. Everyone had his own personal style; my own began with a fevered parking session with Mattie behind the football bleachers. As usual, I got no more than my finger wet, but was left revved up and filled with the adrenaline to run miles. Mattie would always leave a hickey on my neck, not one of those blood blisters that look like the mark of vampires, but her own discreet, tasteful, personal sign.

If ever in my family lineage any black blood was mixed in, the influence showed in how I juke-walked through the gymnasium on the way to the dressing room. The second half of the girls' game would have just begun, the spectators in their seats. I would bop along, chest thrust out, Mattie hanging to one hand, my uniform bag swinging back and forth in the other. I would glance into the stands, nod and smile at friends, hear shouts of encouragement, and know in my heart I was the envy of every male and the great lust of every female.

We weren't the best team in the league, but were far from the worst. We played Terry Sanford again, this time in their gym. The game was a battle. I hit a jump shot with twenty seconds to go that put us one point ahead. A Terry Sanford player stepped on the line inbounding the ball, and suddenly all we had to do was hold on to the ball less than half a minute for victory. Keith Culbreth, my longtime friend, was our ball handler. I'd put the points on the board, and now it was his time to perform. The pass was inbounded; Keith had the ball taken from him in less than five seconds, then fouled the player who had robbed him.

The boy sank both free throws to win the game.

Secretly, and without realizing the fact, I held Culbreth's failure against him for years.

MATTIE and I had separated for the first time, my soul tormented with the doubts and fears that come when a woman claims she no longer loves you. Culbreth and I were going to the beach; I drank almost a full fifth of Wild Turkey during the hundred-mile trip.

I was close to knee-walking when we arrived at the ocean. I floundered in the surf, barely able to stand up in the waves. Some concerned person called the rescue squad. From just beyond the breakers, I cussed the rescue workers, plus a couple of deputy sheriffs who had arrived. Culbreath pleaded with me to come out of the water. Finally, Culbreth got me on shore, tried to hush me as I cussed the law, and pleaded with them not to lock me up. I hung out the car window, flipping the deputies the bird as we drove away.

"Get in the window, Tim," Culbreth told me. "The man is going to lock you up." He grabbed my arm and pulled me down into the seat.

"They ain't shit," I said, slurring my words. "Barney Fife could whip 'em all." I shouted through the window again.

"You better cool it, Tim. That guy is through playing."

I craned around in my seat and flipped up my finger at the last sight of the deputies. I glared at Culbreth. He frowned at me.

"What you looking at?" I mumbled. "You ain't shit, either."

Culbreth didn't answer. A drunk wanting to argue does not like silence.

"Yeah, you scared to death, too," I tried to egg him.

"Always were scared." I thought back to the ball game when he lost the ball.

"I don't know what you're talking about," Culbreth said.

"Naw, you know," I taunted. "Unless you blacked it out of your memory. Got a convenient case of amnesia or something."

Fortunately, my liquor-loosened tongue did not unfairly accuse Culbreth of blowing the game.

In my drunken stupidity, I did decide I wanted to fight Culbreth. I called him every name that might induce anger, even spat several times in his face. A lesser man might have with great justice knocked my teeth down my throat. Culbreth endured my assault, carried me to a motel, and got me in a bed just as I was starting to pass out. I woke up about ten hours later, a hangover raging, bits and pieces of terrible memory surfacing.

Culbreth laughed it off; I stored the memory in the file I will draw from should this good friend ever need aid or rescue.

MY SENIOR year passed, we won some and lost some. Culbreth was next to quit the team. He became hesitant to shoot even open shots out of fear of missing and getting chewed out by Brock in front of the crowd. But I continued to weather Brock's wrath. I was too addicted to the roaring crowd, the newspaper clippings, to give it up. And then when Brock was good, no one was better.

We'd be a few baskets ahead of a team, a rebound would come off, and a fast break would ignite. I'd sail in for a lay-up. We'd steal their inbounds pass and someone would pop in a jumper. Suddenly we'd be up ten points. Brock would call a time-out and run to center court, his hands raised in victory signs. The crowd would thunder their approval, cameras would flash, and for the rest of the game I'd have followed that man into hell.

Brock had his other good points. Once during my senior season, my grades were especially bad, and I was getting sent to the principal's office a lot for skipping class. Brock called me into his office and talked about how he cared about me, wanted me to straighten up. He cited several small colleges that had expressed interest in me and said he would help secure a basketball scholarship from one of them. Many times, I saw him pull a few dollars from his pocket and slip it to a student in need.

But late in the season another happening colored my memory of high school ball. My father, mother, and grandmother came for the first time ever to see me play. Our opponent was Gray's Creek, a small school we usually punished. I remember how my family took a seat high in the bleachers, huddled and small among the huge crowd, not accustomed to large, noisy sporting events. I was terribly nervous at their presence and would have preferred they stayed home.

Gray's Creek was sporting the best team they'd assembled in years. Maybe I was too eager to please my parents, maybe the night was just one of those off times when a shot won't fall, but I wasn't scoring the way I usually did, rebounds were not coming my way. We fell behind Gray's Creek by several baskets. Brock signaled a time-out.

I could see coach's fury in his face as I ran toward the bench. He met me halfway across the floor, grabbed my jersey, and shoved me toward the dressing room. He shouted at me and shook me. I tried to speak but no words would come. Brock shoved me further toward the dressing room, and then he booted me in the butt. From the corner of my eye, through a film of embarrassed tears, I saw my father rise from his seat. Mama reached and grasped his arm. I knew he wished he was within fist's length of Brock.

I went into the dressing room and sat in a chair, debating very hard whether I should be the next person to quit the team. But my rage was even stronger than my humiliation, and if nothing else, I wished to play again to prove Brock wrong. Brock later apologized; in a rematch with Gray's Creek, we trounced them by twenty points. At the end of the season I had earned All-Conference honors. I was offered some small-time scholarships but turned them down and joined the Marines. But in my memory of high school sports, above the trophies and honors I won, I remember most the image of my father standing somber and erect amid that screaming crowd, his face reflecting my humiliation and pain.

MICHAEL heard the crack of the last rifle from high in his tree stand and knew the buck was dead. Something about the sound, no echo, as if the wound sucked up all thunder except that first pop of gunpowder. The hounds sounded different too, a crazed pitch to their baying as they anticipated the taste of blood. Michael hated the hunting club and the noise nearly as much as he hated Monday mornings and the Coca-Cola route he worked. That was no way to hunt—dogs, CB radios, four-wheel-drive trucks; the deer had about as much chance as a gnat against a flyswatter.

Michael was a loner. He preferred the deep woods to a crowded shopping mall, was more comfortable around animals than girls, and did his hunting from tree stands—one man matching wits and senses against one deer. Bow and arrow, black-powder guns, high-powered rifles, he got his limit, and when deer season was over, he studied the woods and deer, where they rested, their paths, where the big bucks congregated to rut. On his bedroom wall were mounted some of the biggest racks taken in the area. Michael's father was teaching him taxidermy, and one day he hoped to mount an entire deer.

Michael listened to the sound of the forest slowly return following the gunshot. He knew he might as well come down from the tree and go home, because every buck in the area must have fled those dogs. But it was quiet here, so peaceful. He knew as soon as he and his father were together again, the fussing would start over, and he wasn't ready for that. Not when he could lean here against this tree trunk where he was alone and comfortable and at peace.

Michael slid to the edge of his tree stand and rested his feet on a limb. He lay back against the small square of plywood and rested his head against a hollow between two branches. He cradled his shotgun against his chest, the muzzle passing beside his ear. Looking skyward, he spied a woodpecker hammering a limb. The sound traveled down the tree and vibrated against the back of his head.

BILL could barely see his son from his own tree stand fifty yards deeper in the woods. He could barely see him through the tree limbs, but he saw enough to know he was lying down. Lying down when he should be wide alert and studying the forest. He cursed silently. That's all Michael seemed to want to do anymore—lie down. Didn't half-ass work, blew every damn penny he earned. Twice already he'd had to make his truck payment to keep the bank from repossessing. The boy was twenty-two and acted more like he was two sometimes. And here he was now lying down in his damn tree stand when an eight-point buck might walk under him at any second. Bill tensed his jaw and clamped it shut to keep from bellowing across the woods.

WHEN the forest in my home county has been reduced to one last acre, my Uncle Bill will be in the middle of those trees, dressed in his hunting camouflage and stalking whatever game has retreated there. He is the very mold of a Southern sportsman.

Bill is a big man, a little round in his belly from the thousands of Coca-Colas he has drunk over the years, his jaw forever packed with chewing tobacco. His arms are thick from moving around crates of soft drinks, his voice loud; with his black hair and sideburns he looks a little like Elvis might today if he'd kept on driving a truck. He is only ten years older than me, so I remember well as a child his weekend visits, a roughneck young teen who detested school and longed to live a life like Daniel Boone. He was quick to act on impulse, and has always been accident-prone.

An alligator bit him once. This was in the sixties when pet stores still sold unusual animals like horned toads, spider monkeys, and baby South American alligators. Bill came for the weekend, lugging a sack stuffed with a few clothes and a cardboard box that contained an eighteen-inch young gator.

The alligator, like most of his breed, was quick to bite. Bill liked to show off by teasing the alligator with a pencil and watching it snap. I had just begun my own interest in reptiles and was fascinated by the creature, its large, slow-blinking eyes, fat belly, and rough hide.

On our kitchen table, Bill fed the alligator small pieces of fish. He had caught a few small perch in the creek behind our house and cut them into small fillets. He'd drop a fillet in front of the gator and watch it bend its neck and gobble down the meat. Watching was better than seeing a Saturday-morning Godzilla movie.

One of the pieces of fish fell on top of the alligator's

head. The alligator shook a couple of times trying to dislodge the meal, but the damp meat stuck fast to his skin. Bill, acting very brave in front of his audience of nephews and niece, slowly extended his hand with the intention of flicking the food off the gator's snout.

Apparently alligators have a wide circle of vision. Bill's finger was an inch away from the morsel of food when the beast lunged upwards and snapped, clamping firmly on a knuckle. Bill shouted and flung up his arm, gator in tow. When his arm reached the zenith high over Bill's head, the gator's teeth ripped out of Bill's flesh, and the momentum slung the reptile completely across the room. The alligator slammed into the wall high above the stove, bounced off, and fell smack-dab into a large pot where butter beans were boiling. He was instantly killed. We stood there in front of the pot and watched the alligator float up and down in the rolling water while Bill cussed, his finger gushing blood. Finally Karen went and got my mother, who fished the gator out of the beans with a spoon. We were not of the finances to throw out a large pot of butter beans and ate them with fascination that night at being flavored with alligator stock. Bill buried the scalded alligator in the pasture after praying it went to hell for biting his finger.

Bill's ability to maim himself has continued all his life. He carries several scars on his hands from knife cuts. Once, soon after he was married and Michael was born, a shotgun he was holding discharged and blew a hole through the couch where a minute before his wife and child had sat. Recently, he was firing a .22 caliber rifle when the bullet ricocheted and somehow fantastically came to lodge between his front teeth. Still, despite his tendency toward mishap, he is a fine hunter, keen of eye and born with the patience to sit motionless in a tree stand for hours in freezing weather waiting out a deer. He has also taught himself the art of taking his kills and mounting them so well that they seem to live again. If I was lost in the Alaska wilderness, he is a man I'd like to have as my partner.

BUT when I think back on my early years, I hear coon hunting, not deer, the haunting sound of blueticks and black-and-tan hounds baying in pursuit of their prey. The sport was my father's favorite and his father's, cold nights huddled close to a campfire while the dogs searched the woods, their voices a mix of barks and yelps as they sorted through the many scents of the deep woods, finally one of the older dogs catching a fresh scent and rending the air with a single long bellow that called pursuit. The chase would begin, a zigzag mile through the bramble of trees and vines that constituted Yellow Island, in the delta of Cape Fear, approximately twelve square miles of some of the most junglelike terrain north of the equator.

Oftentimes the coon would lose the dogs in reed stands or blackberry thickets, but occasionally a coon young of experience, a mother with litter, or one weakened by age would take to a tree. The excited yelps of chase would change then to long, baleful baying as the hounds ringed the tree, some of the younger, foolish dogs trying to climb the trunk. Then it was time to douse the fire and go, cross swamps and reed thickets and brier brambles, crash deeper into Yellow Island, the pitch blackness of night punched through with flashlight beams.

We'd walk single-file, my father at the head of the line with one of the lights, his ear cocked to the direction of where the hounds had treed, Bill second in line, chattering in excitement, me, maybe Bruce, bringing up the rear. Usually after the first hundred yards our feet were soaked and cold, and we feared something would grab us from the darkness at our back. By the time we neared the tree, my feet would be numb, my face and hands scratched. I'd wish mightily I was back at home in front of the kerosene heater.

The hounds would hear the crash of our approach. The old bitch hound would sing mournful deep-lung bellows to guide us, my father would cup his hands around his mouth and holler a sound that assured her he was coming. We would usually find the hounds ringing a massive oak or sweet gum, one with many gnarled branches in which to hide. The flashlights would go up and search the leafless branches, slowly following forks and turns, climbing from the low limbs to the higher ones and if needed to the top of the tree. Sometimes, if we found no coon, we understood that a hole existed in the trunk and the coon was safely tucked away from our lights and gunsights. We would have to forcefully lead the dogs from the tree, because they knew their noses did not lie. But usually as the light beam swept a branch, a flash of green would appear, two tiny lights glowing back at us. As our eyes adjusted we were able to make out the body of the coon. While we stared, he would usually turn his face from us as if in shame and hunker closer to the wood.

Bill always begged to shoot the coon from the tree, but unless the shot was clear of branches, my father did the killing. A wounded coon would jump from the tree and could maim a dog before they overpowered it. Rifle loaded with long hollow-points, my father always shot for the head. The fur would be sold and the coon would be eaten if he was young enough to be tender and the flesh wasn't clotted with blood. The death would also be quick.

I believe the coon knew his end had come. He rarely tried to move out of the light and hide in another shadow, but just accepted the fact that he was soon to return to his place among the stars; his eyes glowed like twin suns in a distant constellation. Often at the sound of a shell being chambered, the coon would turn his face toward the light, his eyes glowing again like guiding beacons. My father would aim between the two small lights and squeeze off a single round that punched through the animal's forehead and scrambled his brain. He would fall like a piece of deadwood.

The hounds would mount him, bury their noses in his fur and shake the coon, taste the blood that dripped from the round hole in his head. Often the older dogs would simply watch, as if realizing their sport had cost another creature his life, and knowing their own time on earth was measured. My father would step in soon and take the coon from the hounds, hoist him and slit his throat to let out all the blood, then place the animal in a burlap sack. He would whoop again, a different noise the hounds understood as a challenge to hunt. The old bitch dog would begin first by leaving the tree and running in widening circles in search of a fresh scent, the other hounds following in their own circles till one caught the odor of fresh game, lifted his head, and again called pursuit. Depending on the night, the weather, and our luck, we might bag four or five coons. The meat is dark and sweet.

Yellow Island was a haven for raccoons and deer, fox and possums, the thick tangles of reed and brier topped by hardwoods, a fortress against man and his hunting tools. For every coon shot from a treetop, probably a dozen slipped the dogs. A savvy buck could shed many racks and live until his muzzle was gray as long as he stayed in the deep woods. At night, from our backyard, I often listened to the hoot of an owl, the lonely song of a whippoorwill, drift over the night from the confines of the dark forest. Occasionally, lights could be seen floating between trees— fox fire or swamp gas—easily explained in the light of day but ghostly and mind-expanding when viewed from a camp-fire. A patch of clover a couple hundred yards into Yellow Island grew lush and green and taller than all the surrounding grass and was spotted with lilies. Rumor said a man had been murdered there and his spilled blood fed the grass. Then there was the Hollering Thing.

The Hollering Thing has been heard calling from deep inside Yellow Island for years and years. A dreadful, screeching cry sounded through the forest some nights, moving rapidly from tree to tree, a noise that seemed to be a cross between an animal's angry growl and a woman or baby crying for help. I have heard the sound with my own ears and liken it to that of male cats fighting. Probably the animal is a migratory bird that rests a few days in the creeks and pools of the forest before flying further south, but when it cries at night, I am not totally sure a soul is not lost in the bramble of that forest, eternally stumbling in search of the gate to heaven.

My dad and Bill ran up on the Hollering Thing one night in Yellow Island. The hounds had treed, but the chase had been short, not the usual circular path of a coon. As they bushwhacked their way to the tree, the hounds bayed in answer to my father's call, but their song was different. Instead of the joyful, deep-throated baying of an accomplished hunt, the dogs sounded mournful, as if they were chained. As my father and Bill neared the tree, two of the younger hounds met them and milled around their legs. My dad cursed the dogs and ordered them back to the tree, but they hunkered down and stayed close behind the men's heels.

The old bitch hound had stood her ground at the base of a large oak, but she ceased her barking when my father and Bill reached the tree. She sat yards back from the trunk, her ears flat against her head, looking into the branches and growling. The hair stood up on her back.

Bill was ready to go home. My father chambered a shell and ordered the younger dogs forward, but they lay flat against the ground and whined. My father and Bill shined their lights into the tree, but found no coon, no living creature in the bare branches. Then they heard the noise begin, that same crying, scolding shriek between devil and woman. The sound seemed to come from the tree branches, but in the light of their hunting lanterns, they found no maker. Even the bitch dog slunk back; the young dogs huddled around Bill's legs and whined. Bill pulled his skinning knife from the sheath and begged my father to leave the tree. My father was never a fearful man, but he said he felt a chill surrounding that tree, and when the cry sounded again from somewhere in the branches, he, Bill, and the dogs retreated at double time until they were clear of Yellow Island.

Later that night in the warmth of the kitchen, sipping cups of coffee, my father explained that they had probably treed a bobcat or even a bear migrating through, that the animal was hidden inside a hollow in the trunk and the strange cry was only its frightened voice echoing between tree trunks and branches. But from Bill's eyes, the way he watched the dark windows and nervously scraped dead skin from his palm with his blade, I knew he had come as close to the Hollering Thing as he ever intended, and in his dreams he would again face that dark forest and the secret she held.

I chose to hunt outside of Yellow Island, in the smaller, more open forests. These woods had been cut over in years past and were crisscrossed with logging roads, the clear forest floor sprinkled with mushrooms and Easter lilies and rotting logs. The logs were perfect hiding places for snakes, box turtles frequented the damp ground, the trees were home to squirrels and doves and songbirds. I had no fear of these woods, they were home only to animals and fairies and the imaginary jungle animals that LJ and I hunted with our spears.

I killed my first bird with a pellet gun. Unfortunately, the bird was a male cardinal of brilliant color. I cradled the dead bird in my hand, watched his head loll to one side, and immediately wished he was again singing in the bush. But I ate the bird, boiled him in a pot of salted water and stripped his tiny bones of all flesh. I killed my first squirrel with a .22, and I ate the creature. I was taught that a hunter ate his prey or he didn't kill it, and I stuck fast to that rule.

In the spring, robins came by hordes of thousands to our farm to pick over the fields where we had scattered hay for the cows. Three holly trees stood in a row beside our hog pen; the birds would congregate in the limbs by the bright red berries. LJ and I and my brothers would stake ourselves under the trees armed with pellet guns and slingshots. The greedy birds would sit on limbs barely higher than our heads, breasts exposed, and ignore us while they gobbled berries. We killed them by the sackful. Probably many people would say it was wrong to kill robins; I'm not sure if it was legal, but the birds numbered in the thousands then, and still do today when they arrive every spring. We'd pull the breast free much like a dove's, then boil the meat in salted water, adding rice. The result was a fine, gamy stew that I sometimes wish for today. Our family appreciated the free meat, and it freed a couple dollars for something else. At LJ's house, the slain robins might be the only meat on the table.

I only went coon hunting once without my father or Bill along, but the episode convinced me I preferred other sport. I was thirteen and not yet allowed to carry a rifle; my brother Bruce and Helmut Clark were my safari companions. The only hound we carried was Joe, the old black-and-tan yard dog who would have no more thought of venturing into Yellow Island than we would. The old dog ran around us in large circles, sniffing the dust, his mind probably recalling younger days when he led the hunt. We walked one of the dirt roads and listened to Joe crash through the edge of the woods. Occasionally Bruce or I would holler in imitation of my father, but the sound did not carry like his voice. We were walking under a large moon, our flashlights flicked off, when Joe suddenly barked, then bayed long and sorrowful like a true black-and-tan.

We stood beside a bean field. Joe tore off across the rows of beans, snapping stems and ripping leaves and running faster than I'd seen in years. We flicked on our lights and ran single-file after him. The old dog stopped midway across the field and leaped against the trunk of a small tree. Even while I was yards away from the tree, I smelled the musky sweetness of ripe persimmons—a treat of coons and possums.

The tree stood no taller than twelve feet. In the branches our lights quickly revealed a fat mama raccoon and three nearly grown babies sitting on their haunches looking surprised. Their snouts were wet and red with persimmon juice.

The young coons were just right for eating, the four hides worth a small fortune to us. Best of all, I knew of no one who had ever taken four coons at one time from a single tree. We stood on the verge of bragging rights that might take years for someone to beat. Unfortunately, we had no rifle.

"You can shake them out and Joe can kill one while we beat the rest to death with sticks," I proposed to Helmut.

"Damn if I'm going up there. My mama wouldn't cook a dozen coons if I brought them home."

I knew he was right. His mother had married an American soldier in Germany and immigrated to America. She continued to cook strange things that involved lots of sausages and sauerkraut. I looked at Bruce and knew he would go up in an instant, but he was three inches shorter than me and pounds lighter, and no decent big brother would ask such a thing.

"All right, I'll go up," I announced. "But y'all got to find some sticks to kill the coons with."

We searched, but in the middle of a bean field there was little to offer. Helmut finally seized a large rock he said would make a good basher, and Bruce pulled up a bean plant, explaining that he would hit the coons with the heavy end where dirt was clotted. I took a long, deep breath and began climbing, Bruce and Helmut illuminating my way.

Coon are known as fierce fighters and have killed dogs one on one. As I neared that mother coon, she bared her teeth and hissed. The younger coons watched wide-eyed; it was probably their first encounter with a human. I decided I would shake the coons from their perches instead of plucking them.

"Gonna shake 'em down," I hollered. "Y'all get ready."

I began shifting my weight from side to side. The persimmon tree wasn't much more than six inches in diameter, and inside a minute, the tree swayed. The coons moved with the tree, trying to counterbalance. I put all my strength and weight into shaking the tree and soon had it whipping like a dog's tail.

I don't know which one of the coon jumped first, but it landed on top of my head, clung for a split second, then bit through my John Deere baseball-style hat into my scalp. I flung up my hands and clawed at the coon, and promptly fell backwards, tearing limbs off and the coon from my head as I plummeted to earth.

Things got busy. I figure now the mother coon was the

one that jumped me, because the other coons leaped as we fell. The fall knocked the wind from my lungs, and though I wanted to cry and cuss, nothing would come out. I heard Joe snarl, then yelp, and Bruce and Helmut shout as they ran in circles trying to clobber the coon. As soon as the coons got their bearings, they made a beeline for the woods, and neither Joe, Bruce, nor Helmut followed. I was still trying to get enough breath to cuss.

We sized up the battle under the light of one flashlight. I had several puncture holes in my scalp that oozed blood, but we figured they'd heal all right if the coon wasn't rabid. Joe had a torn ear. Bruce had two chewed boots where the mama coon went between his legs snapping like a buzz saw, and Helmut had dirt plastered on the side of his head where Bruce had gotten carried away while swinging his bean stalk. We had not a single kill.

Worst of all, we were laughed at. Bill swore we had treed a single possum and let our imaginations get carried away. But the three of us, Joe, and God know we treed four coons that night, regardless if we nailed up the hides. That same tree still stands today in the middle of the bean field, and for lack of a rifle, we would hold the record.

I WATCHED Bill grow up almost as much as he watched me. I remember when he turned sixteen and got his driver's license and quit school soon after. I remember when he went to work with the mattress company in east Fayetteville, when he married Jeanne, a quiet, brown-haired young woman who seemed ill suited for one so big and boisterous. I remember when Bill's son, Michael, was born, how proud Bill was of his boy, how he said he would raise him as a woodsman and hunter.

Years passed, I became a young man. Bill began working for the Coca-Cola plant, fathered a daughter. Michael grew into a quiet, gangly kid. He spent a lot of his free time searching the surrounding fields for arrowheads, and by the time he was an adolescent, had a collection of hunting points, spear heads, hatchets, and pottery that most museums would envy. He was also a gifted artist and with pen and pencil could draw startlingly realistic pictures of Indians and game. Unlike his dad, he was a loner and shunned crowds. He avoided having his picture taken, always moved to the back of the group at family gatherings and hid his face behind someone's head.

As soon as he was old enough to handle a gun safely, Bill took Michael to the fields and woods. They rode the back roads, looking for deer crossings and planning where they would build tree stands. The day Michael, at thirteen, killed his first buck, Bill was so proud he rode all over Fayetteville with the animal strapped to the hood of his truck. As the boy grew into a young man, it was usual to see him emerge from the woods in midmorning on a Saturday after having sat in a tree stand since before dawn, his face and hands painted green, clad in camouflage. More often than most people, he carried a deer over his shoulders. No one will ever know why he turned.

Michael's hunt became different, more deadly. The game was a white powder that could be sniffed or smoked in a pipe. The wilderness of Yellow Island was replaced by the black projects that sprawl on the east side of town close to the river.

FOOT on the brake, the other poised an inch over the gas pedal. The guy riding shotgun for Michael sucked nervously at a cigarette. Two black youths of maybe twenty stood by the truck window studying the two white boys.

"We got the rock if you got the cash," one of the blacks said. "You got a lot of cash, we got a lot of rock."

Michael nodded, thrusting out his bottom lip. "I'm looking for a gram."

"Look no further, my man. Hundred dollars, I got you a gram that'll kick your ass."

"Fellow over on Plymouth Street sells a gram for ninety."

The black nodded his head. "Go buy from him. My shit is a hundred."

Michael reached into his shirt pocket and pulled out cash. He counted out five twenty-dollar bills. The black man watched him count.

"You gonna let me see it?" Michael asked.

The black shrugged and pulled a small bundle from his pocket. The thumbnail quantity of cocaine was sealed inside the clipped corner of a baggie. The black eyed the money and handed the bag to Douglas.

He rammed the gas and the truck peeled rubber and leaped forward and was a half block down the street before the two black men could react. Michael and his rider laughed hysterically, ducked low in their seat in case one of the men shot. Inside thirty seconds, they were out of the projects and roaring toward the river bridge and the country land.

"Gonna get high tonight," Michael sang. "Bet that coon feels like a chump."

Already the other young man had taken a pipe from his pocket. When they were back in the safety of the land they had trampled over since childhood, Michael backed his truck into a dark side road, where they cooked down the coke and smoked it deep into their lungs. Free-base cocaine—ready rock. Beat the hell out of Red Man.

Dope softened the world, took off the rough edges. Bill

had grown to be a perfectionist. Like all fathers, he wanted the best for Michael, but wanted it to come easier for him. He used his influence to get Michael his first job following graduation as a route salesman. While he had grown into a large man, with talents of his own, he didn't have the glib tongue of his father, was not a natural at persuading store managers to stock more Coca-Cola. He was also painfully shy around girls, and while his father had wed at eighteen, Michael preferred the sanctuary of the woods. He discovered another line of coke, a toke or two of ready rock, and the problems rolled back. He could wash the dregs down with a six-pack.

Michael went through several withdrawal programs, but his heart was not in facing the world sober, and he failed each time. He spent more and more hours hunting alone or walking fields in search of arrowheads. He drifted through several jobs, wrecked his pickup, was usually broke Monday mornings.

"Wanna buy my truck?" he asked suddenly one afternoon while fishing on the Cape Fear with a friend.

"Buy your truck?" the friend asked. "Why in the world do you want to sell your truck?"

Michael stared at the lazy water for a few moments as if he was seeing something in the depths.

"Well," he drawled, "I guess it's about time for me to be moving on from here."

A fish struck, conversation ended.

The night was Friday, payday, Michael drank some beer with a friend, maybe snorted a few lines. Sometime around midnight he backed his truck into a dirt road beside a tobacco barn. He lay down on the seat and cradled his head on the armrest. He placed the barrel of a twenty-gauge under his chin and squeezed the trigger.

Bill paced the floor the next morning, wondering where

his boy was. Finally he called a buddy over, got in his truck, and headed for town to search. He spied Michael's truck from the corner of his eye while driving past the barn.

"Reckon ole Mike is sleeping one off," the friend said with relief as they turned into the road. Bill stepped hurriedly from his truck.

Bill fell to his knees after he looked into the cab, pounded the door with his fists, and swore and cried at the sky. He buried Michael with an arrowhead held in one of his hands. A buck is chiseled on his tombstone.

MATTIE cried great, fat tears that coursed down her face and dripped from her chin. Her breasts heaved with each racking sob. I stared at her through the window of the Greyhound, fighting back my own tears, bound finally for Marine Corps boot camp.

My recruiter had come to see me and two buddies off. My mom was there standing silent and sad with my sister and one brother. Bound for glory in service with the finest, we wanted no less than the jungles of Vietnam. The bus driver gunned the engines and began to pull away from the curb. Mattie ran to the window where I sat, her face contorted and shiny-wet. She leaped and slapped her hand against the window, leaving the print of her small fingers in the condensation on the glass.

WE WOULD have joined the Navy. Mike Spake and I and my cousin were in the last months of high school when the idea arose to enlist. My father had served in the Navy, Mike's father had been a career Army sergeant. We were sick of school and of the quiet life of rural North Carolina.

Vietnam was still raging and seemed like high adventure—maybe a deck gunner on a boat in the Mekong Delta. We skipped class and swaggered into the recruiting office on Green Street in Fayetteville.

The naval office was closed; a sign read "Back after lunch." Across the hall I stared into an open door where a tall man sat ramrod-straight in an immaculate uniform of blue, white, and red.

"Come on over here, men," he said, waving a big hand. We walked into his office and stared at walls covered with posters of fighting men in camouflage paint, a large picture of the Marines raising the flag at Iwo Jima. We bit and swallowed the entire hook in less than thirty minutes. After about a week of visits, a film or two watched on the virtues of being one of the proud and few, we signed up for a two-year hitch with our enlistment due to begin in six months.

MATTIE was terribly upset when I told her of my plans. We had been dating steadily for almost two years. She was planning to attend nearby Campbell College and hoped to persuade me to do likewise. My mother worried and fussed at me, immediately mindful of the war. But my father said very little; I could see in his eyes a twinkle of pride, probably the memory of his own departure for the military at seventeen.

The following six months before I had to report for boot camp is etched in my memory as a lost time hazed between wanting to cling to what I knew of home and childhood and the urge to leave all that and walk into the world as a man. To simplify that statement, mostly all I did was goof off.

I finished my senior basketball season, then doodled through my last two months in school. All the teachers knew I was already enlisted in the military, so they let me slide through on minimal work. I skipped class about as much as I attended.

Mike and I were certain we would spent thirty years in the elite Marine Force Recon. In fact, I would probably have immediately joined for four years instead of two if not for my recruiter. He took a liking to me, had seen my picture in the paper from playing ball; I took poisonous snakes to his office and milked them in a coffee cup. He advised us all to join for two years, then reenlist for a bonus if we wanted to continue. We were also certain that boot camp would be a breeze. Hadn't we grown up in the country, worked the tobacco fields, walked miles under a hot sun? We began running every day in formation, would go to the Cape Fear River and float down it on inner tubes, climb knotted ropes to high tree branches.

I graduated—barely—only two months before we shipped out. For the first summer since I was eight I did not labor in the tobacco fields. Mike and I did work some for a local farmer fixing fences and pulling weeds from his fields, but the work was halfhearted. In our minds we were already soldiers, killing machines, warriors for liberty. I dated Mattie nightly; she would cling to me at the door when I finally rose to leave at midnight. We would assure each other again that nothing would change; we were lovers for ever. When I finally tore myself from her and drove off, I would speed through town to find Mike and the other guys at the Prince Charles Tap Room, a topless place, where I would sling down as many beers as possible before the one-o'clock closing time.

Finally the week arrived in mid-August when we were scheduled to leave. The reality of what I had gotten into became more real as we were handed bus tickets and twenty dollars in cash by the recruiter. I had never been away from home for longer than the five days when I traveled to Connecticut as a small child, had not missed seeing Mattie for more than one night in our two years of romance. I walked the fields around home, scratched the old dog's neck, watched and listened to cows low in the cooling air at dusk. Home suddenly seemed more important, those green pastures, the gum and oak trees, even the hated hog pen where I suffered my most dreaded labor.

That last night before I left, Mattie lay with me on my bed, the house empty except for us. We had expected passion, but could not bring it out above our sadness, our fear of what could happen in three months of separation. Mattie repeated her vows of faithfulness, I knew I would be locked away for three months with not even the opportunity to stray. But I knew I would return. At eighteen one cannot fathom death or the demise of one's values and beliefs and loves. I was going adventuring.

"YA GOT three goddam minutes to get off this bus," the drill instructor barked, "and two of them are gone." We had changed buses at midnight in Savannah, and finally here we were at Parris Island Marine Training Depot, South Carolina, a full load of recruits staring wide-eyed at a man offering as much compassion as a rattled rhino.

"Now move it."

We came off that bus as if it were burning—a motley crew, some longhairs, others sporting crew tops, several fat-bodies. Some were young John Waynes, others probably got pushed into mud puddles at school. All of us swarmed into the damp summer night, out to where several more drill instructors were screaming at us to fall into line. We assembled into a wavy formation that only made the drill instructors cuss more and grit their teeth.

I was carrying the orders for ten recruits from North Carolina. When the sergeant asked for those carrying the packets to come forward and center, I rushed forward to the red footprints painted on the pavement, positioned my feet, and locked my body at attention, ramrod-straight. Something was wrong. One of the drill instructors stood before me, wearing a squint-eyed frown. As the seconds passed, I noticed in my peripheral vision only the backs of the heads of the others carrying orders. Then I peered toward my feet and saw that I was standing backward on the markers.

The drill instructor took a couple of steps toward me until his chin was only inches from mine. His breath hinted that he might have had a few beers while he waited. His close shave had grown to black stubble. He shook his head slightly, cracked his lips, and croaked as hoarsely as a frog, "Turn arooouuund, asshooole."

I realized then that the kisses and handshakes were long gone. Like the poster said, there are no rose gardens on Parris Island.

"I got a girl that lives on the hill, she won't do it but her sister will." We sang that little ditty and many others dozens of times over the next couple of weeks, as our platoon ran in combat boots and fatigues, did push-ups, sit-ups, and pull-ups, cried and sweated. Incompetents in the Marines are called "shitbirds," and the worst ones are recycled to newer platoons to begin anew. The thought of being recycled motivated most recruits to stagger that last half mile or push up one more time. One of the shitbirds in our platoon was Private Dewey Johnson, a jug-eared twenty-five-year-old who had already spent five years in the Army. In those first weeks Johnson couldn't even do three pull-ups, the minimum required to graduate. But he tried so hard, hanging there on the bar and straining until his chin trembled, that the drill instructors must have seen enough in him to keep giving him another day's chance. The Marines have a tried-and-true system. In the beginning weeks they try to break you, and if they don't, they come damn close. We sang the Marine Corps hymn with buckets on our heads, did push-ups with our feet placed high on racks, screamed "Yes sir!" till we were all hoarse, pissed in our trousers, ate standing up, prayed aloud for war, and wakened each morning to thrown trash cans and obscenities, warning us to get up and fall out. I actually wished that my dear old grandma would die so I might get to go home for a couple of days. Screwing up brought no second chance.

"Didn't I say beddie-bye, bitch?"

I was standing in my skivvies, hands locked by my side, staring at the forehead of Sergeant Ronny Schmidt, one of our three drill instructors. Schmidt, who hailed from Alabama, was a short, stocky Marine whose face shattered like broken glass whenever he tried to smile.

"Yes sir!" I shouted, knowing all the squad bay was listening.

Schmidt held up the letter he had caught me reading under my covers with a flashlight. "Eat it."

I chewed the letter and swallowed it, after reading only half of the tormented lines my girlfriend had written. Then I braced myself for what was inevitable when you screwed up—a hard shot to the belly, a couple of open-handed slaps to my face. I tasted blood, but didn't blink until dismissed. A good recruit could take a beating. You screwed up, you took your lumps, straight and tall, and learned from it. In a combat situation, a flashlight at night might get you and your buddies killed.

In the beginning weeks they beat us down until we thought ourselves about as worthy as the mud flats that surrounded the island. Life was right to the point, with no fooling around. Once, early in training, a shitbird who was having a very bad time walked to the senior drill instructor and asked to speak. A few moments after he began whispering, we heard the booming voice of the senior.

"What? You're a goddam faggot?" He unzipped his trousers. "Well, here. You prove it to me. Get down there and prove it, scumball."

The sergeant had called his bluff. The next day the shitbird was gone.

Arguments between recruits were also settled quickly. The two in disagreement were given shooting gloves to avoid cuts and were allowed to fight it out while the rest of us sang the Marine Corps hymn to drown out the noise. We lived in a world that was much like the animal kingdom—survival came first, the strong prevailed, the weak were devoured or cast aside.

Finally, at a point about midway, the Marine Corps began to rebuild us into soldiers. A sense of camaraderie began to form in our platoon, honed sharper daily by drill competition between troops, rifle competition, pugil-stick fights, and field days. We began to rely on each other, recognizing that the screwups of an individual hurt the whole platoon. It became commonplace for the stronger runners to grasp the belt of someone about to fall out and keep him moving. Someone with an extra shined belt buckle would think nothing of slipping it to a buddy caught lacking in a surprise inspection. If one man got caught talking, everyone did push-ups. If one man got caught sneaking a smoke, everyone lost the privilege for a couple of days. Repeat shitbirds were sometimes straightened out by other platoon members after lights-out, just like in the movies. If a shitbird screwed up long enough, he was sent to Motivation Platoon for anywhere from a half-day to several days. I can't speak firsthand of Motivation Platoon, because I made sure I was never sent. Most recruits made sure after seeing some unfortunate screwball return with mud covering his body from boot tip to scalp and his eyes holding the dull sheen of the broken.

We also learned discipline—extreme discipline. In time you learned to ignore a horsefly feasting on your nose until they told you to scratch. Standing at attention for two hours, staring straight ahead, became a form of rest. There was no free time at night to go have a beer and shoot pool; we sat on our metal buckets or foot lockers and polished our boots or brass, read our handbooks or wrote home. The weekend passes that other branches of the service allow midway through the training were as unlikely as flying off to the moon. We learned discipline, motivated when necessary by a stiff right or a blanket party—twenty-four-hour discipline that went on to the very end of thirteen weeks.

Private Johnson kept at those pull-ups until he was able to place his chin atop the bar five times, even though most other recruits were knocking out fifteen to twenty. He slept in a bunk beside me. I asked him once late in training, when we were occasionally allowed to talk, why he joined the Marines when he had already been a sergeant in the Army with a cushy job. He was looking at a picture of his wife at the time, and before he answered, he returned it carefully to his wallet.

"'Cause I want her to be proud of me," he said, his eyes carrying a hard glint I had never seen. "Know I'm one of the best."

I rode off Parris Island ten pounds heavier, with hard biceps, a nubby Mohawk running the crest of my head, and the attitude that I was one bad son of a bitch. I was ready, like all boots, to kill the Vietcong with my bare hands. Instead, since the Marines were in the process of pulling out of Vietnam, my two-year duty was spent mostly on training stints in Cuba and Panama—for a grunt jarhead, a situation similar to flooring the gas pedal on a 426 Hemi while the clutch is mashed in. The only combat I experienced was a few hand-to-hand bouts in bars while on liberty.

Five of us were sitting in the Circus Lounge in Fayetteville, all fresh from training, wearing our Marine sweatshirts, sporting whitewalls above our ears. We had come to get drunk and kick a little ass—and where else but right in the home of the 82nd Airborne Division, a bunch of Army chaps who enjoy fighting just as much as Marines.

Mike was in the group, and so was Coleman, who stood six foot five with arms and shoulders like a gorilla's. We drank down several pitchers of draft until our courage was as full as our bellies and watched the topless dancer tweak her nipples and beg dollar bills from the GIs. Finally, Coleman put out his cigarette, wiped his mouth with the back of his hand, nodded, then flung the contents of a half-filled pitcher onto the inhabitants of the nearest table. They put war on our ass. If we had been matched five on five with the 82nd, maybe even five to ten, we probably would have taken that hill. But five on fifty with Uncle Sam's best paratroopers! Lord, I doubt Chesty Puller himself could have led us out of that one. I remember at one point blindly slinging my fists as we worked our way in the direction of the door, thinking, "Schmidt, you lying bastard! Thought you said a Marine was unbeatable. If I can just make it to that door, my shoes are going to smoke."

The law was waiting outside and locked the five of us up. They knew Marines in Fayetteville were up to no good. But we didn't resist them or speak out of line. Even a Marine with a bloody nose respected authority.

On another morning, in the Caribbean, I awoke with a start to find a cow licking the side of my face. After shooing away the beast, I spied my buddy, Richard Cauthen, sprawled a few yards away, still sleeping it off. I only had vague recollections of the previous night—slugging down shots of rum, a fight with a bunch of sailors that spilled out of the bar and carried into the pasture behind the small town of Palo Seco. My knuckles were raw and one eye was swollen and black. We were several hours past the time we should have been back at the site where our company was bivouacked, and we paid for our absence with extra guard duty.

Such adventures slowly taught me that although a Marine was indeed the finest fighting machine on earth, he was made of flesh and blood and had limitations. At the end of my two years I was tired of playing war and being sneered at by my civilian peers, and opted to resume a life that included hair. However, I carried away a measure of pride that I had endured boot camp and survived in the Corps. In subtle ways, I was forever changed. My fifteen-foot jump shot that did the job in high school was replaced by a head-down, elbowing drive for the hoop. For the first time in my life, I could look my father comfortably in his eyes. Since then, I have often seen that pride reflected—from a job interviewer who would glance up from my résumé, nod, and say, "Marine Corps, huh?" or the bar lady who would slide a little closer as if to make her own surprise inspection.

Dewey Johnson struggled out eight pull-ups the day of our final PT test. He smiled when the drill instructor nodded and marked it down. The last time I saw Johnson's face was in 1979, when it was plastered on the television screen along with the other soldiers who died in the aborted rescue mission to free the hostages in Iran. I like to think that on that night, as Crew Chief Johnson sat in his seat on that helicopter, as it bucked and hammered its way through a sandstorm above the desert, he was looking at that same picture of his wife he carried to boot camp, never doubting that she thought he was one of the best.

I RECALL another night years later after I had returned from my hitch in the Marines, after Mattie and I had married, separated once, tried again, only to reach a stalemate where we were fighting if we were not fucking, and even the fucking was a sort of combat.

I lay in bed and thought back to dinner, I'd had a few beers, we were once again arguing about the petty and trivial differences between us. She snapped out some remark, whatever I said I've forgotten but it must have been equally hard, and suddenly she tossed her fork toward my face. I know she was not trying to hurt me, just vent some of that bottled-up rage, but the fork struck tine-first in one brow and pierced the skin just enough to draw a bead of blood. She stared in horror for a second, then wrapped her arms tightly across her bosom and sobbed.

"I can't stand this no longer," she wailed. "I'd rather die than have to stand it."

She rocked slowly, water dripping on her face. I felt the trickle of blood slide down the cleft between my brow. I alternately wished to hug her and comfort her and then to kick her like one wants to boot a cowering dog.

I lay on that hot mattress and heard her slow breaths beside me. Spring was upon Dixie, the wisteria fragrant in bloom, dawn gathering through the window in the east. I lay there and watched the tiles on the ceiling gather shape. I knew it was time to go again, walk out of her life for good and let her find a man who fit her mold of husband. I remembered what she had written in my junior-year school annual: "Tim, I hope you will always be the romantic dreamer you are now, and that you will never settle for that little house on the corner."

I chuckled bitterly at how so often what we admire and wish to possess in a person becomes resentment and heartache in the battles of day-to-day living. I slipped from the bed while she was still sleeping and began packing my few things.

THESE two instances of leaving loom greatest in my mind—a boy going away to cross that division between boyhood and becoming a man, an adult walking away from manhood, his vows broken under witness of God, away from a woman he loved but no longer liked. Eleven years have passed now since I last glimpsed or spoke to her. I find much irony in that as a Marine I did not have to face combat, but the wars between hearts maim and destroy as thoroughly.

———— ▬ ————

I STOPPED recently on my way to visit Fayetteville at the small wooden church I attended as a child. Set under large water oaks, the building seemed as silent and timeless as it did when I was seven. I wanted to go inside the building, but found the door locked. The land had been sold and soon the old church would be torn down. I stood there in the shade and tried to recall the wail of the congregation as they sang hymns, the singsong chant of the preacher, how I would distract myself from the tales of hell and brimstone by listening to summer locusts through the large open windows.

I will say that despite my offbeat strain of interpreting religion, I am not a hard-times Christian who turns to prayer only in time of need. As a sixteen-year-old with a couple too many beers in my gut, I thanked God for getting me home the next morning as sincerely as I had asked his help the night before in staying between the white lines. I was as thankful after tossing in two free throws during a high school ball game as I had been prayerful before stepping to the line. I especially remember one night's experience with ten grams of blond Lebanese hash.

I was a senior in high school, had smoked a little pot, but was out of my league with hash. Especially ten grams. An older friend in college had brought it to me in hopes I might sell a little bit to my schoolmates. The whole deal seemed just another bit of adventure for me. I stashed the hash, sold a couple grams, and waited for the night to sample some myself.

Of course, Mike Spake and I were together. We rounded up another couple buddies and ended up at the house of a fellow whose mother worked nights. We lit a pipe, popped a few beers, and smoked.

I laughed. Laughed from my belly as waves of intense intoxication rolled over my body and mind. Everything was so funny. I believe the phone ringing set me off—this incredibly loud bell that jolted me and reminded me that the world existed. My laughter froze, and as suddenly my mirth changed to extreme paranoia. I stumbled from the table and washed my face under the kitchen faucet. For a few seconds I felt sober again, but quickly the intoxication and paranoia washed over me again in a paralyzing wave.

I weaved from the house under protest from the fellows, the remaining six grams of hash in my shirt pocket. The cold February air sobered me momentarily, but then the horror began anew. I suffered an intense fear that my mind had been irreparably altered and I would never be sane. I slung the grams of foil-covered hash into weeds beside the road and set as straight a course as I could muster for the lights of home a quarter mile distant.

I went straight to bed, lay there praying my head off that I was not forever insane. Sometime later, I drifted off to sleep and awoke the next morning to normality. I prayed just as hard later that afternoon while crawling on hands and knee through the weeds that I might find the hash I'd dumped. I knew without doubt I did not want to smoke any more hash, but I also knew I owed a guy for the drugs. I figured God could understand that.

I found the hash and gave it back. I maybe smoked hash twice more in my life, and then in moderation. My theory has always been that God did not put pleasantries such as alcohol and drugs and nooky in the world to tempt and forever damn mankind, but more as a learning tool to temper how he must live within moderation of the extremes. I live with conviction that a few beers after a long day is a gift from God, but sixteen beers in one night is a betrayal.

THE wages of sin and the afterlife preyed heavily on my mind the summer of my eighteenth year in the weeks before reporting for boot camp. American troops were pulling out of Vietnam, but I expected and secretly hoped to be sent to fight. The gnawing guilt at the back of my mind finally made me dial the number of the preacher at the local Southern Baptist church and request to talk with him. He told me to meet him in his church study at seven that night.

I talked my cousin, Walter, and another guy into going with me. We were all preparing to enter the service, and I explained the added insurance couldn't hurt. From what I could interpret of religion, all we had to do was publicly confess our sins and our belief in Jesus and we were guaranteed a ticket to heaven. Maybe we would have to slack off on the beer a little bit, stop saying "goddam," but we wouldn't have to run the risk of spending eternity in a lake of fire.

The preacher ushered us into his study right on time. I explained that we were soon to be soldiers and wanted to be right with God. He nodded and said we were wise and began reading us scriptures. As he read I studied his fingers—stained from tobacco smoke, although he never lit a cigarette up in the presence of his congregation. After finishing the verses, he asked us if we believed what he had read, and we nodded. He had us each say aloud our belief in Jesus, then he prayed.

"Don't you feel better now?" he asked at the conclusion. We nodded again, although I felt basically the same.

"You'll want to join the church," he said, "and be baptized."

He told us that on the following Sunday during the call to repent, we were to come forward and publicly announce our commitment to Christ. We would then be baptized and fully accepted into the fellowship of the church. The preacher finished by shaking our hands and telling us how glad he was we had come to be saved.

Three days lay between me and the Sabbath. During that time I swung between moods. No big deal—I would march to the front of that church, hang my head and denounce my evil past, and walk guiltless and clean into the rest of my life. But then I would think of those men and women who would stare at me from the congregation—men who kept a pint of vodka under their truck seat, women who circulated gossip as hot as hell's fire, people who had stared at the moon through my telescope lens and lectured me on how the heavens and earth were made inside one week, and how believing in evolution was the same as not believing in God. Would I become a part of that fold? They were good people at heart and in most of their actions, but they seemed bound to such a small world and God. I *did* believe in evolution and a universe that had taken millions of years to create, but did that not reflect an even more powerful God to conceive and develop such an intricate plan? By walking to the front of that church, would I be taking the first steps toward binding myself to a lifetime of following another's interpretations and rules?

The debate raged inside me until Sunday morning. I did not hear the precher's sermon, but instead studied the people around me, men and women and children in washed, starched clothes, faces and hands scrubbed clean. They did not ask much from life, only that it be as long as possible and filled with health and enough money to get by, that their few sins be kept private and their God forgive on a weekly basis. In return they would pass the collection plate, stand and sing hymns, and march into war with any people or nation that threatened that.

"Won't you come forward now," the preacher chanted as the choir broke into the first verse. "Just step out of your seat into the aisle, people will let you by, and come forward. Jesus is waiting."

My eyes were blurred as I stood. I wished the preacher would pop a Marlboro into his mouth and light it and exhale a blue cloud of smoke. I stepped into the carpeted aisle and turned and began walking. The door was oiled and made no sound as I walked outside into bright summer sunshine.

RELIGION has changed much in the South today. The Primitive Baptists have all but died off, and most of the more fundamental churches are viewed with skepticism. The television evangelists did that, all the scandals and crimes committed by these fake men of God, begging thousands of dollars so that their church might have the highest steeple. I believe some of these men are sincere, but their image is severely tainted by their crooked brethren.

I've seen a great change in churches since I was a kid. Partly the influx of people coming here from other regions altered congregations and theologies, partly more wealth and education among the locals. Diminishing daily are the churches that cling to the faith that one almighty God knows all, controls each second in eternity, and ultimately judges the vices and virtues of our souls.

I have attended a church in Chapel Hill that is the personification of the new religion. The congregation is typical of this area—educated, middle-class, and liberal. The minister holds an advanced degree. The bulletin board in the church is filled with fliers for political activism and community involvement. The announcements at the beginning of service remind people of upcoming meetings to protest U.S. support of the Contras, of rallies in favor of abortion rights, and of gatherings of Democrats for Christ. Even the sermon is a mild oration that speaks more of the duty of man to his earth and people than service to a higher God.

These people are sincere and good in their values and beliefs. They hold hands when singing hymns, drink from a common cup during communion, and give freely of their money and time. But I cannot feel a kindred spirit in that large glass-and-brick structure; I have found in time what my father believed—my God dwells in open fields and meadows, his voice heard in the whisper of the wind in trees. I cannot imagine these people stooping to scrub each other's feet.

AS I WALKED around the old church, acorns cracked under my heels. I listened to the whisper of wind in the branches. Granny has been dead now for years, along with most of the people who brought the plates of fried chicken, the pies, the ones who patted me on the head and said how good I was. The church will be torn down soon, a new house or business built on the same ground. Time passes and the marks of our lives leave us like dry leaves blown before a wind. But I will not forget the drone of voices from within that church, the sense of timelessness and age and the patience of their God. I will remember old men who worked weekdays with their hands and stood on Sundays waiting for words from above. Sometimes they hung on that first sentence, eyes searching cracks in the wall, then sat back down saying they had nothing for that moment to say. Those words were maybe their wisest.

JUNE 1989. I wished immediately I could rush from that hospital room after hearing the doctor, jog for miles under the warm June sun until I was far from the smell of disinfectant and starched sheets. Me sick? Hadn't I raced four miles up and down hills the day before I entered the hospital? Just a few weeks ago hadn't I climbed a mountain in the desert outside of Los Angeles and felt good and strong in my lungs and legs? And today this crazy man was staring at me and telling me I had only a few years to live.

When under attack, a person can either draw in his limbs and roll into a ball and hope for amnesty or lash out with fury and strength. I decided in that first minute I would not face this disease in a passive mood, but would confront it as an intruder. I felt more pissed-off than afraid, more hassled than victimized. I remembered the shine of fear in my father's eyes the day he was told he had lung cancer, how on that day he accepted his fate and was dead weeks later. He was a man of habit and ritual. He paid his bills on time, worked when it was time to work, and passed his years all within a few miles of where he was born. His religion taught that a man's life was set and planned eons before his birth and one could not tamper with it. Cancer killed people, and if the doctor said he had cancer, it was time to die.

But as much as I am his blood, my approach to life has always been different. I have been fortunate in having the opportunity to see a lot of the world, and with that education have come to question much of what I am told. I believe that man can direct and affect much of his life, and that hope and positive thinking are very strong medicine. I did not want to be told the worst of the worst, but only what could be if I was lucky and brave. I told the doctor I wanted the most aggressive treatment I could stand, and that I fully believed I would beat this disease and recover. Our eyes locked and a pact was formed.

Chemotherapy—I had heard all the horror stories, loss of hair, vomiting, diarrhea and discomfort. The nurse started my first bag of medicine that night, blue in color, much like antifreeze. I watched the liquid begin to drip down the clear tube into my veins.

I decided to look at the chemotherapy not as a poison that was sure to rack my body, but as a lifegiving medicine developed through years of research. I imagined the chemotherapy melting the myeloma cells away like acid. As the hours ticked away, I formed images in my mind of healthy white blood cells forming like petals opening on a flower. When I was tired of lying down or reading or thinking, I would work out with a dumbbell or walk the halls rolling an IV tree behind me.

Forty-eight straight hours of treatment. I began watching for signs that my hair was falling out. It never did. On the morning I was to go home, a resident stuck his head through the door and smiled at me.

"Hey, I got some good news. Your kidney function looks better already."

I returned home that afternoon to the welcoming of neighbors. In the front yard an oak had died in the time I was hospitalized, her leaves shriveled and brown. I recalled how branches fell from trees when my father was ill.

OVER the summer and fall of 1989, I received six four-day treatments. Never once was I nauseous or unable to eat; I felt no worse than a bout with the flu and rebounded quickly after each treatment. My blood counts and kidney function tests steadily improved.

I will not say this period in my life was a breeze. I alternated sometimes between an almost euphoric optimism concerning the future and cold anger that just when life seemed to be making sense, this had to happen. Late after midnight I would awaken and hear only the sounds of those sleeping, the drip of water from the bathroom faucet, a distant owl hooting. At thirty-six one has trouble imagining his demise when the sun is shining, children play, and birds sing, but in those muted hours between midnight and dawn, I realized how easy it would be to slip out of this life and into the realm from which no one has returned. I often wondered what education or truth could be found in a young father having cancer.

Seven months after my diagnosis of multiple myeloma, a bone marrow biopsy showed no sign of cancer. I had gained a complete remission. I took my family down to Florida to spend Christmas and fish and just plain get away from the memory of the past months.

The first of the year rolled by. My doctor asked me to come in and talk about what he felt to be my best course of future treatment.

"I think you should consider a bone-marrow transplant," he told me, gazing steadily into my eyes as he had done that time in the hospital room.

His words hit me like an uppercut. I had been told from the beginning a transplant was not possible in my case, and I was secretly glad. I had heard the horror stories of such an operation—people isolated for weeks in a tiny room, raging infections, sterility, and loss of all body hair. Even if I survived the operation, the myeloma might not be cured. I had battled for half a year to get into remission, and now I was being asked to undergo an ordeal as ravaging as anything in modern medicine.

"I didn't think I was a good candidate," I said, wishing he would say he had told me a bad joke.

The doctor explained that he had never thought I would reach such a solid remission. He went on to say that history showed that myeloma did not usually stay in remission long, and usually returned with a vengeance. Transplants take best when performed on those under forty with little or no sign of the disease.

"It's not a guarantee, Tim," he explained, "but it's the only possibility of a cure that we can offer you at this time."

He paused. "The decision is totally up to you."

I have never been one to spend much time making decisions. I usually work on how something feels in my gut. I've made my share of bad decisions, but the majority have turned out as good as or better than I planned. I remembered my father lying in his deathbed, unable to control his bowels or his thoughts. I decided then to go for the transplant and gamble on a cure. I wanted to raise my children, write some more books, and grow old and gray with Katie.

A BONE MARROW transplant is among the most difficult and extensive operations in medicine. The patient undergoes several days of extremely intense chemotherapy, then receives full body radiation. The combination of chemotherapy and radiation destroys the bone marrow and any other fast-reproducing cells such as hair follicles and those lining the mouth and stomach. If it works as planned, the bombardment kills all the cancer cells, too.

Once the bone marrow is destroyed, the patient is then given a blood transfusion filled with about a pint of donor marrow. The donor marrow begins to grow inside the bones, eventually producing a totally new immune system minus the malignancy. But while the new bone marrow is growing, the patient is subject to a wide range of infections and ailments.

During the bombardment of chemotherapy and radiation, a major organ sometimes fails. Simple pneumonia becomes a killer. The patient must stay in the hospital for weeks in semi-isolation. After being discharged, he must then stay close to the hospital for one hundred days in case emergency follow-up care is needed. Many transplant patients develop graft-versus-host disease, in which the donor bone marrow attacks the host body. The condition sometimes proves fatal.

I read all the pamphlets on bone marrow transplant and alternated between being enthusiastic and horrified. The first obstacle was to see if any of my siblings qualified as a match.

ALL five brothers and sisters were eager to volunteer. They drove up in two cars from Fayetteville, Mama riding herd as usual, and had samples of their blood drawn. The test results came back in two weeks; Bruce matched me almost perfectly, my next-younger brother, the one I had shared a bed with growing up.

The whole concept of a bone marrow transplant seemed bizarre. Another person's immune system would replace mine; I would develop his blood type, allergies, and immunizations. The donor process for Bruce would be relatively simple and pain-free. He would be put to sleep first. Then long needles would be inserted into his pelvis and about a pint of marrow would be "harvested." The marrow would then be strained and given to me. The marrow cells would migrate to the bones.

Katie and I had researched several hospitals when the bomb was dropped. My insurance company, Blue Cross/Blue Shield, announced it would not pay for the transplant because it considered it experimental. Suddenly, I was faced with coming up with about $150,000. I considered the possibility of trying to raise the money, pondered not even having the transplant if it would leave my family in hock to the future. Fortunately, I learned my two years' service in the Marine Corps would now pay off handsomely.

One Veterans Administration hospital does bone marrow transplants. The hospital is located in Seattle, Washington. Its success record is good, and its staff considered my age and condition excellent for treatment. I received a phone call telling me to arrive in town on April 11 to begin preparations.

I have sometimes pondered why in my life I have always pushed myself into areas that required strong physical and mental stamina. Marine, handler of poisonous snakes, Peace Corps volunteer, writer, outdoorsman—each of these roles hardened and strengthened me in differing ways. I liked to think now that life had been preparing me all along with these earlier adventures for the ultimate challenge of a transplant, and that I would not find in that hospital room anything I could not face.

I talked to my young daughter and son about the possibility of me dying in Seattle. Both were still too young to fully comprehend death, but I was comforted by Meghan's concept.

"Daddy," she told me, "if you die you become a spirit and then you will always be in my heart."

My own heart was full of many spirits when I drove west. I asked myself, "Country boy, what memory might you carry that will protect you and guide you full circle back to the land and people you love?" When I was lonely, I could call up images of Dixie, her land and people and ways. Beyond the Cascade Mountains I would look east and recall any of a thousand Southern spring evenings. The cows lowing as they walk single-file across the pasture to where my brother has put out hay. Frogs singing in chorus from the shallow water of the pond, the cry of one mourning dove blending her sad notes from the bough of a pine tree. If I looked hard, I could see my father's ghost in the shadows of the tree line where he stood watch for those he loved. Strong medicine to lead me back home.

NEW MORNING

TRENCH warfare—the reality of a bone marrow transplant hit me well after I had crossed the border beyond no-man's-land. In stages I learned why the procedure is considered one of the most complicated operations on earth. Along the way, I also saw and learned much about how the body heals in stages, how my family and I deal with stress, and how the human spirit prevails.

I left North Carolina April 6, 1990, on a sunny morning rich under the early blanket of spring. Mama, Kelli, and Karen stood on the front lawn, their arms thrown skyward, as Katie and I drove west. I wondered if I would ever see the homeplace again.

We crossed the United States in a sprint, four and one half days of twelve-hour driving, passing the changing scenery at a sixty-five-mile-an-hour blur. We climbed the Cascades into western Washington and decended into the ever-moist weather of Seattle with two hours to spare before my brother Bruce, his wife, and our children arrived by plane.

A good omen stepped first off the plane—Dr. John Parker, one of my favorite oncologists. By coincidence he was arriving in Seattle for a speaking engagement on the very flight as my family. We exchanged surprised greetings while waiting for Meghan and Christopher to bound down the corridor wearing plastic flight wings and beautiful smiles.

Two weeks of tests. Vial after vial of blood was taken, the strength of my heart and lungs was measured, eyes and teeth examined, more blood drawn. Between tests, we squeezed in sight-seeing, visited the rocky coastline of the Pacific, the massive firs of Olympic National Park. I had always wanted to visit the Northwest, but found myself becoming quickly biased against the region, as much a defense to further spur my determination to return home as real hatred. The days passed under rainy skies; I missed the clash of Southern thunderstorms. I compared fir and cedar with sweet gum and longleaf pine and found the former lacking. Despite my identification with reptiles, I cannot shed readily my home.

D-Day. Pre-transplant day number eight, in hospital lingo, arrived. I began gulping daily 135 small pills of very strong chemotherapy that would begin the destruction of what to now had been a very reliable immune system. The pills were salty, but I managed the three daily doses with food and lots of fluid. Several times my stomach balked and I threw the mass up and had to start over again. My body and nerves coiled slowly like a spring.

Four days later on Sunday, the day I was to report to the hospital to begin the more intense chemotherapy, a seizure struck. I don't remember much except feeling very strange that morning. My stomach cramped; a slight feeling of panic rode me. I awoke on the floor, under a team of paramedics, my mind a jumble of strange thoughts. I felt very cold. Meghan and Christopher stared at me from the corner of the room, their large brown eyes like those of frightened calves.

My mind returned in sketches—a highway exit sign that

proclaimed "Seattle"; questions prompted by the para-medic: "What is your name? Where is your hometown? Do you remember you're preparing for a bone marrow trans-plant?" By the time I was wheeled into the marrow trans-plant unit my memory was intact.

I sailed through the rest of chemotherapy. Despite vari-ous pipes, lines, and hoses carrying drugs and fluids in and out of my body, I suffered no nausea or other ill effects.

DAY NUMBER ONE. The time arrived for transplant. Bruce was put to sleep, his pelvis and thighbones punched close to two hundred times with large needles to suck out more than a pint of marrow. An hour later a nurse walked into my room with a sack of golden fluid that contained the essence of my brother's and my own future. Katie took pictures. The moment seemed hugely anticlimactic after such a buildup.

DAY NUMBER TWO. The Cascade Mountains stood like a wall between me and Carolina, snowcapped and ragged, like the spine of some great serpent lain down to sleep. Through the window of my hospital room I viewed the expanse of the valley as it swept to the hills and higher and higher to bare rock and ice. Towering even above these mountains stood the great hump of Mount Rainier, white and ghostly and so tall that clouds collided with her flanks. And if this wall of stone wasn't enough, to the west lay the whole damn Pacific Ocean. I felt trapped between rock and water, like being sealed inside a cocoon, forced to bide my time like an insect until I could reemerge, I hoped with a new skin, healed and unscarred and cured of multiple mye-loma.

The hall of the bone marrow transplant unit was quiet. Occasionally I heard the phone ring at the nurse's station, the click of heels upon the floor, the desk buzzer where another patient called for aid. From the next room I heard the constant chug of a respirator where a tube had been forced down the windpipe of another man who was not doing too well. The last rays of sun lit the crest of Rainier, and soon the long, long night would begin.

Midnight passed and a waning moon sat over the mountains. The drugs they gave me kept sleep away. I couldn't even hear the nurses, only the hum of the respirator from the next room. I wondered if he was sleeping. We'd checked in at the same time; I remembered talking with the fellow. He was my age, had a wife and two children the same as me. He had leukemia and was given about the same survival possibility as my own. He jiggled his leg as he talked.

My mind tricked me for several days. Yesterday I sat up in bed for an hour and watched a picnic take place on the roof of a lower adjoining building. Katie came into the room and the people and food vanished, and I realized I had been hallucinating. Tonight, in the shadows of moonlight, I thought of what a bad year it had been for several of us east Fayetteville boys. I was diagnosed with rare cancer, Eddie and LJ were murdered, Jeff burned up in his pickup, and Michael blew his brains out. I wondered why I was going through the hell of this operation in an attempt to live when so many friends kept getting picked off like doves on the wing. I remembered poker games and the luck of the draw.

Jeff floated in like one of the clouds. He rolled his truck into a ditch last March and burned to ashes while rescuers tried to get to him. They say when the heat was close he started blowing his truck horn like a trumpet.

"You look all right, Jeff," I told him, suspecting I was really talking to air. I had no fear of his image, for we were always friends.

"I'm fine now," he said. "Getting here was kind a rough, but that's over now. You look sort of tied up yourself."

He waved one luminous arm at the tubes leading from my body, a catheter thrust into my bladder, IVs spliced into veins in my arms and chest.

"Yeah, I'm like a puppet. Pull one of these strings and I jump. Hey, I heard you were blowing your truck horn when people were trying to get to you. I like that."

Jeff blinked off and on for a few seconds. "I was protesting. I had two beers still in the cooler and several miles of open road between me and home. Gave that up and my life trying to avoid a deer."

I thought about what I had read in the paper, how Jeff blew that horn even after the truck cab was a ball of flames. People said the horn got weaker and weaker like the witch's voice trailing off as she melted in *The Wizard of Oz*.

"I don't have a horn in here," I said. "But I have this buzzer that calls the nurses. I got some good lungs, too."

"You keep scrapping, homeboy," Jeff said. "I want you back home riding them back roads. A deer get in your way, run it the hell over."

Jeff faded and I drifted into sleep. A nurse awakened me at five A.M. for vital signs and blood draws.

DAY NUMBER TEN. Getting over the cure was the trick. Getting zapped with chemotherapy seemed mild compared to the war that erupted inside me. A chart on the wall plotted the downward spiral of my blood counts, and they hit zero—no white cells patroling my blood to fight infection, nothing to form new white blood cells. A cold could quickly turn into pneumonia and kill me. Every person who entered my room had to wear a face mask and gloves. My daughter Meghan's eyes floated above her mask huge and worried and sad. My hair started to come out in clumps, and I lost weight and strength. Food tasted like cardboard. My throat got sore, and a rash began on my armpits and groin. I found myself drawing more and more into my inner mind and hanging on to something my friend Jim Seay told me of, a kernel composed of one's secret strength and soul, formed with that first division of cells in the embryo. I remembered his words the night before I left Chapel Hill.

"You're probably going to see rough days out there," he told me. "You just remember that little ball inside your brain. Can't nothing touch it, not pain or loneliness or fear."

I HOPED the fellow in the next room knew he had that same little ball. He needed it. A stream of doctors came in and out of his room all day, and I didn't take that as a good sign. I saw his mother pass by several times, and the worry was etched in her face like someone carved it with a knife. I heard his kidneys were going out.

My mouth and throat began suffering the full effects of the chemotherapy; drooling was less painful than trying to swallow. I got morphine, and all I had to do to get another hit was mash a button on the pump. Midnight had again rolled by when Michael floated in, looking healthy and young like he did before taking his life. Today was one year past the night he tucked a twenty-gauge shotgun under his chin.

"Better go easy on that dope," he advised me. "It'll make you crazy."

I found it strange he was worried about my morphine. When he killed himself, he had gotten pretty deep into cocaine.

"You look good, Michael," I told him.

"The big man doesn't hold none of what you do down here against you," he answered. "I kinda like it where I am now. Nobody on your back."

Michael was lying on his back when his father found him. He had nestled down in his truck seat with his head cushioned on the armrest. Using the same shotgun he hunted squirrel and dove with, he rested the weapon on his chest and squeezed the trigger. The blast drove his head backward so violently it dented the door panel and sprung the latch.

Michael floated back into a deep shadow at the sound of a nurse walking by. He reappeared with the silence. "This thing get too tough for you, all you have to do is close your eyes and let go," he said. "Easiest thing in the world. Man, it don't hurt a bit."

He was gone in the morning, along with the moonglow and shadows. The pain in my throat seemed better each time I remembered how he had pressed that gun barrel against his Adam's apple.

DAY NUMBER EIGHTEEN. My new marrow grafted, and over the next five days my blood counts reversed and started up. The doctors said I was strong enough to become an outpatient. My legs were weak and my head spun when I stood, but the thought of getting out of the room filled me with renewed strength. I had another motivation—yesterday the fellow in the next room died, and I needed to distance myself from the smell, sight, and sounds of the ward.

He went hard. I could hear the sound of his respirator

through the wall, his labored breathing as he tried to pull in life. His family came in and out through the day, faces streaked with tears. Finally in midafternoon, with his wife, mother, and children beside him, he stopped fighting. I stayed awake most of last night to monitor my own breathing. I did not look into dark corners for fear of inviting in his ghost.

I KNEW I was required to stay in Seattle a full one hundred days before my doctors would allow me to cross those mountains and return to the pines and sweet gum of my homeland. I knew I had many obstacles to face, trials to endure, setbacks to face. Pneumonia was a real threat, the worst danger period still weeks away. I would have to coax and pamper my new immune system for months before I could call myself recovered. I planned to focus on that pure ball of primal strength and self, hold to it and wish upon it like a star.

Somewhere along the way I hoped to come to terms with why two men of equal age and worth could walk into a hospital ward and only one walk away. I would question myself as to what lies behind a man's will to live or not to live, why one man blows his horn like Gabriel enraged while another lies down with a gun.

But mostly, I planned to play the cards I have been dealt and not dwell on too many "what ifs." Bury the dead, this world is for living.

DAY NUMBER TWENTY-FIVE. I did great the next two weeks. My new marrow grafted quickly, my blood counts of new white cells and stem cells that manufacture the blood components bounded. Bruce was allowed to return home.

My full sails soon collapsed in the doldrums. I noticed first that the soles of my feet were getting tender. In a few days, blisters formed as if I had been walking on hot coals. I was suffering from a slight case of graft-vs.-host, a struggle between the new marrow and my host body. A rash began on my face and began to creep down my body. Soon it covered my neck, armpits, chest, and groin.

But most frustrating of all, my platelet count began to fall, the clotting factor of blood. Bruce had to be called and asked to return to Seattle to be milked of his own platelets to keep me from reaching a state where I might hemorrhage internally. My other blood counts, which had been rising steadily, faltered, dipped and rose, then began to spiral down. I realized more and more that I would not skip through this operation, but that it would be the most trying, exhausting, and dangerous situation of my life. I might even die.

Two more men in the unit developed complications. One was my age, the other only twenty years old. Both had done well in the beginning, but then their lungs and kidneys began to go out on them. They were put on respirators to keep their lungs pumping. Through the grapevine, I heard that for them it was just a matter of time. On daily walks through the hallways of the transplant unit, I passed their rooms, and though I wanted to avert my eyes, the sight was fascinating. The men reminded me of octopi with all the life support cords leading from them. The respirators hissed like snakes. Family members were either huddled around the bed or sleeping sprawled in chairs. The men lay on their backs, chests heaving for breath. When they were awake, their eyes flitted from side to side like birds.

I feel shame in myself that I found some relief in their death. The odds stack up that one out of three die from marrow transplants, and human nature would naturally rather see those statistics manifested in another. I felt sadness for these men and their families, but did not want the same loss reflected in my own children's faces.

These weeks were a hard lesson in reality for my daughter, Meghan. She attended a part-time school that was populated by children of patients in the three hospitals that perform marrow transplants in Seattle. Several times she saw classmates check out of school and return home because a mother or father died, a little sister or other family member. In her eyes I saw the reflection of my seizure, her bewilderment over a father suddenly bald-headed and jowly from medicine and often hooked to machines. She missed her friends back home, her cat and dog. One day as she sat by my bed, her eyes were unusually sad, her small brow furrowed with thought.

"What's wrong, baby?" I asked her.

"Nothing," she answered. She drew circles with a crayon on a piece of paper.

"You look mighty sad."

She sighed. "Daddy, will summer still be there when we go home?"

"Some of it will be."

In her eyes I could see her mind working. "Daddy, why did you have to get sick? If you hadn't gotten sick, we wouldn't have had to come out here."

I could not answer her question, only hug her to my chest. Still, her kisses and hugs remained genuine, and she was another strong motivation for me to get through this maze and return to her a strong father.

Christopher was still too young and full of exuberance to be greatly affected by the changes. "Pop" looked funny to him, he liked to rub the stubble on my head. Once he asked me, "Pop, if you get dead, will God hang you on a cross?"

I wanted to laugh, and had no answer for him either. I

found in him another great motivation to live, for he would only have fragmented memories of me if I died, no real sense of who his father was.

In Katie, I have seen more vividly the range of emotion, the conflict, compassion, pain, and commitment adults are aware of and must bear.

DAY THIRTY-THREE. We celebrated our ten-year anniversary early in June. My wedding band is the only material object I have ever kept track of for a decade. I gave her stones for the occasion—sapphire-and-diamond earrings. When we married I was too broke to afford a band. The earrings were given in love and appreciation, but also in honesty, that in their sparkle and flash one would glimpse and remember something of me eternal.

In my illness, Katie has seen a strong reflection of her own father's early death from cancer. She was eight years old, was never told he was even dying until his soul had departed. That poor preparation has haunted her through life. In me, she married a vigorous man who seemed immune to such a fate, and I can occasionally see and understand in her eyes a sense of betrayal. We come from vastly different backgrounds—Katie from the upper end of the middle class, a direct descendant of ancestors who grew cotton and owned slaves. Her father and uncle served in the war as officers, then returned to a country ripe for business and industry. Her people are college-educated, professional; they work hard to maintain a life-style that allows sailboats and house help and international vacations. They face life with bold smiles and exuberance, buoyed by the safety that a little extra financial comfort allows. I came from a background just as hardworking and honest, but from the lower scale, tempered by years of living paycheck to paycheck. Katie and I approach most decisions and obstacles with a K-Mart-vs.-Calvin-Klein balance, but yet through argument, compromise, and occasionally one party throwing up hands and giving in, reach at least a truce if not a full solution or agreement.

One day early into the transplant, Katie brought a banner into my room that had been signed by many of my in-laws and their friends in Memphis. The banner read, GO TIM, GO! in large red letters.

"Where do you want me to hang it?" Katie asked.

"Nowhere," I answered.

Every time I entered the hospital for treatment the past year, I received such a banner. Their effort is well intended, but I am just not the sort of person who likes brightly colored banners.

"Just hold it against the wall for a second," I instructed Katie. "I'll swear it stayed up there a week."

Katie shot me a cold stare, but did as I had asked. She folded the banner and put it in her purse.

Katie is pragmatic, a person ruled by laws. She reaches most decisions through a committee effort with her peers, acting then on advice, rational and planned execution. My own approach is often to go on gut feeling, try to knock aside obstacles and act on my sense of truth and conviction.

During recovery, one of Katie's first questions each morning was what my blood counts had climbed to. I had learned that these statistics were like a roller coaster from day to day and not a concrete indicator of one's improvement.

"I didn't ask," I answered. "I figure if something is important, they'll tell me."

Katie didn't speak. After a few minutes she left my room. I could hear her through the door asking the nurse for my counts. She soon learned to bypass me and go straight to a doctor with her questions.

Katie liked conferences. Her family sent me banners and humorous cards. My family members phoned and talked for long minutes, but their voices dripped like the rain with worry. Two differing people, two differing approaches to life forged by reality.

I found as I went deeper into the transplant, I was at last confronted with a situation where no back exit existed. I have always been a man of fantasies. After returning from the Peace Corps, I harbored a private fantasy for the next few years that if the conflict of marriage and meeting the demands of middle-class living proved too much, finally I could escape to the French Foreign Legion, where I could change my name and be another man for five years. The day I became ineligible at thirty-five, I worried. My cabin in Fayetteville will always serve as a beacon to me, a last sanctuary where, if only in fantasy, I might live in solitude.

But I could not turn from this transplant. Tough it out, keep my mind intact, hope my body held up, and endure. The only other option was death, and at this point in my life, I did not recognize death as an escape, fantasy, or solution.

DAY FORTY. I continued treatment as an outpatient. As the weeks rolled by, a unique comradeship formed among the surviving patients. Henry Sanchez, Jesse Boyle, Barney Carter—they became to me more than just names. As we made it through the early danger period and became outpatients, we stopped fearing friendship, and instead explored our common bonds in background, in military service, and in facing death at a young age.

"I never hesitated getting this transplant," Sanchez said. "If I hadn't gone for it and five years from now I was dying from cancer, I'd hate myself."

I agreed. I had easily decided I would rather risk dying

now. I figured my children would suffer less losing me when their memories were short.

The other patients and I shared similar complications and setbacks. When a virus showed up in someone's blood, a spot on his lungs, we knew his fear. When someone needed a transfusion, we all knew it meant sitting for four hours and watching the blood slowly drip. When the doctors made rounds and entered the outpatient treatment room, we all sat up and tensed for possible bad news. We talked of new patients entering the program, of our favorite nurses, and of our plans once we were home.

"I got a cabin down in Oregon where I can stand at the door and see Mount St. Helens," Barney said. "I've shot elk in the forest not a hundred yards away."

"We're gonna try and buy a little motel unit on the coast," Jesse said. "I got to get out of diesel mechanics because of the chemicals. I'd like that, working with people, not a lot of pressure. Just a few rooms is all we need."

I told them of wanting to go canoeing, just drift down the Cape Fear for a few days on that slow water, set some catfish lines at night. I swore never to complain of the Southern humidity again. We complimented one another's children, cheered one another on, and confided the problems of dealing with family members.

I went through nearly three weeks of extreme discomfort with bladder irritation. I rushed to the bathroom every twenty minutes and pissed clots of blood the size of my thumbnail. The burning sometimes bent me double. Nights were worse, lying in bed trying to sleep, listening to sounds and thinking. Just as I would begin to drift off, my bladder would call again. I discovered that the basin on the wall of the bedroom served fine as a urinal and saved me the extra steps in reaching the bathroom.

"Will you please stop peeing in the sink," Katie

pleaded. "Don't you know that is disgusting? I have to clean after you."

I would not even waste energy arguing with her. She would never understand how trivial I considered her complaint. I did not tell her that sometimes I simply draped a towel across my stomach and urinated lying in bed.

Despite the discomfort, the fear, the weeks of boredom in recovering from a bone marrow transplant, I did see good come from it. I gained several new friends and found my sanity, body, and marriage able to survive another test of endurance. I also discovered my little brother Bruce as a grown man.

How fitting that the person I shared a bed with for the first fourteen years of my life would turn out to be the only one of my siblings to match me perfectly in bone marrow. Also, quite ironically, in the years following childhood he and I had grown the farthest apart.

We shared no middle ground in the years following our first marriages. With Karen I found the comfort of an older sister, in Kelli I doted on the baby of the family. Keith and I discussed and debated the facets of life, Danny and I talked sports. But with Bruce, there existed a gulf, not born of conflict or disinterest; I had simply left home at eighteen and never really returned to live in Beard, he was married and a father at nineteen. Our worlds were so different.

In Bruce, I often glimpsed my alter ego. We look much alike, but the similarities seemed to stop there. As a teenager I had often stopped short of sex with girls out of fear of how a child would anchor my life. I lived under a self-control that Bruce seemed never to consider.

I was home from the Marines on leave when I heard through the grapevine that Bruce was planning to get married. I finally cornered him in the bathroom and asked him if it was true.

"Yeah," he admitted, his face drawn. "I was going to tell you."

"Does Mama know?"

He shook his head. I asked what could I do to help.

"Nothing," he answered.

Bruce was lying on his bed staring out the window when he told my mother the news. He didn't look her in the face.

"I guess we're going to get married this weekend."

"Get married!"

"Yeah."

"Well, this is kind of a quick decision, ain't it?"

"We'd been talking 'bout it for a while."

They were married a few days later at her house. She was sixteen. Mattie and I were married a year later after careful plans following four years of dating. We had bridesmaids and ushers and a reception afterwards. Our marriage didn't last as long.

When Bruce left Linda, she had given him two children and lived with him seven years. His departure was as unexpected as his marriage. My mother had come to love Linda like a daughter, and when she called to tell me the news, she could hardly talk.

"Said he didn't love her no more," she explained. "He said he was in love with someone else. Tim, he just sat there and cried in my arms."

I drove to Fayetteville that night and parked outside the truck terminal where Bruce was driving part-time for Roadway. I wanted to tell him I was behind him no matter what his reasoning for leaving was. I sipped beer and waited for two hours, but when he finally drove in, we didn't talk more than five minutes. Like my father, he had never been one to express his thoughts.

He went through a rough period following his divorce. Linda had the children. He quit the fire department and started driving a truck full-time. The woman he had left home for proved to be little more than a home wrecker, he drank and smoked a lot, spent all his time either working or alone in his small house. About that time Katie and I left for the Peace Corps, and for two years I only heard of him through my mother's letters.

Now my bones were infused with his marrow. I needed his platelet transfusions so a vein would not burst in my head or my lungs start to bleed. He did not hesitate a second when the call came, but boarded the next flight out, leaving once again a demanding job, many unpaid bills, and an unhappy second wife.

I had reached a low point in morale. I was less than halfway through the required one hundred days of recovery time spent in Seattle. I knew that even the hundred days was not concrete and I might have to stay much longer. Rain fell daily. My routine was to get up, force down some breakfast, and report to the hospital, where I might sit for treatments that lasted from two to nine hours. My strength declined, my muscle tone softened until I could hardly rise unaided from the toilet. Small bruises formed in clusters over much of my body, and my neck looked like it was covered with hickies. The inside of my mouth was tender with blood blisters. The combination of drugs fogged my mind as if I was under a perpetual hangover. For the first time in my life I began to understand how people could choose death over life. I forced myself to remember my commitments to the children and all my plans yet unfulfilled.

DAY FIFTY. Bruce walked into the bone marrow unit like a gangbuster, looking strong and healthy, wearing a cowboy hat, his black mustache as large as a bandit's. I noticed how his arms were almost twice as thick as mine. Later that day a bag of his platelets was pumped into me, and for the first time in a week I was not in danger of sudden hemorrhaging. But moreover, a chunk of home had been returned to me; we passed the hours recalling tales of our childhood spent in the fields and woods of Beard. For the first time in fifteen years we were simply brothers, and not pushed by the demands of children, bills, and women.

The days stretched again into weeks, and I still required platelet transfusions. Bruce coached me daily, said my counts would improve anytime, constantly played down my concern about his losing his job or having problems with his wife. He joked with other patients and spent time with their families. People smiled when they saw him come through the door. I realized more and more my quiet brother possessed sensibilities and talents I had never imagined, I understood gradually how as a fireman he had been able to enter a burning building and fight the flames with only a water hose.

DAY EIGHTY. As my days ticked off, my resolution to return home on time deepened. Three weeks shy of the departure date, my platelets began to improve. I began to gain weight, and my muscles strengthened. Finally, once again Bruce was told he could return home. He had spent a total of three months in Seattle and I had never once heard him complain. His arms looked like a drug addict's where he had been stuck with needles.

He left me a note on the mattress where he slept. I found it the day after his departure.

Tim,
   I'm not much for expressing my feelings. That is one of my faults I will one day overcome I hope. I am wurst at spelling

which you are finding out now in this note. I just wanted to tell you that I am glade that I was the one to match with you and was able to give you my marrow. I would also give you my heart if it would help. The time I spent out here gave us a chance to be together as brothers should. I will always cherish this time we had and hope we can stay close and not drift apart as we have in years past. . . .

I finished the note reading through tears. He *had* given me his heart, or at least a part of it that I will carry with me, the same as I carry his marrow in my bones and his note inside my wallet.

My days in Seattle ticked down to single digits. Barring any complications, I was given the green light by my doctors to return home at the end of the week. I became paranoid over every spot on my skin, every sneeze or cough. I also was aware that no one had died on the floor in two months and the law of averages would sooner or later turn. I had only four days left till my flight when one of the newer patients began to have respiratory problems.

I remembered seeing him on the day he checked into the floor for preliminary tests. He was thirty-two and had already won two previous bouts with cancer. His brother was his donor, a truck driver like Bruce. His mother was a likable, talkative woman not unlike my own.

He did well in the first days of his transplant. Like me, his blood counts initially plummeted, then rebounded quickly. His mother bubbled over with enthusiasm. He often walked the hallways, his face set with grim determination that made him set one step after another. But I also noticed a fear in his eyes, a jerky movement there as if he was constantly scanning 360 degrees to see where the next danger would come. He was almost due to be released as an outpatient when a fungus showed up in his lungs. He seemed to have expected the infection, as if in his dreams he had been foretold he would not escape this time. Within a few days his lungs had deteriorated to the point where a respirator tube had to be shoved down his windpipe. He died on the morning I left on the plane.

DAY ONE HUNDRED ONE. The sun was shining on Seattle as the jet banked sharply and turned east. Mount Rainier stood as snowcapped and towering as she had looked four months earlier when I rode in. I held Meghan's small hand and assured her she would go to sleep in her bunk bed that night. I settled down in my seat and began reading a paperback copy of *All Quiet on the Western Front.* The book helped the ten-hour flight pass quickly. The novel also showed me that no matter how tough my ordeal had been, it paled when compared to what some people had suffered through.

We arrived at Raleigh-Durham Airport at midnight. We rode home with the windows of the car open. The night rang with the sound of frogs; heat lightning lit the horizon. The air was hot and sticky and sweet like perfume.

WHAT is left of this strange summer in my life is at least predictable. The days will be hot, thunderstorms will roll in to cool the evening. Meghan will begin first grade in a couple of weeks, Christopher his preschool. Katie will once again manage her office and her demanding schedule of meetings and international travel. She pushed all those responsibilities aside for four months to administer to me. I already hint to her of buying another python to begin building a new edition of The Last Great Snake Show.

My future is not so predictable. No sign of myeloma

exists in my body now, and it may never return. But it may at any time. I will not dwell on that.

I dreamed of my ancestors the second night I was home. I was at another of the reunions at the Primitive Baptist church, but all the people there except me were long deceased. Kingfish spoke to me.

"Boy," he said, "the people who count are going to remember the good things you did long after they forget the bad. You're bound to mess up some, but in the long run that'll all be forgiven."

I woke up and stared at the dark ceiling and thought of these people, and for each of them I could remember some virtue that outweighed their losses.

HIS hounds raged. The old bitch dog stood with her forepaws on the wire, her head raised high in the air and her mouth open in a long bellowful howl. The younger dogs milled around in the pen, yelping and nipping one another, occasionally breaking into a chorus of deep-throated bays as if hot on the trail of a raccoon that had doubled back from the high ground toward the river. But the old dog wrapped her long, wet tongue around the air and blew the sad notes that told me the hunt had treed, the old man had reached the water.

My grandfather died in a hospital fifteen miles from where his hounds were penned. In his last minutes, his pulse and blood pressure went to zero, and he sat up in his bed and began calling his dogs, his mind having returned to a better time. The doctor stood back from his bed and watched, fascinated as my grandfather's voice split the afternoon hospital quiet and reverberated. I could not hear, but his hounds did and tried to come to him. The old man's eyes said he stood under a cypress tree in bottomland that smelled of moss and mud, and when his last shout rolled up from his throat and slowly faded, the light went out in his eyes, he slowly settled back in his bed like a great tree falling, and he died. The bitch dog knew, she cut off her own bellow as suddenly as if her throat had been sliced with a blade, she turned and lay in the dirt, and in seconds all the other hounds quieted.

Dying usually comes with vigor in the South, often with struggle, as if the spirit is reluctant to leave such a fair land for a region uncharted. Of the people I have watched fight terminal disease, most faced death as they had life. Some accepted the verdict with bitterness and silence as if dying was just one more final addition to a lifetime list of failures. Others went with shouts of joy, their eyes turned to a vision of Jesus coming down to retrieve them. Others raged and fought to the last breath, either afraid of dying, reluctant to leave such good times, or not satisfied with what they had yet done on earth.

The South has given her share to the worms. A goodly portion of the Revolutionary War was fought on our turf, we were devastated by the Civil War, and in the foreign wars we have lost more sons than any other region of the country. Plagues thinned our Southern ports and hurricanes washed some of them off the face of earth. But we have learned to bury our people, mourn for them a proper period, and continue with life. Lonely family cemetery lots rest under groves of oak trees, the grass and stones well tended across generations. Funeral wakes and family visitations are often grand affairs with everyone bringing food and drink to share. Picture albums are opened to pages showing the deceased in young finery. Unless the death has been especially senseless or tragic, the person's faults are ignored and tales are recalled of the good times and deeds.

A couple of days after my father died, probably a hundred or more people came to gather at the homeplace and praise the life of a good man. They sat in circles of lawn chairs or ganged in tight bunches, depending on the memory they shared. Occasionally men drifted off to their cars to down a beer or shot of whiskey. I remember no one crying openly during the funeral, for we all knew Reese had gone to a place of open fields.

We buried him without ever opening the coffin for viewing. The family decided we wanted to remember him before the waste of disease. I can see him come across the field on an early evening, cows following at his heels and lowing, a bush ax slung across his shoulder where he had been clearing land.

The South has her share of ghosts. Souls so full of life take their time in departing—some hover only for a few minutes or days, some stalk and haunt for eternity.

The day after my father was buried, Katie saw him in his bedroom. She was passing the door on her way down the hallway when she glanced into the room and saw him standing at the window. She took several more steps before realizing she had just witnessed his funeral. She stopped and backed up to assure herself it was only me or one of my brothers, but the room was bare, the window offering a clear view of the pasture.

Years before, Granny Baggett died of her own lung cancer, an independent woman who passed away alone in her hospital bed.

I visited her a few days before she died. I was twenty-one, fresh out of the service and soon to be married. She had moved to Wilmington to work for a private doctor before the disease struck, and she lay in a dark room in the local hospital, a private nurse filling her water glass and helping her turn when the pain got bad. We exchanged small talk. I was rising to leave when she took my arm and pulled me close and whispered:

"You behave yourself, hear?"

Her words were not accusing, only spoken with love and the knowledge she would not be around to remind me later. I hugged her and left, went to the rest room and blew my nose, partly from the stench of medicine and illness and partly to stifle tears.

Three nights later, I was out with two cousins who were going the next day with my mother and me to visit Granny. They left me at about two in the morning at my parents' house. Soon after I was home, the hospital called to tell us Granny had just died. I drove over to my cousin's house early the next morning to tell them that Granny had passed, and we would not be driving to Wilmington. As I spoke, they stared at me in bewilderment.

"We know," one cousin said.

"Oh, okay, I answered. "Someone already called?"

Their dismay deepened into frowns.

"What are you saying? You told us last night when you were getting out of the car. We were shocked that you had been with us all night and hadn't said she'd died."

My face flushed, and I leaned against the wall. "What the hell do you mean? I didn't know she died till the hospital called after I was asleep."

The room was very silent as we stared at each other. I've never figured out the voice that spoke through my tongue, but I guess as Granny's spirit passed, she stopped by long enough to whisper in my subconscious she had departed that dark room. It was like her to worry we might make a useless trip, spend gas money and subject ourselves to the danger of the road. She's fishing somewhere right now, dressed in loose jeans and a man's flannel shirt. The fish may be biting well or only nibbling, but she's happy.

The old people's dying was expected, often a relief for the deceased and those left to bury them. Ashes to ashes, dust to dust. But when the children die, the youth and young people, Southerners particularly mourn. We believe in the wisdom of old people, the learning and tradition passed down in their teachings and stories, and with the death of a youngster, a young man or woman not allowed to "live," we feel particularly cheated and sometimes question the will or sense of God.

Billy Van died in the flaming wreckage of his uncle's gas truck at age nine. He was the first of my friends to die; I found no solace or security in being told he was taken home early to be an angel. I have never forgotten he was supposedly heard screaming from inside the flames. His uncle died from his burns, trying to rescue the boy.

A good dozen schoolmates died before age thirty. One beautiful young girl hanged herself in a tobacco barn at seventeen over an argument with her boyfriend. Another buddy broke his neck diving in White Lake two days after high school graduation. He languished in a wheelchair for ten more years, smoking pot through a long rubber hose and recounting tales of when he used to date and drive his car fast.

The list goes on. Last spring a fellow I used to camp with as a kid and later share beers with drove his car into another vehicle at high speed late at night. He was "feeling no pain" at the time, and I hope he was just as numb when he went through the window and was crushed in the wreckage. Then like an old gun slinger, Eddie Brown got his, the childhood poet dead with a knife hammered literally into his skull. Jeff O'Neal burned up in his truck. Worst to me, L. J. Williams was murdered last spring, my black childhood friend beaten to death in what people suspect to have been a bad drug deal. Keith and I attended his funeral only weeks before I was to leave for Seattle. We were the only white people there, as his father was the only black person to attend my father's funeral.

My own battle with bone marrow cancer seems trivial and easily beaten in comparison to such sudden tragedy. Still, I have been unable to find any more sense in a man having cancer at thirty-six than in being crushed, burned, or beaten to death. I have wondered if that first cell might have turned on me years ago when I rejected a career as a Pepsi salesman, the cell multiplying slowly but grotesquely as I wandered further from the taproot of my heritage. Might not the trade cost years of a man's life in discovering the earth—and be worth that price if in the end he is able to return home with his knowledge? I should stop guessing and charge forward into whatever I have left in this world. Whenever my clock should wind down, I hope I will find peace and strength as Franklin McLaurin, a distant cousin, was able to do when he died in his late thirties.

Franklin was known by all as Duck, a name given to him for his flying skills in high school basketball. I was only a child when he performed, but remember tales of his leaping ability. He grew into a gangly red-haired man who farmed the land of his ancestors. He was terrified of snakes, and I remember backing him up in the local store several times when I walked in with a chicken snake or king snake wrapped around my neck. He was only in his early thirties when he was told he had intestinal cancer.

Duck was helping raise two children, supporting a wife, working full-time as a postal man, and farming on the side. After the initial shock of being told he had only a few months to live, I believe he buckled down and decided to prove the doctors wrong. He turned back to the life he had led, planted new crops, and brought in the harvest for several more years.

His disease slowly caught him. In his last months when the cancer spread, he often went to the dusty fields to plow wearing an oxygen mask. He planted a large crop of soybeans in the fertile bottomland close to my parents' land. As the bean plants grew taller, Duck's own life seemed to slip quicker from his body. His wife would tell of finding him sitting early mornings in front of the window where he would see the sun rise over the fields. He was told he might pass on any moment, but he kept rising each morning, willing himself through another day. His pain and labored breathing, the weariness in his face, made many who loved him wish he would just turn loose, relax once, and let go, but he kept his vigil.

His beans matured in the early fall, the pods hardened and turned brown. Duck could no longer operate a tractor, and some of his black field help began the harvest. At noon, Duck asked to be taken to the field.

Getting him there was a problem. All his oxygen equipment had to be loaded into the car, extra help taken along to support Duck. But he was loaded up and driven down the dirt road to where two combines moved in wide rows, gleaning the beans and throwing plumes of chaff into the air. He got out of the car and walked into one of the fields and examined the beans, made sure they were mature and hard and of good market value. He watched the harvest for an hour, then asked to be driven home. There he took off his oxygen mask and died peacefully in the early afternoon while the clear fall sun was still in the sky.

EPILOGUE

I DRESS and am out of my tent while the sun is still somewhere over the Atlantic. My propane stove is hissing and heating up water for instant coffee sweetened with honey, a breakfast of grits and salted ham. As I break camp and pack the canoe for this final day's run, dawn begins to roll up and I catch my first view this year of Venus blinking through the nude boughs of trees.

The river flows by me. I have always likened rivers to life. They roll on and on, seemingly unaltered by man or time. We can dam one up, but she will flow over the concrete or around it and back into her original banks. She might rise with the rainfall or run slow in time of drought, but she remains, year after year after year.

I was on the river before the sun crested the horizon. This trip is finished now, and the faster I make the ocean, the happier I will be. My arms and shoulders are strong, my wind good. As the day opens, for the first time in this journey I can see my reflection in the water. I don't look too bad. A little worn and ragged, but I'm alive and happy, and I have remembered many who lost that claim.

I paddle hard, and in a few hours the water begins to widen and deepen. The river rolls on and on, and like life, I can ride her for a while—

you can—but not always. She will continue for centuries beyond us. Around a sharp bend in the channel, the river suddenly opens into a wide bay. I dip my hand in the current and taste sweet rainwater that fell pure from the clouds, flowed through the fields and forest to now mix atoms with the ancient, primal water of the sea.

WE ARE sons and daughters of the land, our heritage tied to fields and woods, the call of hunt, the spiritual transition of the seed that cracks the hard earth and grows into weed, food, flower, or tree. I have carried in my wallet for seven years a plastic sandwich bag filled with plain dirt scooped from the pasture behind the homeplace. It has traveled with me through Africa, Europe, and much of America, a talisman that whispers to me the song of mourning doves, wind in longleaf pines, the low rumble of thunder from a summer storm that has recently passed and soaked the dry fields. I hope to waltz slowly to that tune the day I lift above this bright land.

I have told you of home.